Crossing the Zorn

Crossing the Zorn

*The January 1945 Battle at Herrlisheim
as Told by the American and
German Soldiers Who Fought It*

Edited by
EDWARD MONROE-JONES

McFarland & Company, Inc., Publishers
Jefferson, North Carolina, and London

LIBRARY OF CONGRESS CATALOGUING-IN-PUBLICATION DATA

Crossing the Zorn : the January 1945 battle of Herrlisheim as told by the American and German soldiers who fought it / edited by Edward Monroe-Jones.
p.   cm.
Includes bibliographical references and index.

ISBN 978-0-7864-4712-1
softcover : 50# alkaline paper ∞

1. Herrlisheim, Battle of, Herrlisheim, France, 1945.
2. United States. Army. Armored Division, 12th.
3. Germany. Heer. Panzer-Division, 10.
4. World War, 1939–1945 — Personal narratives, American.
5. World War, 1939–1945 — Personal narratives, German.
6. World War, 1939–1945 — Regimental histories — United States.
7. World War, 1939–1945 — Regimental histories — Germany.
I. Monroe-Jones, Edward.
D756.5.H47C76   2010   940.54'214395 — dc22   2009050019

British Library cataloguing data are available

©2010 Edward Monroe-Jones. All rights reserved

No part of this book may be reproduced or transmitted in any form or by any means, electronic or mechanical, including photocopying or recording, or by any information storage and retrieval system, without permission in writing from the publisher.

On the cover: "Purple Heart Lane," east of the town of Rohrweiler, Alsace-Lorraine, France (National Archives). American flag, Iron Cross and helmets ©2010 Shutterstock

Manufactured in the United States of America

*McFarland & Company, Inc., Publishers
Box 611, Jefferson, North Carolina 28640
www.mcfarlandpub.com*

Acknowledgments

The following American and German veterans of the Second World War have been both gracious and unrestrained in their description of events that were often traumatic and personal. The author expresses his gratitude for their patience in honing description to most accurately portray events as they actually occurred. In alphabetical order they are:

Robert Arrasmith, Erwin Bachmann, Wilhelm Balbach, Frank Conway, Charlie Fitts, James Francis, William Funke, George Hatt, Ernst Storch, Bernhard Westerhoff, Andy Woods, and Fernand Zilliox.

The author recognizes the written accounts of American and German veterans who contributed descriptions of personal events to various journals and newsletters of their respective divisions. These written accounts were used as corroboration of other relevant information.

The author is grateful to M. Joseph Voltzenlogel, mayor of Weyersheim, for his interest in and deep knowledge of Alsatian geography relevant to the events of January 16 to 20, 1945; to Irmgard Diekmann for her many hours of translation from German to English; to Dennis Denholm and Eric and Stephanie Zilliox for translation of French to English; and to Laurie Berg for her work in preparing maps of the battle area.

Appreciation is extended to the Department of History at Texas A&M University and particularly to those few professors who were so helpful in criticizing the initial drafts of the work.

Table of Contents

Acknowledgments   v
Preface   1

Part I : Roads to Alsace

Introduction to Part I	7
1. Texas and Le Bec Hellouin, December 1943	8
2. Russia and Spokane, December 1941	15
3. Vienna and Fallingbostel, November 1942	21
4. German POWs and the Frundsberg Division, June 1943	24
5. Camp Barkeley and Russian-Occupied Poland, April 1944	30
6. Normandy, August 1944	39
7. Camp Shanks, New York, September 1944	45
8. Zutphen and the SS *Empress of Australia*, September 1944	49
9. Operation Market Garden, September 1944	55
10. The Salisbury Plain and St. Pölten, October 1944	59
11. Le Havre and Beyond, November 1944	65

Part II : Alsace

Introduction to Part II	75
12. Bining, Rohrbach and Roeschwoog, December 1944	78
13. Schweighausen and La Breymuhl, January 1945	91
14. Althussheim, January 1945	107
15. The Steinwald, January 1945	115
16. East of the Zorn River, January 1945	121
17. Herrlisheim, January 1945	131
18. Weyersheim, January 1945	152
19. The Bruchwald, January 1945	159

Part III : Beyond Alsace

Introduction to Part III   171
20. Oberhoffen and Heidenheim, February–May 1945   176
21. Stalag XI-B and Berlin, April 1945   185
22. Michigan, Texas, Mississippi, Niedernhal, Vienna and Fachingen Lahn   194

Chapter Notes   201
Bibliography   209
Index   211

Preface

In January of 1945 Hitler tossed the dice for the last time in his Operation Nordwind. It followed on the heels of the failed Operation Wacht am Rhein, later known as the Battle of the Bulge. When a corps of Patton's Third Army diverted to the north, its southern flank, guarded by the Seventh Army, was left open to attack. The American 12th Armored Division, a newly formed and untested unit, was held in reserve and in early January moved to fill the void. Meanwhile, the 10th Waffen SS Panzer Division, which also had been held in reserve, was pushed across the Rhine River where it established a bridgehead south of the village of Offendorf. The area was marked by the small towns of Herrlisheim and Weyersheim, which were separated by the meandering Zorn River/Canal. The two divisions were thrust into a hasty confrontation which was intended by both sides to be an easy offensive. The clash of arms was violent and staggering to Americans and Germans alike, but it was overshadowed in history by the headline stories of the Battle of the Bulge.

Writers of history are lucky in having the opportunity to know people who have played a pivotal role shaping the history of which we write. Although I did not know it at the time, research for this work began in 1987 when I first interviewed General Heinz Harmel for a previous work, *Before I Sleep* (1991). I was able to spend many weeks over several years with this veteran of the Waffen SS, and through lengthy discussions I became familiar with his division's combat record. Through General Harmel I met and became friends with a few other Frundsberg veterans, and over time I recognized combat in Alsace as singular, both in terms of its importance as Germany's last offensive of the Second World War and as a defeat for them at the hands of American youngsters who had as their only real weapon their grit to see it through. By all rights, the tough soldiers of the Waffen SS should have taken the town of Weyersheim on January 19, 1945, but a few Americans stopped them at the Zorn River. My curiosity about the Americans of the 12th Armored Division led me to the division's museum in Abilene, Texas, and to several veterans of the division who had been the young men with the fortitude to meet the Germans in the dismal winter of January 1945. This work is the story of both the American and German soldiers of that January, told as they remember it and backed by documentation from written sources of the time. The story is told, as much as possible, in simultaneous time sequence so that we can visualize what was happening to the Americans and Germans who were destined to meet in Alsace.

Operation Nordwind was a major German offensive that involved many German and American divisions spread over the entire area of the French Alsace. The description of battle contained herein was delimited to an approximate 30-square-mile area marked on the south by the Steinwald Woods, to the north by the town of Drusenheim, to the west by Weyersheim and to the east by the Rhine River. These were the dimensions of the January 1945 killing ground.

Little has been written about the January battles to the east of Weyersheim, and I spent many months searching for obscure, out-of-print books in German and English as well as hours in the U.S. National Archives and the German Military Archive in Koblenz. While these sources were of value, it is the firsthand accounts by veterans of the battle that turned the present work into a vivid, personal saga of soldiers at war. Their stories include family, training and combat. Remarkably, the American and German veterans who told their stories held nearly identical Christian-based values and had held them even as young men fighting one another.

To understand the geography of the combat zone I walked the fields in the winter of 2004. They lay fallow under a frozen week-old snow as they had in 1945. Surprisingly little had changed. The ruins of the waterworks were covered with vines, but the red brick walls still guarded the intersection of La Breymuhl. The houses of Herrlisheim had been rebuilt, except for the residence of the Zilliox family, and it was in their barn's cellar that the 17th Armored Infantry Battalion command post had resided during the battle for the town. These good people welcomed my inquiry and were not only forthcoming in their recollection of the battle, but were most gracious in their hospitality.

The mayor of Weyersheim, Joseph Voltzenlogel, took time out of his busy schedule during my visits in two successive years to accompany me in my reconstruction of events to the east of that town. He was also present some years before when veteran George Hatt met his old enemy Bernhard Westerhoff in Weyersheim.

In 1943 and 1944, young Americans were graduating from high school and undergoing basic training while the Germans were fighting the Russians in Poland and the British in Normandy and Holland. How the green Americans were able to defeat the experienced Germans was a unique story that has never before been told. From the German perspective, it was a fight for their country at its border. For the Americans it was a matter of learning on the job. Heroism was abundant on both sides and the frozen fields were filled with valor. It became apparent to me that I was writing, not so much about a pivotal battle in Second World War history, but about how a few youngsters on each side, thrown into combat, became extraordinary soldiers. I was amazed that after establishing a rapport with them, they were able to remember the events of so long ago as if they had happened last week.

Still, it was necessary to corroborate memory before recording it as history. Time tends to distort memory, and for that reason it is most accurate when rendered as writing as soon after an event as possible. Post-action debriefings and reports have great credibility because of their immediacy. Long-term memory, as is the case with veteran soldiers remembering events that took place over fifty years ago, may be diluted by time. It is only human to repress unpleasant and ugly memory and to retain events of levity.

Military history is most often portrayed at high decision-making levels. The generals become the focus of attention while the enlisted men are accepted as vehicles for carrying out the generals' decisions. But when the generals err, it is the men in the foxholes who take up the slack. Such was the case in Herrlisheim.

January 1945 was a bitterly cold month, and the battles that took place in the Weyersheim-Herrlisheim area during that month were dramatically affected by the weather. It was the common soldier who fought the cold as well as the enemy. The battles east of Weyersheim must be told from the enlisted man's point of view, because it was he who experienced the inhuman conditions that winter.

It is respectfully submitted that only through their memories of that traumatic month can history gain an understanding of a little-known but crucial battle in the Second World War.

The Zorn River/Canal irrigates fields of French Lower Alsace, north of Strasbourg. It runs essentially northeast to southwest and separates the towns of Weyersheim to the west and Herrlisheim to the east. It is fed by the Moder River and, while not wide, its sloping sides render it impassable except by bridge.

Herrlisheim and Weyersheim are similar to other small towns in the area. Like their neighboring villages, their names are distinctly German despite their location in France. This is attributed to the ambivalent history of the region: over several centuries, Alsace has alternated between German and French control. Other town names in the area carry the same German influence, including Gambsheim and Drusenheim. This is not to say that the people of the area consider themselves to be anything other than French. Indeed, they are fiercely patriotic to France and were so in January of 1945.

Few Americans have heard of Weyersheim or Herrlisheim, even though they were the sites of a critical battle during the Second World War. The battle remains emblazoned on the memories of those young American and German soldiers who fought each other in the streets of Herrlisheim and in the fields between the two towns.

The terrible winter weather of January 1945 brought agony to both American and German combatants and to the civilians caught in the great conflict. This is their story; one of ordinary young men going about the business of war.

Part I

Roads to Alsace

Introduction to Part I

The year 1943 saw the formation of two military divisions, one American, one German. The American division was, in large part, made up of college students, and the German division was made up of seasoned political soldiers of the Waffen SS. These two fresh divisions were to be thrown into a deadly combat at war's end where the untested American soldiers would stand up to the experienced Germans.

The soldiers who made up these divisions went to war with the sure knowledge that what they fought for was worth the sacrifice. Their stories are like those of all soldiers: full of optimism, humor, suffering, fear and pain. A look into their world, as it was then, starts in 1943. It was Christmas. The American division, the 12th Armored "Hellcat" Division, was in its initial stages of development, while the German division, the 10th Waffen SS "Frundsberg" Panzergrenadier Division, was in the final stage of training.

1

Texas and Le Bec Hellouin, December 1943

Charlie Fitts was a student in the Army Specialized Training Program (ASTP) at Texas Agricultural and Mechanical College in College Station, Texas. Texas A&M was founded in 1876 as the all-men's Agricultural and Mechanical College of Texas. It produced a prodigious number of military men, with nearly 20,000 serving in the Second World War. The entire graduating classes of 1941 and 1942 went into the military.[1] For reasons unknown to Charlie, the Army only allowed its officer-cadet students a weekend pass for the 1943 Christmas holiday.

Charlie described his circumstances: "I had first reported to Fort McClellan, Alabama, in the spring of 1943. Another young private had thrown his duffel bag onto the top bunk of our barracks, so I took the bottom bunk. He was Bobby Fryer and we became instant roommate buddies. We were both chosen to be students in the Army's ASTP college program and, in August, we went to Texas A&M with aspirations of becoming Army officers. In the fall we started classes and did well academically. The world was in front of us and our spirits were high. We looked forward to going home for Christmas, but the Army didn't see the need for such frivolity.

"Upon receiving news from their son Bobby that he would only have Christmas day off, his wealthy parents reserved a suite in Houston at the famous Rice Hotel. Bobby invited me to accompany him for Christmas in Houston, a short distance from College Station. I accepted. I had sent gifts in the mail to my parents and sister Harriet in Meridian, Mississippi, so there was no reason for me to stick around the barracks. We were met in Houston by Fryer's parents, who laid out the red carpet for their son and his friend in the military. After a four-course Christmas Eve dinner served by the hotel in the Fryer suite, we settled into comfortable chairs while Mr. Fryer poured an after-dinner liqueur. They wanted to know all about me. I told them about my family in Meridian, Mississippi; my father who had contracted tuberculosis during the Depression and how my sister and I had gone to work while in school so the family might survive. My high school education, including prowess at football, was really quite ordinary, and my brief career in the military was even more common, but Mr. Fryer wanted to know how I felt about the war."[2] The people of America had viewed the news of Germany's invasion into Poland with great alarm. It was the beginning of the war and something that stood out in everyone's mind.[3]

Charlie thought back and said, "I remember September 2, 1939, as a special date. My father had taken me down to Perdido Bay, Alabama, to do some fishing. I loved being with my dad, but he didn't have much time for leisure, so our fishing trips were special for me. We rented a rowboat and all day pulled fish into the boat while talking about life in general. I was nearly sixteen and my dad took this opportunity to talk to me about Christian values that have remained with me as a part of my life. We also talked about Roosevelt and the New Deal, about America and what it meant to be an American and about how important it was to show respect for God and country.

"When we tied the boat up at the dock we saw a crowd of men at the bait shack. Dad and I went over to the men. They were quiet and a voice came from a radio. A man turned, held a finger to his lips and pointed to the radio. I leaned toward the sound trying to hear the commentator, Gabriel Heatter, I think was his name. The voice was telling about Germany's invasion of Poland. Not a word was spoken by any of the listeners. When the station interrupted itself for a commercial, a heated argument began

Private First Class Charlie Fitts, a member of the 66th Armored Infantry Battalion which attacked the Steinwald Woods the morning of January 16, 1945 (Fitts collection).

among the old men. I listened with interest as some wanted to get into the fight to help beat the Germans into the ground. They pointed fingers skyward as they tried to out–shout one another. Those who seemed more thoughtful said that it was just another European war like all the rest. America should mind its own business, they said. Meddling in matters that don't concern Americans is just plain dumb, they said.

"On the drive home I asked my father about what it all meant. My dad had served as a Marine in the First World War. He thought that America would stay out of the European war as long as possible, but in the end it would have to pitch in to beat the Germans, just like in the last one.

"After a pause, Mr. Fryer said, 'And your father was exactly right.' Bobby's father called it a night, so my buddy and I flopped into luxurious beds. Those beds were like floating on a cloud.

"The next day was Christmas and I followed the Fryers into the lobby where an enormous tree stood in the center of the polished floor. Bing Crosby sang 'White Christmas.' The radio music came from hidden speakers around the walls. Everyone became quiet when the traditional American Christmas favorite 'Silent Night, Holy Night' was sung by Kate Smith."[4]

In the town of Lubbock, Texas, F. George Hatt, Jr., was in line with other young Army officer cadets of Texas Technical College. They were frantically calling on the pay phone to tell their parents they wouldn't be home for Christmas. Founded in 1923 as Texas Technological College, it was a part of the Texas state college system. In 1943 it embraced several military training programs, including Army Air Corps preflight training, the Navy's V-12 program and the Army Specialized Training Program (ASTP).[5] Edward Waszak, himself an ASTP student, described the program: "The initial group of ASTP students was made up of students already in college who joined the Reserves in order to stay in school. The balance came from Army enlisted men all over the country who applied for ASTP and passed the tests. Some were selected by their commanding officers based on the enlisted man's score on the AGCT test [Army General Classification Test] when entering the service."[6]

George Hatt remembered the day he too was denied leave for Christmas 1943: "I had waited in line for the only pay telephone in the dormitory. I dialed home and put a finger in my ear, as I fought to hear the instructions of the long-distance operator. It was my father who finally answered. I had no explanation for the Army's refusal to let us go home for Christmas. My dad, Mr. F. George Hatt, Sr., was sympathetic. He vowed that the family would keep the Christmas tree and unopened gifts until I came home. It was a quick conversation, because other ASTP students were waiting to tell their parents similar bad news."[7]

Private First Class George Hatt, Jr., a member of the 17th Armored Infantry Battalion which attacked Offendorf on January 16, 1945, and Herrlisheim on January 17, 1945 (Hatt collection).

When George Hatt finally was granted leave in late December, he hitched a ride to north Dallas. He told of his homecoming: "I didn't bother to knock. I was too breathless from running the last two blocks to my house. I stepped into the hallway, sweating in my uniform. With hair trimmed high and a ramrod posture, I was the object of family admiration. My mother ran to me despite being almost blind. She hugged me as she had done so often in my youth. The rest of the family stood to one side as mother inspected me at close range.

"The family moved into the living room. The droopy Christmas tree still stood with shiny balls and hanging tinsel. Presents were under the tree and hadn't been disturbed since my telephone call the night before Christmas. We settled into chairs and I remember the approving nods from my parents and brother when I told them that in a year I would be an officer in the Army. It was important to me that my father agree with my decision to go with ASTP. He was a successful dairy products distributor in the Dallas area and was in the habit of making sound decisions.

"After dinner we sang Christmas songs even though it [was] long past. Mother played the piano. 'Silent Night, Holy Night' brought tears to her eyes, but she played the piece flawlessly."[8]

The quiet evening hours in America were not shared by the soldiers of the Waffen SS in occupied France. For them, the Christmas season was a matter of stealing a few hours of enjoyment in a climate of war. The German soldiers were far from their families, were homesick, and were tired from the months of training. It was a melancholy time, a time for song and daydreaming of home while letting the abundant French wine soften the reality of their circumstance.

Technical Sergeant (Oberscharführer) Bernhard Westerhoff told of that Christmas Eve. He had decided to let his hair down and celebrate with his men: "I hoisted a case of French wine onto my shoulder and carried it up the cellar steps. I heard piano music sweeping from the tavern above. It was my fourth trip into the French cellar to replenish the party's spirits. I could have assigned a private in my 6th Company to bring the wine from the cellar, but on this special Christmas occasion I wanted to personally serve my men. My comrades cheered as I set the case of Bordeaux onto the tavern counter.

"I looked at the faces of the men who made up my family away from home. A layered haze of cigarette smoke hung in the tavern dining room. I had arranged for a variety of French puff-cakes to be served. They had been prepared by Le Bec Hellouin's best baker from ingredients supplied by our company lead cook. The French pastries were accompanied by Dutch cheese and dark German bread and butter. Washing the heavy food down with first-rate Bordeaux could be considered an insult to the wine, but it was Christmas, and in a time of turmoil was to be excused. A pause in the endless 1943 training allowed my men to vent their pent-up spirits. They smoked, laughed, punched each other, and toasted whatever popped into their minds. I watched wine glasses being raised and their contents drained in tribute to nearly everything except the war. A piano sat in a corner and a Frundsberg soldier with open collar and hanging hair banged its keys. A few jazz lovers hovered around the instrument listening and weaving in time to the raucous tempo. No one took note of the Reich's ban on such music."[9] The Reichsführer SS concentrated most of his energy on the

Sergeant Bernhard Westerhoff, commander of a Mark IV medium tank which attacked Drusenheim on January 16, 1945, the waterworks at La Breymuhl on January 17 and Weyersheim on January 19. He was the sole survivor of a hit from the Vickless tank at the Waldgraben Canal east of Weyersheim (Westerhoff collection).

various training and political indoctrination programs of the SS, leaving him little time for restrictions on music.[10]

Bernhard went further back in his memory to recollect his 1937 entry into the Waffen SS, which was then called the Verfügungstruppe, or VT for short. "I was fed up with the National Labor Service. I knew what I wanted. I would join the Navy. On my way to the Navy recruiting office, I saw a poster advertising the VT. In a moment of inspiration I walked in and signed my name. I watched other men being turned away and didn't give myself much chance of being accepted, but I was tall and muscular and therefore hoped for the opportunity to prove myself."[11]

Bernhard was lucky to have been chosen for the SS, because shortly thereafter, recruitment was curtailed. Hitler simply said, "The SS should not recruit too much."[12] Bormann then directed Himmler, who reluctantly slowed the pace of recruitment.

Bernhard continued his narration: "I remember that the SS barracks outside of Munich were modern five-story buildings with shining floors and shouting sergeants. When the basic training was completed, I lined up with fellow young soldiers and took an oath of allegiance to Adolf Hitler. I spent several months guarding the Soldiers Memorial in Munich's Odeons Platz and standing guard in Hitler's Munich domicile called the Braun Haus. When Hitler took over the Sudetenland I was assigned to the Deutschland Regiment in a small village. I stayed with a wonderful family that treated me like one of their own. As I look back on it, my stay in Czechoslovakia was thoroughly delightful."[13]

The initial organization of the Waffen SS consisted of only three regiments, "Deutschland," "Germania" and "Der Führer." The Leibstandarte SS, which was equivalent in strength, was a personal guard unit and thus not initially a part of the Waffen SS.[14]

Bernhard said, "When the VT became the Waffen SS its redesignation wasn't of importance to me. I had no way of knowing that my life would be shaped by that organization. When I had been assigned to the Deutschland Regiment I had been trained on the Model 34 heavy machine gun, and my company took orders from Captain [Hauptsturmführer] Freiherr von Reitzenstein. I thought that any person with so distinguished a name must be a competent soldier."[15]

Bernhard Westerhoff played a small role in the invasion of Poland. Stein wrote that the contribution of the Waffen SS in the invasion of Poland in 1939 was modest, but not negligible. The major part of the Waffen SS was shipped to East Prussia during the summer of 1939 and organized into regimental combat groups attached to larger Army formations.[16]

Bernhard's perspective was personal and intense: "They trundled us into Poland on September 1, 1939, in trucks that threw up clouds of dust. We met only slight resistance from riflemen. By the end of the first combat day, we had advanced to Uniszki Zawadsky, nearly sixty miles from our jump-off point at the Prussian border. Colonel (Standartenführer) Felix Steiner, our regimental commander, ordered us this way and that, requiring Captain von Reitzenstein to order us to mount our vehicles, move to a new area, dismount, dig in and set up machine guns — only to be told to move again. I wasn't an officer, but I was smart enough to guess that both Steiner and von Reitzenstein were learning their trade just as we were learning ours.

"I manned my machine gun as my comrade Private First Class [Oberschütze] Erich Adam grabbed a fresh belt of ammunition. A bullet struck Erich in the chest. I jumped to his aid and held him in my arms while trying to stop the bleeding. Erich's head sagged onto his chest and I was immobilized from shock and grief. I looked into Erich's face with a devotion I hadn't recognized until that moment. The noise of battle faded from my hearing. That was the first time death had taken a friend. I was suspended in time, like a man free-falling through space.

"A short time later I was struck in the leg by shrapnel. I was sent back to Germany where I went through surgery and recuperative therapy to get my knee back to normal. When released from the hospital I was allowed a week of leave. With cane and uniform I went home to the town of Scheidt. My mother cried with happiness at seeing me, cried with concern at seeing the cane and cried with anguish from the knowledge that my visit was only temporary. My family had been poor. My mother had taken in laundry to make ends meet before the war. Then my father joined the Nazi Party. He was rewarded with a low-level administrative job and from then on my parents lived a better life. My father greeted me with a mighty ten-fingered handshake and a slap on the shoulder. For a week I was the king of the household. My mother pampered my appetite and my father asked me endless questions about the fighting in Poland. After that the family ignored the war and I caught up with the gossip from the village."[17]

The invasion of Poland was viewed by most Germans as a justifiable action. The German public had been duped by the Gestapo and the Reichsminister for Propaganda who together created a fictitious scenario to convince the German nation that Poland had been aggressive toward Germany. Görlitz wrote, "In August 1939, German preparations were complete, and the press duly began to lay down the required barrage of stories concerning the maltreatment of Germans by Poles. There was no official mobilization, merely an acceleration in the rate of call-up. Incidents were manufactured by the agents of the SS and Gestapo. This new threat of war filled people with a kind of dumb fear."[18]

Bernhard's memory returned to Christmas Eve 1943 as he painted a verbal picture of the evening's strange mixture of emotions. "I heard from the opposite side of the room the voices of men singing a Waffen SS marching song. Their pounding boots on the tavern floor and expanding voices soon were too much for the piano player who gave up his solo concert in favor of the unanimous singing. I joined in with gusto. I liked singing the many marching songs and prided myself on my steady pitch. Soon the tavern was shaking with stamping boots and slamming fists as the march carried my wine-soaked merrymakers to a resounding climax.

The men demanded to hear their favorite wartime song, "Come Back to Me (Komm Zurück zu Mir)." It was a haunting melody that spoke of home and a girl who waited for her lover to come back from the war. The piano player softened the keys with the gentleness of the music and soon the men were humming and singing the words in whisper-like tones. Recordings of the song were often played on wind-up gramophones, and it was sung in French as well as German. Some of the men mouthed the words, being too lost in memories to sing.

"A mud-smeared motorcycle messenger entered. Striding to the bar, he asked a man leaning on the counter to point out the top sergeant. I was listening to the music and not in a mood to be interrupted, but the muddy messenger looked so pathetic that I walked to a table and pulled out a chair for the lad. He was all business and wasted no time in pulling from his dispatch case an envelope which he handed to me. As the messenger turned to leave I recognized him and grabbed his arm. I demanded that he stay and join in the festivities, but the messenger shook his head.

"I was feeling the Bordeaux and I threw my arm around the man's shoulder, something seldom done by a sergeant in the Waffen SS. We sat down at the table where the messenger's glass overflowed from my unsteady hand. Men again gathered around the piano as several seasonal German songs were played. They sang 'Home, Your Stars (Heimat Deine Sterne)' and 'When the White Lilac Blooms Again (Wenn der Weisse Flieder Wieder Blüht),' both of which told of home and the loneliness of being away.

"I knew the young man and called him by name, Private Ernst Storch. Through several glasses of wine I explained that the young lad's previous job as 'Donkey Führer' was terminated through no fault of his own.* It seemed that Storch had been caught in an unfortunate love affair involving an artillery sergeant and the lady of the local dairy. The lady was the wife of a French prisoner of war in Germany and it had become my reluctant duty to bring the affair to a close. I did so with the delicacy that the situation demanded, including the transfer of Storch. The young soldier nodded his understanding. We two Frundsbergers shook hands and saluted.

"No one paid attention to the brief conversation. Storch left the tavern amidst the continued Christmas singing. It was now late and I rose from the table. The men again became quiet as the pianist began to play 'Silent Night, Holy Night.' It was the German traditional 'Stille Nacht, Heilige Nacht.'"[19]

---

*See story in Chapter 4.

2

Russia and Spokane, December 1941

In preparation for a possible attack on Russia, General Halder set up a seminar on the problems of attacking the huge nation. He pointed out that the facts of geography made two separate deployments necessary, since the proposed front, which ran roughly north to south, was divided by the Pripyat Marshes. He proposed three Army groups, two of them striking into the area of Leningrad, Minsk and Smolensk, while a third was to occupy an area from Kiev south into the Ukraine. Hitler gave orders as early as August 1940 for Germany's troops in Poland to be prepared for an attack on Russia. This involved railway lines, roads, airfields and quarters to be constructed. Ten infantry divisions and two tank divisions were moved east in this month alone.[1]

At 4:45 A.M. on June 22, 1941, the men in Bernhard Westerhoff's Deutschland Regiment prepared to attack. Columns of tanks, personnel carriers and trucks crossed the Russian frontier. The German Army had 2,434 front-line tanks in 21 panzer divisions at the beginning of the Russian campaign.[2] The Deutschland Waffen SS Regiment was a part of Army Group Center under Field Marshal Fedor von Bock. One hundred eighty-three divisions attacked on a vast front of nearly 3,000 miles. Attacking from Poland were von Bock's Army Group Center, comprising the 2nd, 4th and 9th Armies and the 2nd and 3rd Tank Armies, these being under Generals von Weichs, von Kluge, Strauss, Guderian and Hoth.[3]

Bernhard's job, as a member of a machine-gun crew, was a microscopic part of this vast land armada. After a week of fighting it seemed to him that it was more of a race than a battle. The Russian soldiers surrendered at the sight of the Germans, who rolled along heading for Moscow. The campaign proceeded with precision. At Minsk, Army Group Center fought the first of those great encircling battles that were to inflict such heavy losses on the enemy.[4]

Bernhard remembered the exhausted but euphoric temperament of the men: "I ran and walked from one location to the next while carrying the barrel of the machine gun. No sooner would we get our machine gun set up than we would be ordered to move to the next location farther east. Sometimes personnel carriers were available and on these occasions I jumped aboard as the carrier moved into an endless line of equipment churning dust on unpaved Russian roads. The men groused at the summer heat, dust and flies. Their sleeves were rolled up and the dust stuck to our moist skin. I was itchy and uncomfortable, as were my comrades, who smoked and swore as we bounced along the road. Still, we were winning and that fact made it all worthwhile.

"The trucks halted at a nondescript town called Jelna-Bogen. We jumped down, and squad leaders met for a last-minute briefing on the coming attack. At a signal, the platoon sergeant ordered our machine guns forward to a new position. I picked up the barrel and started running. It was August 4, 1941.

"An explosion nearby thumped my body and I was launched sideways. Coming down on my stomach, I was stunned and it took a minute before I tried to stand. When my legs failed to respond I lay there feeling a bit awkward because the pain hadn't set in. My friend approached and told me to lie where I was. Blood was oozing through my shirt. I had taken a piece of shrapnel in my back from an exploding Russian shell, although at the time I only knew I had been hit. I lay on my side, unable to move. The machine gun crew captain patted my shoulder when a medic came to my aid. After telling me to get into shape and return to the squad, he squeezed my shoulder and rushed off toward the enemy.

"I was taken into a church where a doctor examined the wound, and immediately set up for surgery. After a day lying on a cot, I was taken to an airfield where I was hoisted into the slanting fuselage of a Junkers 52 transport. A nurse sat in the jump seat as the plane's three engines roared. The tail lifted and the main wheels thumped hard on the pitted grass field. At last the plane lumbered into the air. It landed at Minsk. From the airdrome, I was transported to a waiting train. After a day's train ride, another ambulance took me to a permanent hospital in Ziechenau, in the southern part of East Prussia."[5]

A young lady named Ilse Schultz had lived her quiet life in the city of Tilset, East Prussia, where she worked for the police department as a clerk and stenographer. She related her contribution to the war effort: "When a few other girls in the police department volunteered at the local military hospital, I went with them. We took the train to the hospital and were given instruction on caring for patients. I became a nurse's aide and performed routine duties in the care of wounded soldiers — writing letters for those who couldn't use their arms and adjusting bedding for those in pain. I helped the medical staff by changing linen and feeding those needing help with eating. Every day I moved down the ward, talking to patients, trying to cheer them up, holding their hands and comforting them. I spent only a few minutes with those needing minimal help and up to twenty minutes with those in great need."[6]

Bernhard's memory of his hospital ward was as follows: "When I saw that Ilse spent a long time with severely wounded men I exaggerated my condition. It was selfish, I knew, but I loved talking to her and would try to find some excuse for a little extra attention. I made sure that each time she stopped by my bed I was clean shaven and my hair was combed. I reasoned that if I were presentable she would be less inclined to move on to the next patient. My wound healed to the point where I was allowed to leave the ward and visit the garden. It was late summer and the trees offered shade while the flowers were still in full bloom. Each time I wandered the gravel paths, I unconsciously looked for Ilse. On my fourth visit I saw her. She sat on a bench with another nurse's aide. They talked and she didn't notice me. I pretended to smell a rose. I was crushed to think that she didn't recognize me out of the ward. I was frustrated and didn't know my next move, so I simply approached her and stood at her side without speaking. She looked up and smiled. I relaxed a little. I sat beside her and was introduced to the other girl, but I couldn't take my eyes off Ilse.

"After our first meeting we met regularly in the garden. We talked and strolled the winding paths through the bushes and flowers. At ten o'clock every evening the curfew alarm sounded. Rather than a whistle or horn the signal was the wistful recorded singing of 'Lili Marlene,' played over hospital loudspeakers. Its haunting melody and words conveyed wounded men's thoughts to home and happier times. For

Sergeant Bernhard Westerhoff and his bride, Ilse Westerhoff, on their honeymoon in Vienna, Austria, 1942 (Westerhoff collection).

me it signaled the end of a visit with Ilse. On September 20, 1941, I was declared by the doctors ready to return to duty. I held Ilse's hand and promised to write, as all soldiers do, but for me it was no idle promise. I had already thought of Ilse as my wife."[7]

In that same month in America's Northwest, a seventeen-year-old farm boy, Robert Arrasmith, tended to his chores and thought of the fall semester at his high school in the state of Washington. Typical of young men at the time, he took an interest in politics and world events. The fact that he lived in a rural community didn't detract from his intense monitoring of the war in Europe. He described afternoon bull sessions at Birnbaum's Pharmacy on Seventh Street, "We talked about maybe going to Canada and joining the R.C.A.F. Or maybe going to England where we could join the Eagle Squadron of the R.A.F. We all thought that was the best choice, because we all wanted to fly Spitfires as soon as possible. We detested the Huns we'd seen in movies. They wore black uniforms inside their Messerschmitt fighters. We only knew them as Hollywood had portrayed them, and agreed that the Germans needed to be blasted from the skies.

"Billy Cobb was a maverick. He insisted that the real war was fought on the ground and that to be a real soldier meant joining the infantry. I could see no logic in this. News clips of trenches in the First World War with young men going over the top to certain death had no appeal whatever. To be a pilot seemed the most adventurous and romantic way to fight the enemy. But I was shocked when a girl told me I was too big to be in airplanes. At the time I dismissed the comment as coming from a girl who knew nothing of such matters. Later, I found out that her brother was in the Army Air Corps.

"Weekends were a break from school, but the family always had chores and I had to work each Saturday from dawn to dusk. Sundays were reserved for church and I was thankful that my family was religious. During sermons I dreamed of flying Spitfires, but I worried about my size. Being on a farm we always had lots to eat and so I had grown a lot. After church I was allowed to bring a friend to Sunday lunch, usually chicken with potatoes and lots of vegetables.

"One Sunday in December 1941, I invited Billy. Upon arriving home from church we adjourned to the living room where I twisted some radio dials to get the best reception. As mother fixed lunch, Billy and I sat on the floor in front of the big mahogany Philco radio. The local station's program was hardly started when it was interrupted by a dry, flat voice making the startling announcement 'Japanese planes have attacked naval and Army installations at Pearl Harbor, Hawaii.' Billy and I looked at each other in amazement. I jumped to the radio and quickly tuned to NBC for confirmation. Every station was now overriding programs to bring Americans the news that the nation was under attack. Mom and dad came into the living room. My father had a grim expression and mother held her apron. Between announcements, we talked excitedly about the bombing. Billy and I hated the Germans, but now it seemed the Japanese were deserving of some of our hate.

"The European war was forgotten as we tried to imagine just where Pearl Harbor and the Philippine Islands were. After hearing how the Japanese had been in Washington, D.C., talking about peace while their airplanes were bombing American ships, both of us vowed to get even. On Monday, President Roosevelt delivered his declaration of war speech to Congress. Two days later Hitler declared war on the United States, but no one paid much attention. I knew that America would be fighting both the Germans and Japanese, but now it was the war in the Pacific that was uppermost in importance. There were a few Japanese students at my high school and they seemed very nice,

Private First Class Robert Arrasmith, a member of the 56th Armored Infantry Battalion which attacked the waterworks at La Breymuhl and Herrlisheim January 8 to 10, 1945 (Arrasmith collection).

but now we knew them for what they really were, backstabbing non–Christians who were out to destroy America. At least that was my thinking then.

"I wanted to join up right then and there, but I finished high school at the insistence of my father. In June 1942, I caught the bus for Spokane. The intervening months were bleak for Americans who read depressing headlines in their daily newspapers. Not a single American was left behind as the nation transformed itself into a giant arms manufacturer. Each person was in the military, working in war industry or producing food on American farms. Rationing, food stamps, war bonds, victory gardens and ride-sharing became the instant focus of Americans.

"I was big, muscular and fairly intelligent, but to tell you the truth, I wasn't very worldly. When I stood in line at the Army recruiting office in Spokane, I watched those around me. The guys bragged about how America would whip the underhanded Japs in a matter of months. I had to agree that a nation who built second-rate tin toys couldn't be much of a military power. I had never thought much about my size and was surprised that so many willing young men who had stood with me in line were turned down because of physical problems. I was accepted into the Army without reservation. A sergeant looked at me and told me that I'd be perfect for the infantry.

"It was the end of my dreams about the RAF and flying Spitfires. I was a patriot above all else, and wherever the Army needed me is where I would go. I was accustomed to physical labor. My only problem during basic training was the Army's insistence on following rules. It seemed to me that my every waking moment was regulated by some Army rule. Do this and do that. On the double. Hurry up and wait. On the farm I'd known what had to be done and when. I had always had a sense of responsibility. It came with growing up on a farm. The Army was convinced that every recruit had no instinct other than how to avoid work. It went out of its way to make sure that every second of every day was covered by a rule. In that way, low-life recruits couldn't get away with anything.

"It didn't take me long to realize that I was being driven by sergeants whose aim it was to push each recruit into the same mold. After a month, every man in my barracks looked alike, used the same profanity, hated the drill sergeant with equal fervor and looked for the same assignment that would involve the least work.

"Basic training came naturally to me. I didn't *want* to run the fastest, go through the obstacle course with the most ease or shoot the straightest—I just did. The farm had made me into the optimum Army recruit. Because of my size I was invited to box in the Army's Golden Gloves tournament. I accepted and punched my way around the ring and thoroughly enjoyed myself. No one had taught me how to box. I had never really been in a fight while a high school student. It seemed natural to circle the opponent, look for an opening, then hammer the poor man's jaw with a straight right. My sergeant was proud of me and my buddies slapped me on the back after every bout. I loved the popularity that went with boxing. It seemed like a good way to spend my time in the military. The war seemed a long way off. The sergeant told me it was vital for the war effort. Good for the men's morale, he said. I trusted his judgment and was getting accustomed to the daily routine of sleeping late, eating the best food and getting lots of exercise.

"The sergeant told me that I was going to box a tough customer. The man's name was King Kong, explained the sergeant, but he said that I shouldn't be afraid of the man's face. It seemed that the name had arisen from his features. He looked like an ape and boxed like one. The sergeant had a worried expression when he suggested to me that King Kong was just a big bluff.

"When I stepped into the ring I was stunned by the man's size. The referee called for me to shake hands with the monster. I tried to see his eyes, but couldn't. The eyebrows were so bushy and the eyes so sunken I wondered how King Kong could see. While in the corner I hoped that my agility would be enough to overcome King Kong's enormous strength. The gong sounded and I stepped from my corner. He came at me like a freight train. The bout lasted less than a minute, the time it took King Kong to find an opening. I flew out of the ring. It was the end of my military sojourn into the life of a professional boxer."[8]

3

Vienna and Fallingbostel, November 1942

In 1942 a youth named Ernst Storch, a native of Vienna, was released from school to watch a parade of soldiers from Germany. He related his first flirtation with the military. "I heard some older people grumbling about the 'New Order,' but most of my schoolmates seemed elated at the racket of bands playing martial music and flags with swastikas hanging from balconies. I told my parents about what I'd seen. Father held his opinions to himself, but he was delighted at the upturn in his German-made silverware sales since the Anschluss. Mother was irritated that I found the marching soldiers exciting. The school curriculum had changed and National Socialism became one of the subjects that were mandatory for graduation. Still, there hadn't been all that much change in my daily life since the arrival of the Germans. I played soccer, skated in the winter and rode my bicycle with my friends through the narrow streets of urban Vienna. I lived in an apartment less than a mile from where Mozart had resided, and our section of town hadn't changed much from his time. I attended the commercial academy in Vienna, but my heart was no longer in it. All was going well for Germany, and my fear was that the war would end before I and my friends had a chance to get in on the adventure. I learned about guns, discussed the exciting times with my friends, played sports and studied in school to keep my parents happy. I passed the Matura examination and graduated. My friends kept talking about the exploits of the German Waffen SS. Their enthusiasm was fueled by street posters of marching men in sleek black uniforms. We sometimes watched the Waffen SS soldiers walking the streets of Vienna, and they always walked proudly like they owned the world. I noted with special interest that most of the time these Germans had Viennese girls on their arms.

"On my 18th birthday I announced my intention to join the Waffen SS. My father was noncommittal and my mother was furious. She pleaded and begged me to remain as I was. I listened and tried to comfort my mother, but my mind was set. I applied and waited for the results. I was six feet tall and sort of skinny, but the recruiters only looked at height. A letter said that I had been accepted into the Leibstandarte Adolf Hitler. This was a special honor. I was exuberant, Father was proud and Mother, although being skeptical, was impressed. This was the beginning of my new life.

"Basic training outside Berlin was tougher than anything I could have imagined. When I was physically stretched to the limit, I often thought I should have listened to my mother. I stood in line at the medical clinic. The men were stripped to the waist. They were pale, but their lean bodies had muscles that had been hardened during endless calisthenics. I moved to the marks on the floor and raised my left arm. The medic asked me my name and blood type. Then he examined my record. Another medic tattooed the blood type on my inside upper-left arm. I stood motionless and looked straight ahead. At a final, formal ceremony I stood in ranks together with my new comrades. The words spoken by officers were meant to underline the single most important concept of basic training: obey without question. Our oath to Adolf Hitler and the Reich included the phrase, 'My honor is sacred.' I didn't realize how that oath and tattoo would become such a burden."[1]

Elsewhere in the Third Reich, Bernhard Westerhoff had been transferred to Fallingbostel in northern Germany. He recalled, "I wrote my fifth letter to Ilse Schultz without receiving a reply. The letter was [posted] to Tilset, but I was unaware that upon her return to work she had been temporarily posted to Salzburg, Austria, where she had become ill with jaundice. When finally I received a letter I was shocked that it had been postmarked Salzburg. When I read that she was ill, I became even more alarmed. I immediately took the letter to my superior officer. He granted me special leave to visit [the woman] I had described as my fiancée.

"The railroad ride from Fallingbostel to Salzburg seemed even longer than it was. The train ground through the countryside as I mentally urged it to go faster. When the Salzburg station came into view, I was first at the exit door. I hitched a ride in a PKW Kübel to the hospital."[2] The Kübelwagen, or Kübel, was a light utility car made by Volkswagen. It had four doors and a soft, convertible top.[3]

Ilse described seeing Bernhard: "The sight of him was intoxicating for me. I couldn't imagine how he had come all the way from northern Germany. I alternately sobbed and laughed at his exited talk. Before the day was out, he had proposed marriage and I had eagerly accepted. My jaundice cleared under the onslaught of my happiness. My supervisor gave us permission to go to Berlin where Bernhard and I completed the forms for marriage including my documentation of approved ancestry. After a few days our application for marriage was awarded."[4] The SS controlled every aspect of a soldier's life, including sexual habits and marriage.[5]

Once the Waffen SS gave its permission for marriage, it also gave the couple its blessing. This meant leave and transportation for the bride and groom and a honeymoon at government expense. Bernhard explained his marriage and honeymoon: "We were married in Ilse's hometown of Tilset, East Prussia, in her family's residence on November 21, 1942. My parents had made the journey to Tilset and both families enjoyed a traditional Lutheran ceremony and reception. From Tilset we took the train to Vienna to spend a week-long exile from war and worries. On our first night in the city, the air-raid alarms sounded and we had to sandwich ourselves between an elderly man and wife in a shelter. The gray-haired man and woman gushed with good cheer when they learned that their elbow-neighbors were newlyweds. Married life was a world away from my normal routine. We spent most of our time talking of trivialities and family. We spent quiet hours planning postwar vacations in the Alps and drawing mental pictures of where we would live after the war. At last Ilse departed for Salzburg and I returned to Fallingbostel where I was promoted to technical sergeant. My comrades hoisted a few beers on my promotion and I couldn't wait to write a letter to Ilse explaining our good fortune. I became a father on February 13, 1943. My son was born in Tilset, where Ilse had returned after being released from her nursing responsibilities. Ilse named our son Volker Bernd Westerhoff."[6]

A new Waffen SS panzer corps was being formed. It would have two panzer divisions, the 9th and 10th. Major General (Gruppenführer) Paul Hausser, one of the most experienced senior officers of the Waffen SS, was to be the panzer corps commander.[7] Experienced soldiers whose duty it would be to train recruits were drawn from existing Waffen SS units. Bernhard Westerhoff saw an opportunity. "I was transferred on February 23, 1943, to the new 10th Waffen SS Panzergrenadier Division. Two days later I was on a train for Würzburg where I learned the theory, mechanics and tactics of tank warfare. At the end of my training on the Panzer IV, I received an entry into my official record that I was qualified to be a tank commander."[8]

Ernst Storch also read the announcement of a new Waffen SS division being formed in France. He said, "I had accompanied my parents on several trips to France and had always been fond of the people. I completed the request form for the transfer and was surprised by the speed of acceptance. I traveled to southern France and there was assigned as motorcycle messenger for the 6th Company of the 10th Regiment, 10th Waffen SS Panzergrenadier Division."[9]

In America, the 12th Armored Division was also being established. In the spring of 1942, Lieutenant General McNair, commanding all Army ground forces, had authorized the new armored division. The division was formed at Camp Campbell, on the Tennessee-Kentucky border, with a cadre of officers and enlisted men drawn from other units. Its first commanding officer was Major General Carlos Brewer, who was an experienced and dedicated officer. He organized his division and set up a training program that initially consisted of military courtesy, discipline, sanitation, first aid and drill. The training emphasized physical stamina with seemingly endless endurance marches. Each man was assigned a specialization in addition to his primary duty. For example, one might be an infantryman with a specialization as a member of a mortar team or an assistant driver/mechanic for a half-track personnel carrier. Many of the original cadre of non-commissioned officers came from the 2nd Cavalry Division, which was disbanded.[10]

American divisions that relied upon horse-drawn transportation were not only used in the First World War, but were integral parts of the Army's structure up to and including the first part of the Second World War. The 2nd Cavalry Division included regiments of horse-drawn transportation supported by scout cars, jeeps and motorcycles. These regiments contained African-American units making the 2nd Cavalry Division one of the first divisions to be racially mixed. In the latter months of the Second World War the 12th Armored Division also contained units of African-American soldiers who proved themselves in battle. The concept of a horse-mounted attack or reconnaissance unit was displaced by the advance of mechanized vehicles. German forces used horse transportation throughout the war; however, no American horse regiment or division saw combat in the Second World War. The Army deactivated the 2nd Cavalry Division while it was located in Oran, North Africa. Accordingly, its non-commissioned officers were dispersed to other units. Since the 12th Armored Division was being formed in the spring of 1944 it became the recipient of many experienced 2nd Cavalry soldiers. These men would become the cadre of trainers for the ASTP transferees into the 12th Armored Division.

4

German POWs and the Frundsberg Division, June 1943

The U.S. Army had a need for impressive-looking men to guard the thousands of German prisoners of war (POWs) who were expected to begin streaming into New York and other ports on the eastern seaboard. With scant food, little ammunition and no protection from the scorching Tunisian sun, the Germans and Italians of the Afrika Korps had surrendered on May 12, 1943. After their surrender they waited in huge barbed-wire holding pens staked out on the North African sands near Oran.[1]

By June 1945 more than 425,000 Axis POWs, including about 371,000 Germans, were housed in more than 650 POW camps across the United States. These were divided into 125 main camps with 425 branch camps. One of the largest was Camp Hearne, Texas, where 4,800 prisoners were housed.[2]

The provost marshal general, the United States Army and the U.S. government established its policy of prisoner-of-war treatment from the Geneva Convention. Those captured early were known as Afrikaner, veterans of the Afrika Korps. When the POW program began in 1942, only 36 military escort companies with about 325 men per company had been used. But with the decision to accept 50,000 POWs from the British, the Provost Marshal General immediately requested the activation of an additional 32 military police companies to bring the ratio of guards to prisoners to one American guard company per every 1,000 prisoners, or one guard for every three prisoners. This ratio was quickly reduced to about one guard for every ten prisoners as the influx continued. Camps were built in nearly every state, from Maine to Florida to California and the Northwest. Many were attached to regular Army training camps such as Camps Chaffee, and Robinson, and Fort Ord, California. Ships of every character had been pressed into service as troop carriers for American and Canadian soldiers heading to England. Loaded on the eastbound voyage, they were empty on the return trip to the United States and Canada. It was a natural outcome of this system that the many prisoners of war should be transported to the U.S. on these otherwise empty ships. The ships were modified somewhat for these trips, with access to decks prevented by barbed wire. Crossing the Atlantic was uncomfortable for the prisoners due to lack of space, ventilation and exercise. They landed at Camp Shanks, New York, and Norfolk, Virginia, and there boarded trains for their final destination.[3]

While other young men had gone off to foreign countries to fight the Axis powers,

Robert Arrasmith had turned in his boxing gloves in favor of going to military police school. There he had learned the rudiments of police work and control of war prisoners. He described his new duties: "I had been told early on that I was to be assigned to duty as a guard for the thousands of German Afrika Korps prisoners to be brought into New York on returning troopships.

"After completing Military Police School the Army sent me to New Jersey, where I was told that I was to wait for the next convoy, which would bring the hard-core of Nazi fanatics. My job would be to escort these Germans from New York directly to prisoner-of-war camps. While awaiting the arrival of the Germans, I spent two weeks in New York performing duties as an MP. I walked the busy streets with a fellow military police soldier. With polished boots, armband and nightstick I tried to look imposing. The fact that I was, in reality, just a farm boy was kept hidden by my intentional scowl. Sometimes I was called upon to quell raucous behavior of drunken sailors. I seldom had to use force. I relied upon my farm-developed muscles. I found that by simply lifting a disorderly sailor off the floor and allowing the offender to swing by the shoulders, I could temper the man's aggression.

"When the ships arrived in New York, I was lined up with the other MPs. We were ordered to off-load the prisoners and march them onto buses. The debarkation was deliberately timed to take place around midnight. I was told this reduced the possibility of friction between curious civilians and the prisoners. I found both Germans and Italians to be obedient and respectful. After hounding drunken sailors it was a welcome change.

"The prisoners boarded buses with black-painted windows. We traveled to New Jersey where we transferred the prisoners to trains. Strangely enough, the trains' windows were clear, peacetime glass. The dim-out of the eastern seaboard was duplicated by the train, which allowed only two low-wattage bulbs per car. I watched the prisoners cup their hands and press their faces to the windows. They couldn't see much, but their whispers registered an excitement to see America for the first time. A few didn't condescend to look at the country of their enemy. They sat erect, staring straight ahead in the hope that others would follow their example. Few did. Those must have been the die-hard Nazis.

"There were two guards at each end of every railroad car as well as two roaming guards to handle any unexpected problems. The prisoners sat two to a seat exactly as if they had paid full fare. We guards had M-1 rifles cradled in one arm while the other arm manipulated cigarettes and matches. When the smoke wafted to the Germans they looked longingly at us. We had been warned not to interact with the Germans, but it was difficult not to be friendly. I smiled, but the faces of the other guards were resolute.

"The train slowed in mid-morning. We were somewhere in Pennsylvania. The rolling hills were green in summer 1943 and leaves of poplar trees shimmered in the hot wind. It reminded me of home. Long white fences surrounded cows in pastures and curtains in open farmhouse windows waved in the breeze. I wished I was back on the farm. It must have been a scene of envy for those Germans. They seemed enraptured by the American countryside. It was an image of peace, an image they must have remembered before the war. Some of the Germans talked, but most seemed lost in thought.

"The train halted on a little-used siding and we allowed the prisoners to detrain and relieve themselves in the brush along the railroad bed. I expected trouble, but the Germans jumped into a double rank at my command. They took their seats on the train without comment. All seemed to be going well and I began to relax. My fellow guards broke down and shared their cigarettes with grateful prisoners who smiled and gestured their thanks. By the time the train approached its destination, I saw the enemy from a different perspective than what I had been taught. I discovered that the Germans were not much different than me. They wore a different uniform, but pictures in their wallets of family and loved ones told a story of simple guys who were soldiers.

"On my third trip from New York to the west I became an old hand at my job of escorting Germans across America. I spoke not one word of German, but some of the prisoners spoke English and they were keen to know about America. I considered myself the Army's official tour guide for German prisoners of war. Actually, it was a toss-up as to who knew more about American geography, but I never told the Germans that I was really just a kid from a farm. I never contemplated what I'd do if the Germans wanted to escape. They seemed content with their lot and took every opportunity to sing their lusty folk songs. I thought that it was a strange war that caused these amiable men to kill Americans.

"I noticed that the Germans were very good at marching. They seemed to take marching and all that went with it very seriously. I wasn't used to giving orders. I often had to line my prisoners up or march them from here to there. I found that my gentlest suggestion was like the trigger of a cannon. I would move my finger up and down to indicate a desire for the men to form into ranks. They would jump into the most military-like ranks where they would stand rigidly until I again moved my finger for them to relax a bit.

"On one journey the train stopped at a small town where American girls handed the prisoners sandwiches and coffee through open windows. I never knew if the girls' friendliness came from a misconception that the Germans were American soldiers or was simply an enthralled reaction to the smiling faces and outstretched hands. They didn't seem to take notice of the Germans' gratitude expressed as *Danke schön* rather than 'Thank you.' By the time the train reached its destination there was hardly a German who didn't want to settle down to a postwar peace in the very spot they then occupied.

"I was told that when the Germans were in prison camps they were allowed to work in the fields and packing houses. I guess some caused trouble and wanted to escape, but most lived from day to day waiting for the war to end.

"The Army eventually realized that as long as the prisoners were doing so well under such minimal supervision it might as well transfer me to a more productive job. I viewed the transfer with a certain amount of anxiety because I had never really been a soldier."[4]

While some Germans ended their military careers in American prisoner-of-war camps, other Germans in Europe took their place as the Nazi war machine continued to expand its forces. In France during the spring and summer of 1943, the 10th Waffen SS Panzergrenadier Division was beginning its training. Its first commanding officer was General (Oberstgruppenführer) Lothar Debes, who was relieved on November 15, 1943, by General Karl von Treuenfeld. Commanding the 10th Regiment was Lieutenant Colonel (Obersturmbannführer) Otto Pätsch. Captain Leopold Franke was 6th Company commanding officer.[5] Second Lieutenant (Untersturmführer) Hans Quandel was second in command and Master Sergeant Edmund Erhard was in charge of Bernhard's platoon. The heat in southern France in July and August wasn't conducive to the constant training. Westerhoff recorded the difficulties involved: "The summer fields provided fresh fruit and the men had their fill of melons, grapes and oranges. Soldiers were often restricted in their diet to bread, cheese and wurst. The sudden change to fruit in such abundance had the predictable result. Extra latrines had to be built under the supervision of Sergeant (Unterscharführer) Utsch who was responsible for sanitation. In fact, the problem became so acute that a permanent job of 'latrine kommando' was established where a designated man inspected the latrines on an hourly basis to make sure they didn't overflow. He was stuck out there by himself with his head down, peering into dark matter that repulsed the bravest of men. Three other men were kept busy digging fresh latrines. None of these jobs was appetizing and each was reserved as motivation to work hard, learning the jobs of a tank crew member. Those who slacked were assigned as latrine-digging orderlies. These outcasts worked hard because they knew that if they were singled out by Utsch they might wind up as latrine kommando, the lowest of the low jobs.

"In June 1943 we were in Angoulême in southern France. During times of relaxation we sergeants talked of our tank training and of the merits of one tank over another. When I wrote to Ilse I was almost ashamed of my comfortable lifestyle when so much serious fighting was going on in the east. I told her of my daily routine and she told me of our baby son and of her life in Tilset.

"On July 16, we moved to Souprosse, in southern France. The company had just settled into its new encampment when a British bomber appeared overhead. Its engines were smoking and sputtering. I watched the plane as it dove toward the earth. The men's eyes were intent on the doomed aircraft when several parachutes opened. Privates First Class [Oberschütze] Willi Helm and Herbert Wrobel volunteered to take a PKW and go looking for the crew. I gave them permission and off the men went, bouncing down the road in anticipation of bringing some British airmen back to our camp. The two men were gone for two days and Leo Franke was taking it out on me. I assigned Privates First Class Ernst Storch and Albert Schehle to conduct a search for the two missing soldiers. They too sped off down the same road taken by Helm and Wrobel. Another full day passed before the four Frundsbergers presented themselves to the company commander sans prisoners."[6]

The story was recorded in Westerhoff's journal: "It took an hour for the men's story to come out. Helm and Wrobel had not been able to locate any fliers, but had located a farmer's smokehouse. Looking inside, they had found a dozen hams curing and aging while hanging from the rafters. Helm and Wrobel discussed the situation and drew the conclusion that a portion of the hams should be donated to the war effort. For one full day the two men gorged themselves on the best ham in France. When they couldn't eat another piece, they discussed the best way to cover their absence. They agreed to offer two hams to the company's Chief Cook, Ludwig Reisenberger, as a peace gesture. When Storch and Schehle went hunting for the two delinquent men, they saw the PKW and entered the smoke-shed with good intent to bring the men back to the camp. Upon listening to Helm's explanation of their inability to resist the luscious hams, Storch and Schehle decided to join them. When they too had eaten their fill, Schehle suggested that it would be wise to get back to the company as soon as possible. Leo Franke wasn't amused by the story. Whether or not the company commander had decided to make an example of the four young men wasn't known, but Storch and his comrade Schehle received the same punishment as the two culprits who had perpetrated the original theft."[7]

Ernst Storch related the story in his own words: "I remembered my father's insistence on truthfulness. I had crossed the line and was willing to take whatever the company commander could hand out. Franke announced the punishment to all in ranks. This would be a lesson for 6th Company. The four Frundsbergers would perform strenuous calisthenics while wearing gas masks. Two hours of punishment each morning for four days. The first two hours were nightmarish. With [our] arms flailing and legs jumping, the warm sun heated our work uniforms. Perspiration built inside the gas masks. The glass visors fogged. Condensation clogged the intake. I fought for every breath. I felt like I was drowning as I kept up the drill. When the two hours ended on the first morning and I ripped off my gas mask, I felt near death. The worst part of the punishment was the terror of knowing that the drill would be repeated the next morning, the next and the next. Comrades sympathized, but one thing was clear — Leo Franke wouldn't tolerate pranks involving theft of civilian property. If he had intended to make a point he certainly had achieved his purpose. The escapade came to be known as 'The Great Souprosse Ham Attack,' and it was the last of such indiscretions."[8]

Ernst Storch spoke of his assignment as milk delivery boy: "I had been assigned to 6th Company, but my duties as messenger didn't take me into contact with Bernhard Westerhoff until that Christmas Eve when he explained the dairy incident. From my perspective the incident was a tragedy. Each messenger in 6th Company was assigned his own motorcycle, and I took pride in my machine. I cleaned and polished it at every opportunity. I reached between small parts and wound a rag around the drive shaft to make sure all the hard-to-get-at parts were clean. After I mastered my motorcycle and was proud of my job, the motorcycle was taken back. I was crestfallen and respectfully asked my superior, Sergeant Fritz Stief, why I had been deprived of my messenger duty. The explanation was slow and painful. It was explained that I was to remain as messenger, but my duty would be to deliver fresh milk to the platoons of 6th Company which were close to the dairy. I was to pick up the milk at the local dairy and make the rounds on a daily basis. I asked how I was to make these deliveries, since a motorcycle didn't seem likely. Stief held a straight face and said that I was to make the deliveries using a donkey and cart. He said I was to lead the donkey and cart on a route determined by Chief Cook Reisenberger. Stief added insult by calling the miserable job 'Donkey Führer.' I was dejected, but I determined that I would make the best of a bad lot. The next morning I faced my donkey. The summers working with animals on farms outside Vienna gave me confidence. I was not intimidated by the defiant look on the donkey's face. I made it clear to the donkey who was to be in charge. I shouted my rage into the animal's large ears. The donkey seemed indifferent to my invectives, but I felt better for having given someone a piece of my mind. That first morning I pulled the donkey along a road to my first stop. The milk sloshed in metal cans as the two-wheeled cart bounced over ruts in unpaved roads. After the first day of my duties, I discovered that the men of 6th Company actually envied me for my cushy job. In addition, they were appreciative of the prompt deliveries and offered me cigarettes and chocolate for extra rations of milk. After a week on the job, I fell into a comfortable routine of rising, eating breakfast, walking to the dairy and having a second breakfast with the dairy's family. This included two young, blossoming French sisters who took upon themselves the task of teaching me the French language. My school French quickly expanded to conversational quality and after a month of this leisurely routine, I hoped that the war would pass me by. Sergeant Stief thought I had turned the milk delivery job into a milk cartel. I knew nothing of the dairy other than my French lessons and breakfast. How was I to know that some sergeant had a yen for the senior dairy maid? I guess he filled the vacuum created when her husband had been taken prisoner at the fall of France. Stief abruptly separated me from my donkey, from my female friends, from my second breakfasts and from my daily milk rounds. In consideration, I was given a new motorcycle and a new rag. It was a Puch 250, a single-cylinder, light, single-seat motorcycle. With four speeds, hand clutch, and foot shift, the motorcycle could speed up to eighty-five miles per hour, though a rider would be foolish to do so. The dairy debacle's fallout reached Bernhard since he had been assigned as the company's new sergeant-major. And that's how he came to pour wine for me at the Christmas Eve celebration in Le Bec Hellouin."[9]

5

Camp Barkeley and Russian-Occupied Poland, April 1944

In May 1943 Charlie Fitts lined up at the Meridian, Mississippi, bus station with other young men who also had graduated from high school that spring. Charlie recounted how the Army changed his life: "As I boarded the bus my name was checked off by a man in uniform who looked as anxious as I. My family waved good-bye while I searched for a seat. At Fort McClellan, Alabama, I went through thirteen weeks of basic infantry training. What had seemed as a noble adventure in the beginning turned out to be a daily struggle for survival. The key, I learned quickly, was never to speak unless spoken to and never to expend an ounce of energy unless it was demanded by the sergeant. I learned never to stand when I could sit and never to sit when I could lie down. The mental challenge was minimal, but the Army funneled its recruits through a schedule of physical brutality. As I stood at attention in ranks, I learned to play mental games while staring straight ahead. Tricks like that would serve me well later on. I accepted my new life without much complaint and, toward the end of basic training, noticed that my body had become hard and fit.

"Post-basic training included a lot of classroom work. One series of lectures was on leadership. I considered myself barely a soldier and couldn't see how I would ever do anything except follow orders. However, I thought the subject matter was interesting. During leadership training I and my fellow soldiers were told that we would all go into the Army Specialized Training Program. I asked one of my buddies and learned that ASTP was a program designed to turn qualified enlisted men into officers. I guess I did well on some of the tests we had taken back at Fort McClellan. I looked upon the turn of events with mixed feelings. On the one hand, I would be going back to school and I had had enough of school. On the other hand, the school was the famous Texas Agricultural and Mechanical College. This was an opportunity that couldn't be ignored. I knew my parents would want this.

"I boarded another bus, this time bound for Texas. At the end of the Army's college program we would be officers, and this had a certain appeal. I imagined how the gossipy old men at Greenhagen's hardware store would look up to me when I came back to Meridian in my handsome officer's uniform. So, in College Park, Texas, I buckled down to academics in the fall of 1943. I was determined to excel in the engineering curriculum. It couldn't be denied that Texas A&M was much more difficult than Meridian High School, but academics had always come easy to me. I attacked the tough course work by nightly study from seven to ten.

"At this point in the war, it became obvious to the Army that it had been a little late in establishing its officer training program. Accordingly, in February of 1944, it ended the ASTP, and we students were notified of our downgraded future. We were to be dispersed to bases and units throughout the country and would serve out our time in the military as enlisted men. Just when I was convinced that I would come out of that war with a real education, the Army pulled a fast one. I was destined to do my duty as a private first class. Of course, I was disappointed, but I shrugged my shoulders and resolved to do my best in whatever capacity the Army might find for me."[1]

George Hatt had continued to pursue his studies and military training at Texas Tech while the Army took stock of its officer training program. What it needed in the spring of 1944 were men who could carry a rifle. Both Charlie Fitts and George Hatt were swept up into the Army's new manpower priority. George tells of how, after years of reserve military training, he was to serve as a private first class: "In March of 1944 I felt really let down. I and my fellow ASTP friends grumbled and moaned, but there was nothing we could do. The Army had double-crossed us and that was that. The day after the fall of the ax, lists of names were posted at the commandant's office in the Texas Tech ASTP Admin Office. They were alphabetically arranged and each man's name was followed by the name of an Army facility. I looked halfway down the list and found that I and a number of other Texas Tech men had been assigned to Camp Barkeley, near Abilene, Texas. We were to be a part of the newly formed 12th Armored Division."[2]

Camp Barkeley was named after David Barkley, a First World War hero, but somehow the name acquired an extra "e." It was constructed in early 1941 and was the training center for many men before the camp was allocated to the 12th Armored Division. The division consisted of tank battalions, armored infantry battalions, artillery units, engineer units and various staff. The armored infantry battalions were the 17th Armored Infantry Battalion (AIB), the 66th AIB and the 56th AIB. Each of these had about 1,000 men. After some transfers of battalions to other divisions during the formative period of the division, the tank components were the 23rd Tank Battalion, the 43rd Tank Battalion and the 714th Tank Battalion, which had been transferred and then returned to the division. The original regimental-type organization was dropped in favor of battalions operating under combat commands. Major equipment included 186 medium Sherman tanks, 77 light Stuart tanks, 54 self-propelled 105-millimeter howitzers and 501 half-track armored personnel carriers. There were also 3 field artillery battalions, the 493rd, 494th and 495th as well as the 82nd Armored Medical Battalion and the 152 Armored Signal Company. These were augmented by an armored reconnaissance battalion and an armored engineer battalion.

James Francis described the influx of ASTP men: "In April and May 1944, 1300 GI's from the disbanded Army Specialized Training Program (ASTP) joined the 12th. These were ex–college students, all privates and privates first class, most of whom had never seen a tank or any other armored vehicle, so they were given jobs where they could do the least damage while learning what was to be expected of them. This brought the division strength up to 11,000 men."[3]

George Hatt continued his narrative: "The train to Camp Barkeley was slow and uncomfortable. It deposited me, in my private first class uniform, on a siding that required a mile's march to the receiving center. While I marched in route step with my Texas Tech comrades I looked at the barren landscape. The fact that I might be thrown in with men who were just off the street meant that I would be in for more basic training. I shuddered to think that this would be a repeat of what I had experienced over the past six and half years in several reserve training programs of the Army.

"The receiving center was staffed by young officers who devoted themselves to finding job slots that would take advantage of each man's particular talents. I sat in a folding steel chair as I listened to the officer behind the desk explain how the Army was going to take care of me. Taking the officer at his word, I went into some length to detail my long association with the Army. I emphasized my three and a half years of engineering education. The officer asked me what I wanted to do in the 12th Armored Division. I eagerly replied that the Army should take advantage of my engineering knowledge. The officer seemed impressed by my explanation and left his desk to consult another officer on how the Army could capitalize on my unique capabilities. He returned and announced that he had found the perfect job. I was to be first echelon mechanic on a half-track. I was speechless. I had only a vague idea what a half-track was and I wasn't sure of what 'first echelon' meant. Furthermore, I really didn't know much about auto mechanics. True, I had once helped my father work on an inboard motor for the family's boat, but that hardly qualified me as a mechanic. Nevertheless, I accepted the assignment since I had descended so low in the Army's hierarchy that I couldn't sink any lower. To top it off, the first echelon mechanic job turned out to be a rifleman in a company of the 17th Armored Infantry Battalion with added responsibility as an infantry squad's half-track assistant driver. My military career had taken a nose-dive from commissioned officer to foot slogger."[4]

The division put out a weekly newspaper. It was called the *Hellcat News* in tribute to the division's adopted name. An article appeared describing the classification process that George Hatt had just endured: "March 30, 1944. Approximately 1,300 former ASTP men were welcomed into the 12th Armored Division last Saturday by the Hellcat commander, Maj. Gen. Carlos Brewer. The former ASTP students were classified immediately after they began arriving here last week, the division classification section working day and night until the task was completed."[5]

There was no bright lining to the dark cloud of Camp Barkeley insofar as George Hatt was concerned. He described his dismal life in the following terms: "It didn't take long for me to learn that my prior orientation to the Army via a college curriculum fell far short of what real soldiering was all about. In college I had learned about military science from the lofty perch of a textbook. Camp Barkeley, in the spring of 1944, taught me that soldiering was a daily war against wind, dust, insufferable heat and insects. Creatures like scorpions and snakes were apt to make their homes in tent and bedding. I learned to run, crouch and lie on sand-covered, hard-pan earth. I put up with grit in my clothing, boots, cot and food. Camp Barkeley's blazing sun, dust and bugs conspired to melt a man into the Army's common denominator of infantryman. In my continual condition of fatigue from the daily grind of calisthenics, drilling and marching, I was tempted to surrender to whatever force that had done this to me. And I would have, were it not for a squad leader, Staff Sergeant Charlie Ruma of St. Louis, who had ultimate and unassailable authority over my life. Sergeant Ruma had no patience for a slovenly barracks, cot, duffel bag or uniform. It was his duty to prod his men never to retreat from their losing battle against the elements.

"Finally, I accepted living in tar-paper barracks with cots and thin, lumpy mattresses. I learned that I was to be a mortarman. This could theoretically have set me apart from other soldiers, but my status as half-track mechanic/assistant driver and member of a mortar squad couldn't disguise the reality of carrying a rifle wherever I went. I liked to sleep, but the Army's sergeants devoted a great deal of time to keeping me awake. I found that I could sleep while lying under a half-track with arms raised and holding a grease gun. It was an awkward rest, but it was better than nothing.

"Having been issued an M-1 Garand rifle, I was taught to make it an extension of my body. The Army looked upon the weapon's allocation as a loan. It went to great extremes to ensure that as long as I possessed the M-1, I would maintain it in accordance with the Army's standards. I could clean it, oil it, shine it, take it apart, assemble it while blindfolded and inspect each part for wear and cleanliness. I carried it wherever I went while on duty. This included field exercises during which the rifle became dust-filled and grimy. The oil that lubricated my rifle acted like a magnet for Texas' powdery dust. And since the platoon sergeant had an obsession about how clean I kept my rifle, cleaning it became a daily evening chore that competed with my meager sleep.

"Above the mess hall was a sign that proclaimed, 'A good soldier is a man who wants to be a good soldier.' I took the sign seriously. I dedicated myself to it. It wasn't enough to just slide by. Somewhere in my roots I had acquired the habit of giving whatever I did my very best. One day Sergeant Ruma told me I was an asset to the platoon. After that I began to take pride in being a good soldier. If there was a limiting factor in what I could achieve at Camp Barkeley it lay only in the stamina it took to keep going under conditions that were designed to test the toughest of men."[6]

George Hatt's memory of Camp Barkeley was shared by others. "Camp Barkeley was not a very hospitable place. It was unbearably hot in the summer with constant winds that blew sage and gritty sand along hard-pan terrain. In addition, armadillos, rattlesnakes, skunks, mesquite and prickly pear cactus made the pace of physical exercise all the more difficult."[7]

James Francis of the 23rd Tank Battalion wrote, "In summer the temperatures at Camp Barkeley were in the hundreds. After several hours in the blazing sun, the armor plate on the tanks got hot enough to fry eggs. In addition, the tanks threw up clouds of dry red dust when moving. The dust penetrated every tank in the column except the lead tank. Sweaty faces and bodies were soon covered with a muddy layer of grit. Fatigue uniforms for the tankers at Camp Barkeley stank from a combination of grease, oil, dirt and sweat. The tankers boiled them in huge pots of water to which was added a mixture of harsh lye soap and gasoline. The pot was stirred with a broom handle. Another pot of boiling water served as a rinse."[8]

Private First Class Andy Woods, also in the 23rd, had similar memories: "The heat, wind and dust at Camp Barkeley was pervasive. The windows in the barracks had to be left open at night because of the heat. This meant we were all victims of the dust riding on the constant wind. Since we slept only in skivvies, when we were awakened in the morning we would be covered in off-white dust. Our bunks were also white except for outlines of our bodies which remained brown, the color of our bunk cover."[9]

Like George Hatt, Jim Francis and Andy Woods, Charlie Fitts had been assigned to the 12th Armored Division. Charlie described his impressions: "I got off the train, marched to Camp Barkeley and was herded into an auditorium along with the others from Texas

A&M University. We saw a training film that introduced us to the 12th Armored Division.

"In the months ahead I withered under the Texas sun as the Army prepared me to be a competent infantryman. I listened to my company commander [urge] his men to greater heights of rugged soldiering. I had already been through basic training at Fort McClellan, but here I was once again taking the insults of my platoon sergeant, who left no stone unturned to mold our young minds into rock-hard numbness. And I accepted the admonishments of my squad leader, who knew little more than I about the vagaries of United States Army life. The old-timers who knew the routine contemptuously viewed us ASTP recruits as pampered college boys. I suffered this brand with the rest of the ASTP soldiers, even though I had less than a semester of college.

"I was in the 2nd Platoon of C Company in the 66th Armored Infantry Battalion. A platoon was made of five squads: three rifle squads, a machine-gun squad and a mortar squad. Having a keen eye from my boyhood squirrel hunting, I became the mortar squad's gunner. This may have struck a prestigious note in my ego, but I, along with the rest of my mortar squad buddies, were, most of the time, in close proximity to the ground. The infantryman was forced to 'hit the dirt' when hypothetically fired upon, which was when a sergeant called out the evil words. This meant that I spent a great deal of time lying flat on the hot, arid ground. I didn't particularly mind lying down, since every opportunity to rest was gratefully received, but I never got rid of the thought that a scorpion or snake might attack me when I was so immobilized. Finally we were ready for the big show. We looked forward to the coming maneuvers in the field where we intended to put what we had learned into practice."[10]

Private First Class Andrew F. Woods, gunner in the Guitteau Sherman tank during the January 17 attack on Herrlisheim and loader in the Vickless Sherman tank after January 21, 1945 (Woods collection).

The final phase of training consisted of exercises in the field with combined units. These day and night training episodes culminated in pitting one division against another in a final maneuver that would test the fighting competence of each battalion, company, squad and soldier. It was to be the final test of competency and combat readiness for the 12th Armored Division, but the exercise was marred by the unexpected. James Francis of the 23rd Tank Battalion described what happened: "While we were out in the field, Corps Headquarters conducted an inspection of our barracks and did not like what they saw. The field test was abruptly halted and the men returned to sweep and scrub for many hours through the night. There were a lot of unhappy soldiers."[11] The men believed they were ready, but their confidence was shaken by this incident.

George Hatt described the culmination of the field exercise: "We were satisfied that we had proven ourselves. Now it was time for the grandstand review. Camp Barkeley's training finale was passing in review. Every soldier qualified to leave for overseas combat duty assembled with his buddies in the company street. Each company then marched smartly to the assigned places at the parade ground. I lined up in my creased uniform, stood at attention and marched in the 17th Armored Infantry Battalion to the sound of the division's band. The line of march started with the 92nd Cavalry Reconnaissance Squadron, followed by the 17th, 56th and 66th Armored Infantry Battalions. Strung out behind these were the three tank battalions, service units, an armored engineer unit, armored field artillery units, medical units, combat command units, and headquarters units. The commanding officer, Major General Carlos Brewer, looked proud in his many medals as he stood on the reviewing stand. He saluted every time the colors passed before him, which was often. His arm jabbed the air in a flurry of respectful reflexes for the flag of his country."[12]

There were a few days off, particularly when the men waited to be deployed. Abilene was the only nearby town which afforded soldiers a chance to relate to civilians. On weekends and evenings soldiers with passes took the camp bus into town for what entertainment it offered. It was a morally upright community, and the men ate hamburgers and watched movies in an air-conditioned theater.[13]

George Hatt remembered Abilene: "We waited for the Army's next move, and while waiting were allowed to visit the town of Abilene. The bus ride into town was not long and I looked out the window at the hot, dry landscape. I blended in with the thousands of other GIs who ambled the main street of the cowtown of yesteryear. We normally wound up in a theater that had a canvas hanging from its marquee. It advertised the theater's best asset, air conditioning. It was late summer and the Texas heat remained oppressive. We watched a newsreel on the fighting in Normandy. The outdated newsreel showed Americans taking Cherbourg in June and General von Schlieben looking straight and haughty in his long black leather coat standing as a prisoner before ragged American soldiers. But British general Montgomery's forces had been stopped by two Waffen SS divisions between the Odon and Orne rivers. On our way back to Camp Barkeley one of the men in my squad wondered aloud about the German Army. He offered his opinion that its reputation was probably overblown and that Patton would be in Germany before the 12th had a chance to fight. We all nodded our heads in agreement."[14]

Private First Class Andrew F. Woods had been assigned to Sherman medium tanks upon his arrival at Camp Barkeley. Like many others he had been a victim of the ASTP program, but unlike others he had an impressive background in tanks before ASTP. Andy had joined the Army in October of 1942 and was immediately sent to the 11th Armored Division at Camp Polk, Louisiana. He endured 6 weeks of basic training, then was assigned to Tank Maintenance School where he learned the design and function of the Grant tank. When the new M-4 Sherman tanks came into the Army, he learned about them as well. The company bulletin board carried a notice of opportunity for the ASTP, and Andy took several tests, all of which placed him at the top of the acceptance list.

In May of 1943 Andy had gone to Baton Rouge, Louisiana, to attend Louisiana State University. He was only there for a short time before the program was shifted to Texas A&M University, at College Park, Texas, where he took a tough engineering curriculum. It lasted only one semester. He was sent to Camp Barkeley where the officers could not ignore his experience in tanks. In a letter of November 2, 2007, he described his introduction to Camp Barkeley. "I had been trained in medium tanks, and so it was natural that I should be assigned to a tank battalion with appropriate training. Many of the old timers had come from the cavalry and they considered anyone who had not done so as unworthy. On top of that, some of us had come from ASTP and that branded us an even lower subspecies. The better we did on tests the lower our status. We became known as 'Quiz Kids,' after a popular radio show of the time. Since we had lived the cushy life, according to our sergeants, it was only right that we should get the lousiest jobs to be handed out.

"I sort of rolled with the punches. After all, they were partially right. We had had it pretty good at Texas A&M, even if it had been for such a short time.

"In September of 1944 we all boarded trains and headed for Camp Shanks. That was the end of Camp Barkeley and the beginning of some real soldiering in tanks."[15]

While the 12th Armored Division completed its training in late August of 1944, the Frundsberg's training had ended five months earlier, in March. The II Waffen SS Panzer Corps was ready for combat.[16] On March 24, General Alfred Jodl at Oberkommando der Wehrmacht (OKW) wrote in his official war diary, "The 349th Infantry Division continues to suffer heavy losses due to overwhelming Soviet strength. Accordingly, it has been ordered to retire for refit. The II Waffen SS Panzer Corps with its two divisions are immediately ordered to the eastern front. It is authorized to use all available rail transport."[17] Fast-moving events in Russian-occupied southeastern Poland changed the II Waffen SS Panzer Corps' orders while the divisions were in transport. General Zeitzler conveyed the OKW's intent that the corps was to remain on the eastern front.[18] During March the Russians gained ground toward Germany. Williamson wrote, "Hitler agreed to allow the II Waffen SS Panzer Corps, which consisted of the elite 9th and 10th Waffen SS Panzer Divisions, to be rushed to the Eastern Front. These two divisions, though untried in battle, were elite units of the highest standard. They were manned primarily by native Germans and equipped and trained to a high level. The units were built around a cadre of personnel from tried and tested units, such as Das Reich and Leibstandarte and had been fortunate enough to be allowed a full year of training. The 10th Waffen SS Panzer Division was commanded by General Karl von Treuenfeld."[19] In southeastern Poland, an area which had been occupied in 1939 by the Soviet Union, the II Waffen SS Panzer Corps became a part of the 4th Panzer Army, which had been assigned the task of relieving the hard-pressed 1st Panzer Army.[20]

The division was transported east, toward the fighting in southeast Poland. The Soviets were trying to take Lemberg, 300 miles southeast of Warsaw, and were pushing hard in that direction. They had two Wehrmacht divisions nearly surrounded and it was the job of the II Waffen SS Panzer Corps to extricate them. Upon arrival at Lemberg, Paul Hauser, the corps commander, planned to move his two divisions into attack position with the 9th Hohenstaufen on the left and 10th Frundsberg on the right. The 100th Jaeger Division and 367th Infantry Division would protect the Waffen SS right flank. On April 4 the two divisions approached Halicz and moved over the Dnjestr River.[21]

General von Treuenfeld of the Waffen SS stood at the Podhajace River's edge and examined the order to attack Russian positions in and around Buczacz. His intention was to build a bridgehead over the Strypa River and to attack from there.[22]

The 1st Panzer Army, which included the 10th Waffen SS Panzer Division, was facing the possibility of being surrounded by the Soviet forces. Already, the 22nd Panzergrenadier Division was sending an alarm for help.[23]

The precarious position of the Frundsberg Division was unknown to the division's

General Heinz Harmel, commanding officer, 10th Waffen SS Panzer Division during Operation Northwind (January 1945), in which he was ordered to defend Offendorf and Herrlisheim and to attack Weyersheim (German Military Archives).

tank commanders who, full of confidence, furiously pounded the Soviet T-34 tanks, temporarily holding them in check.

After a month of continuous and heavy fighting the 10th Waffen SS Panzer Division was placed in reserve. It was the end of April 1944, the weather had grown mild, and Bernhard Westerhoff in the 6th Company worked in shirtsleeves to bring the equipment back into shape. While lounging under a large, tent-like camouflage net strung between trees, the men ate their noon meal of stew with meat and vegetables. Captain Horst Klinkmann, the temporary company commander, came to them and announced that General von Treuenfeld had been relieved and that their new division commander would be General Heinz Harmel.[24] Von Preradovich, who edited *Die Generale der Waffen SS*, wrote, "At age twenty-one Heinz Harmel joined the small German Army of 100,000 men allowed under the Versailles Treaty. His first and only assignment was as an assistant cook and dishwasher. After only three months, during infantry training he was injured by a flying splinter of iron. It lodged in his eye and caused him to be discharged. Until 1935 he tried his hand at several jobs, concentrating on physical training. In 1935 his temporary employment as chief of the Army's sports program ended.

"On February 10, 1935, he joined the Verfügungstruppe at the recruiting office in Hamburg. Because of his earlier short stint with the Army and his affiliation with the Army in the physical training department he was assigned as squad leader in the first company of the Germania Regiment. He was given the rank of technical sergeant. During 1936 and 1937 he assumed more and more responsibility in Das Deutschland Regiment to which he had been transferred. Then in 1937 he became an officer with the rank of second lieutenant. At last he was making enough money to support a wife. He was assigned to the Munich area and in April 1937 married Irmgard Müller. He was promoted to Major in 1938 and was assigned to the Der Führer Regiment stationed at Vienna. This was his honeymoon year with enough time to spend with his bride while performing his duties in the newly organized Waffen SS. He ascended through the ranks and served in several units fighting on the Eastern Front. He earned the German Cross in Gold and the Knight's Cross with Oak Leaves and Crossed Swords. In April 1944 Heinz Harmel took command of the 10th Waffen SS Panzer Division. In that same year he was promoted to lieutenant colonel and then to brigadier general [Brigadeführer]. He was commanding officer of the division until April 1945, when he was relieved of command."[25]

Harmel arrived in Lemberg on April 27 and from there sent a message to his subordinate officers that he had relieved von Treuenfeld of command. He was only 37 years old. He was known as the "face of soldiers in the Waffen SS." He had come from the enlisted ranks and so knew the heart of the common soldier. In the Deutschland Regiment he was known as "*der Alte*," the "Old man."[26] Heinz Harmel was not the only soldier in his thirties to command a Waffen SS division. With him were Theodor Wisch,

Karl Ullrich, Joachim Rumohr, Otto Kulm, Fritz Klingenberg, Georg Bochmann and Hugo Krass.[27]

On June 8 OKW ordered the II Waffen SS Panzer Corps to anticipate orders for transfer to Normandy. By June 10 some of the division's staff was already leaving the eastern front for France. On the same day, the entire division began its withdrawal from positions around Buczacz to march back to Lemberg, where trains awaited their transport to France.[28]

On June 11, 1944, Hitler ordered the cancellation of a planned offensive near Kowel on the eastern front and the immediate transfer of the II Waffen SS Panzer Corps to France.[29]

Word came down to the company level that the division was to be transferred to France. The men had known of the Allied landings in Normandy, but had been too busy on their own front to worry much about them. Now they were to return to France to help stem the tide of the advancing enemy. After a short rest the men began loading their division onto flatcars and boxcars.[30]

Bernhard Westerhoff remembered the rail journey: "The train ride from the miserable eastern front back to Germany was an opportunity for rest. We sprawled over seats, aisles and vestibules of every car. We were a far cry from the exuberant young men who had made the trip from France.

"Out the window was Halberstadt, which had been bombed the day before. Smoldering fires still sprang up and the train passed youngsters in Hitler Youth uniforms fighting fires with hoses and axes in a congested railroad yard. My Hitler Youth days had been sports, camping and a zeal for adventure. Now, the boys fought fires as bombs dropped in their midst."[31]

6

Normandy, August 1944

The American soldiers of the 12th Armored Division had learned the basics of war at Camp Barkeley during the summer of 1944, but during that same hot summer the German soldiers of the 10th Waffen SS Panzer Division were fighting a bitter contest against determined Allied forces. The Germans had been caught off guard on June 6 when an Allied armada landed strong forces on the beaches of Normandy. Field Marshal Rommel's immediate reserve, the 21st Panzer Division, was quickly committed. The two other panzer divisions which he controlled were in the wrong place; one was beyond the Seine River, and the other was even farther away, beyond the Somme. The Panzer Lehr Division and the 12th Waffen SS Panzer Division, though both in Normandy, were also at some distance from the battlefield and still under OKW control, which meant in the practical sense that they could be released only with Hitler's permission.[1]

Also out of play but struggling to the scene, the 2nd Waffen SS Panzer Division had begun the long journey from Toulouse, the 17th Waffen SS Panzergrenadier Division had started from south of the Loire and, closer at hand, the 77th Infantry Division had left St. Malo.[2]

Bernhard Westerhoff and the other men of the Frundsberg Division approached the critical area of combat. The men rode on tanks and marched northward through Dreuy in the area of St. Jean, then through Châteauneuf, Digny, La Madeleine, Le Mage and Longny. It was a long march, and during the day the men of 6th Company had to dodge into the woods when Allied planes appeared.[3]

The II Waffen SS Panzer Corps did not arrive in Normandy until the end of June. On reaching the battle area on June 25, both the Hohenstaufen and Frundsberg divisions were fed into the line between Caen and Villers-Bocage. Their arrival was timely, coinciding as it did with Montgomery's Operation "Epsom." This was the British drive to take Caen. The attack opened with massive artillery and naval bombardments, but what initially seemed to be good progress deteriorated quickly into a vicious battle for every meter of ground as the German defenders fought tenaciously to blunt the Allied advance. On June 29 the newly committed II Waffen SS Panzer Corps managed to recapture the critical Hill 112, west of Caen.[4] Between the Odon and Orne Rivers was terrain suited to a strong defensive line. The embankment hedgerows, sunken farm lanes, woods, coppices, stream beds, ditches and strong, stone-built barns and farmhouses which lay beyond the cornfields had been integrated into a barrier nearly five miles deep.[5]

Harmel's orders were to establish positions between the Odon and Orne Rivers with the Hohenstaufen Division on the left. The Frundsberg Division was to prevent the British forces from moving south after they had overrun Caen. He took his units over a bridge at Évrecy-Bach. Once over the Odon he placed his battalions to face northwest in positions southeast of Eterville-Maltot.[6]

The 6th Company assumed positions southeast of Maltot. Bernhard Westerhoff wrote, "It was June 26 and the assigned sector seemed quiet for the moment. We went to work digging our tanks into defensive positions. The Normandy soil was rocky and full of ancient roots, but the morale of the men was high, the food plentiful, and weapons were in abundance. Chief Cook Reisenberger's ingenuity continued to serve the men of 6th Company. He and his assistants scoured the farms and managed to bring pigs and chickens to the field kitchen. The meals were first rate and the men didn't mind all the hard work in preparing their positions.

"Ships at sea periodically sent salvos of shells into the area occupied by 6th Company. The British were shooting wild, but the explosions were earth-shattering. The ground jumped and from the sides of foxholes loose dirt dropped into the men's boots. I had never experienced anything so profound, but I and my comrades hunkered down in a hole we had dug beneath our tank and waited for the barrage to lift. Despite being bounced about in the foxholes we survived surprisingly well. Some even slept through the bombardment, but some of the young replacements were shaken by the violent bursts that caused swimming-pool-size craters.

"Tanks of 6th Company were commanded by different soldiers according to the availability of tanks and number of experienced crewmen. Little, if any, attention was paid to whether or not a tank commander was a noncommissioned officer such as a sergeant or a lower rank commissioned officer such as a second lieutenant. During June and July 1944, the seven tanks of 6th Company were commanded as follows: Lieutenant Theo Hegemann, Technical Sergeant Bernhard Westerhoff, Sergeant Reinhard Seifert, Second Lieutenant Herbert Wenning, Corporal Ludwig Kroells, Corporal Horst Franke, and Corporal Rudi Schwemmlein."[7]

Ernst Storch was informed by an officer that he could turn in his motorcycle since he was being assigned as a tank crew member. He related how he was introduced to tanks: "For a moment I thought that I would be going back to Germany for tank training, but the officer took care of my faulty thinking by adding that I was to be a gunner in 611 tank. I said good-bye to my motorcycle, then walked to the newly organized field kitchen. I ate hot bread, jam and wurst, then peeled a hard-boiled egg and stuffed it into my mouth as I looked for 611 tank. The tanks were scattered about in what looked like a random disposition, but they were all pointed north. Each was buried under foliage and netting.

"I asked a group of crewmen where 611 tank was hidden. They stood in a circle smoking and talking. One pointed to a Panzer IV that looked identical to all the others. Only the number on the turret was different. The cannon barrel was depressed and two men with a long pole were shoving it into the barrel. I watched without asking any questions as I circled the Panzer IV inspecting the tracks. They were wide and heavy. Eight road wheels supported the tracks with two wheels coupled to each of four pivoting leaf-spring suspensions. It looked to me that this huge beast would probably ride like a derailed locomotive. I longed for my motorcycle. Without asking for permission, I climbed up on the engine compartment, lifted the top turret hatch and peered into the dark interior.

"A voice came from within the tank and I saw a body emerging. The young officer said his name was Theo Hegemann, tank commander. I wanted to salute, but Hegemann got down to business by proclaiming me as his new gunner. He immediately started his first lecture with a description of the tank and its mission as a destroyer of Sherman tanks. The lesson pressed on until dark, when the tank commander slapped my shoulder and gave his first formal order, to stop work and eat dinner.

"Hegemann seemed like an amiable soldier who didn't look much older than I, but I knew that the tank commander would expect perfection. It was a little frightening to think that five men in this tank would be depending on me to kill an enemy before the enemy killed all those in this Panzer IV. I certainly had no idea that my job would be almost as important as the tank commander himself. I dedicated myself to not [letting] Hegemann down. At every opportunity during daylight hours I studied manuals and sat in my seat peering through the optical sight. I memorized the weak points of the Sherman so that I could put a shell exactly where I wanted it to land. I knew I was going to have to learn on the job. The first time I would fire this cannon would be in combat. Fortunately, there would be other tanks around me with gunners who knew what they were doing. The more I worked and trained in the Panzer IV the easier it became. I could never say that I loved my new environment, but I found the crowded space strangely accommodating. On the motorcycle I had been alone and hadn't realized how strong human interaction could be. As I learned the technicalities of my new job, I also learned to be a team member. Each man in the tank was part of a smoothly functioning unit. Commands from Hegemann were instantly put into action. I learned to train and elevate the gun to the position dictated by the tank commander by cranking two well-balanced wheels. Each had a full hand grip, and one grip had a trigger to fire the cannon. On the floor plate was a button for the coaxial machine gun. The more I practiced, the faster the turret moved and stopped on the target. With eye to the scope I could judge range and match it to the range coming from Hegemann."[8]

Perrett wrote, "Elevation of the Panzer IV main and co-axial armament was by means of a hand wheel operated with the gunner's left hand. Traverse could be either manual or powered, and a selector lever switch could be turned to whichever system was required. The traversing hand wheel was located immediately to the right of the elevation control and included a release latch. It was sometimes linked under the gun to a hand crank which could be turned by the loader. If the turret was being traversed manually, the gunner could produce 1.9 degrees per turn of his wheel and the loader 2.6 degrees. If the power traverse was engaged, power was supplied via the rotary base junction to a motor located on the left of the turret, the speed of the motor being controlled by the traverse hand wheel through a chain and sprocket. Using this system, the maximum rate of traverse obtainable was 14 degrees per second. The main armament was fired electrically by a trigger on the traverse hand wheel and its recoil was controlled by a hydro-pneumatic buffer system. A loader's safety switch and misfire lamp were also installed."[9]

On July 10 the British advanced from the Maltot area. The Frundsbergers tried to hold them with their dug-in Panzer IVs. Tank commander Hegemann ordered a counterattack with his few tanks by saying, "We'll make our own small gesture!"[10]

In defending hill 113, the dug-in Panzer IVs destroyed 28 Sherman tanks at a cost of 4 German tanks in a single engagement. Harmel knew that even at that loss rate he could not hold out in his present position for more than another week or two at the most.

Field Marshal von Kluge ordered the II Waffen SS Panzer Corps to pull back from its position. The 271st Infantry Division came into the area held by the 10th Waffen SS Panzer Division. There was a mutual respect between the Waffen SS men and the men of the Wehrmacht. Lieutenant Martin Pöppel of the 6th Parachute Regiment said that the men of the Waffen SS were front-line soldiers "just like us."[11]

The British attacked with flamethrower tanks on July 23. They had come again from Maltot over the road that was the graveyard of so many Shermans. Bernhard Westerhoff explained what he called the Cauldron of Normandy: "I sat in my Panzer IV that rested in a wide ditch. Only the tank's turret was above ground level. It had tree branches attached to it and was therefore nearly invisible. Only the muzzle flash could give our position away. When the British tanks appeared, we allowed them to approach within 100 feet before all the hidden tanks of 6th Company hit them simultaneously. I ordered my gunner to train on the seventh tank in column. It took only a few seconds. My gunner pulled the firing trigger and the 75 millimeter-long cannon recoiled from the shot. I saw the tank explode. I ordered the turret swung to the next tank. Again the cannon blazed. Other Panzer IVs were pounding the Shermans. The destroyed British tanks burned while the surviving tanks turned and fled to the rear. But although we had suffered only one loss I knew it was only a matter of time before the British made more determined attacks until we would eventually fail to stop them."[12]

By July 29 the German positions were breaking. On August 1 the division fell back to new defensive positions near Vire. Lieutenant Colonel Pätsch, commanding officer of the 10th Regiment, scrambled to set up a defensive line near Aunay sur Odon.[13]

On August 6, the Frundsberg Division withdrew to more defensible positions in the area around Mortain. It was hilly country and marked by forests and fields. The town of Mortain lay on a hillside with small farms in the valley below. As the men made their way south they tried to stick to the forests by day, traveling on the roads only at night. They met resistance and detoured into the countryside to the west. Dodging artillery fire, they reversed themselves to trek east through dense woods. They were able to avoid being totally surrounded only by following a creek that ran through a steep valley near Mortain. The Frundsberg forces in the valley of Mortain tried to hold their positions. With the 2nd Waffen SS Panzer Division protecting its southern flank, the division turned east in its continuing withdrawal. On August 7 the division lost its last tank.[14]

The division had entered Normandy on June 29, 1944, with 13,500 men and ample tanks. By August 11, during the fighting around Mortain the division had a strength of 6,500 men and no tanks. This was a 50 percent loss in men, but an 80 percent loss in overall ability to fight since without equipment the division was feeble.[15]

On August 10, Bernhard led a task group in an attack on hill 266, north of Barantan. The group fought hard and held off the Americans coming from the west and south. By August 14, the company had made its way farther east, to the village of L'Épine Orbière. There it was attacked by the Americans and splintered into pockets, which fought against great odds. The men continued a fighting withdrawal to the east toward Argantan. Before the company crossed the upper Orne on August 16, Lieutenant Hegemann was killed near Poutanges.[16]

The Frundsberg Division was no longer halting to establish a defensive line. It was now a matter of hitting the enemy with designated units while others continued the retreat to the east. The division was being pinched by the Americans, who had cut off their southern movement, forcing them to move east. Harmel received orders to move east as rapidly as possible. He was to take his men through Cambrai, then to drive northeast and cross the Seine River south of Rouen.[17]

Bernhard Westerhoff continued his description of the Falaise bottleneck: "I crouched and ran for a wooded area a quarter mile ahead. A Volkswagen amphibious car came from behind with its tinny horn blaring. Standing next to the driver was a Wehrmacht major who shouted for the men to get out of his way. I thought the man must be insane, but he seemed invulnerable to enemy fire as the little car darted into the woods. Still, the sight of the brazen officer gave heart to the men who were nearly at the end of their strength. I entered the woods and deemed myself safe for the moment. I walked more slowly and approached the Schwimmwagen car, which had stalled. The officer rose from the passenger seat. He weaved as he got out of the car and stood holding onto it to steady himself. In his hand was a half-empty bottle of Calvados. He shouted that his trusty steed had bitten the dust, and with that he set the bottle on the car and proceeded on foot, his driver close behind. I grabbed the bottle before its contents could drain. I raised the bottle in salute and took its last swig. The officer and driver of the Schwimmwagen were nowhere to be seen, so I inspected the little machine. It was full of bullet holes, one of which had punctured the gas tank. I whittled a plug and pounded it into the hole.

"In spite of the pulverized body, the little Volkswagen air-cooled engine started right up. I siphoned some gas from a few wrecked trucks and hit the road. It was daylight, and my flight was a moment-by-moment sequence of terror. Soldiers rode bicycles, buggies, horses, cars and trucks. They used anything that moved. Those not able to find a preferable means of transportation shuffled along in a dazed semblance of walking. I realized that two tired soldiers had somehow mounted the Schwimmwagen and were clinging to the car's rear. I said nothing, but hoped that the two men could hang on while I whipped the car around obstacles. For all I knew the noose may have already been completed and my quest for freedom by pushing east may have been in vain. Nevertheless, I continued to drive like a man possessed, shifting gears, whirling the steering wheel and yelling at people to get out of my way.

"I entered St. Lambert. The stream of retreating men had compressed itself into a knot of surging humanity. We were packed together in a jostling, thundering herd of men heading east. By now the Volkswagen had given up and I was on foot with all the rest. I looked up and saw Harmel standing on the steps of a church. He seemed indestructible as he shouted encouragement to his stricken men in their hour of desperation. Above the noise of the stampede a murmur of defiance rose from the columns of trudging men. Onward we pushed, through the valley of death between Mont Ormel and Chambois."[18]

The Falaise Pocket was about 30 miles long and 15 miles broad. Its southern edge was commanded by the U.S. Third Army, its tail by the U.S. First Army, its northern edge by the British Second Army while on the British left the Canadian First Army was working to close the pocket at Argentan.[19]

By August 22 the Hohenstaufen Division had only 460 men and a few tanks left. Frundsberg had no tanks or artillery and only four weakened battalions of infantry amounting to less than 500 men.[20]

Bernhard concluded his description of the "Cauldron": "I came to a bridge and lifted my head to see what surrounded me. There at the entrance to the bridge stood Harmel in camouflage jacket and trousers. After having seen him at Cambrai it seemed that the man was indomitable as he waved each truck and troop of marching men onward. In defiance of my fatigue, I stiffened and stepped into a march, rather than my plodding of the last fifty miles. We crossed the Seine River at a bridge between Rouen and Elbeuf on August 25, 1944."[21]

7

Camp Shanks, New York, September 1944

As August 1944 drew to a close, the U.S. 12th Armored Division was finally deemed ready for combat. The men of the 23rd Tank Battalion knew they were about to leave Camp Barkeley when they were issued boots. James Francis wrote, "At Camp Barkeley the men had worn shoes with leggings, but in preparation for the move to Camp Shanks, New York, the men were issued combat boots."[1]

George Hatt's 17th Armored Infantry Battalion was under the command of General Riley P. Ennis, and it was he who organized the transportation of CCA to Camp Shanks. The first contingent of soldiers to board trains for Camp Shanks rode in cars of the Atchison, Topeka and Santa Fe Railroad. It took many trains to move so large a load. It was a long, arduous trip with neither air conditioning nor, for most, sleeping accommodations.[2]

The train that transported George Hatt to New York was identical to that which carried Charlie Fitts, Andy Woods and Robert Arrasmith. The division was heading north to a debarkation point in New York. The men assumed that the division would soon head for Europe. The train carrying the 17th Armored Infantry Battalion with George Hatt was the fourth to make the trip to Camp Shanks. Andy Woods' train was four days behind that and Charlie Fitts was riding in the second train behind that of Andy Woods. Every day marked the arrival of at least one train at Camp Shanks.

The three-day train ride to New York was filled with rotating poker games, hunched bodies over rolling dice, masculine voices singing "Don't Fence Me In" and letter writers who were oblivious to the racket around them. A few men read pocket books or looked out of windows, but these were the lonesome few.

When the train pulled into small-town stations along the way, the men were overwhelmed by the generosity of ordinary people who passed a variety of homemade food through the open windows. The tedious but otherwise pleasant train ride was capped by a one-hour march to Camp Shanks.[3]

Charlie Fitts and the men of C Company, 66th Armored Infantry Battalion, were in the seventh train heading for New York. Like the others ahead of it, each carriage was crammed with eager soldiers playing cards, shouting at one another and trying to outdo one another in the profanity department. The train passed through little towns in prairie states where children waved at the passing soldiers behind the train's soot-stained windows.

Charlie remembered his new quarters and the few days before he boarded a ship for England: "Upon arrival at Camp Shanks I surveyed the interior of the barracks. It may have been the standard Second World War temporary military barracks, but it was an improvement over Camp Barkeley, according to any soldier's scale of comfort. We had access to our iron-framed beds and sleeping during the day wasn't forbidden. I concluded that the war must be almost over and that the Army had gone soft on its men since they wouldn't be needed. Why else would I and my buddies be treated to such opulence?

"Camp Shanks was close to the country's largest city and I strolled with my buddies down cavernous New York City streets while looking up at tall buildings that blotted out the sky. For me it was all mysterious and magical. We came back to Camp Shanks with stories of unending delights from Radio City Music Hall and Times Square to a nickel Staten Island ferry ride and a subway ride to Brooklyn. Others had similar stories. Some men had danced at the Stage Door Canteen and rode on the Coney Island roller coaster. Others had simply sprawled in horse-drawn carriages in Central Park and gawked at girls on Madison Avenue. Still others had spent their time drinking at Jack Dempsey's Bar. A few were even treated by patriotic citizens to dinner at the Stork Club. We were welcomed wherever we went."[4]

Unknown to most of the enlisted men, September 19, 1944, was the day Major General Roderick R. Allen relieved General Carlos Brewer. The relief was occasioned by the age of General Brewer. Although at age 50 he wasn't an old man, the regulations of the time prevailed. General Allen was a competent, rugged soldier who had a great deal of experience. He is described in *The 12th Armored Division Association Book* as follows: "He was born in Marshall, Texas on 29 January 1894. He graduated from Texas A&M in 1915. He was commissioned Second Lieutenant, Cavalry on November 29, 1916 and promoted to First Lieutenant on the same day. He was assigned to the 16th Cavalry from 1916 to June 1917 and from June 1917 to July 1919 he was on duty with the 3rd Cavalry, A.E.F., in France. After his return to the United States he was personnel officer in the Office of the Chief of Cavalry. Promoted to Major in June 1928, he attended the Command and General Staff School and in 1932 was an instructor in the school until 1934. He was a graduate of the Chemical Warfare School, the Army War College and the Naval War College. He was on duty in the G-3 Division of the War Department General Staff from 1936 to 1940 and was promoted to the rank of Lieutenant Colonel. In July 1940 he was assigned to the 1st Armored Division

General Roderick Allen, commanding officer of the 12th Armored Division during the division's movement into the Alsace, attack on Herrlisheim and defense of Weyersheim (12th Armored Division Memorial Museum Archives).

and in October was made Executive Officer of the 1st Armored Brigade. In April 1941, he was made Commanding Officer of the 32nd Regiment, 3rd Armored Division, and promoted to Colonel. In January he was assigned as Chief of Staff of the 6th Armored Division and in April was given CCA, 4th Armored Division and promoted to Brigadier General in May. On 1 November 1943 he was made Commanding General of the 20th Armored Division, promoted to Major General on 23 February and assumed command of the 12th Armored Division on 20 September 1944. During his Army career, General Allen was outstanding as a marksman. In 1921 and 1922 he was a member of the Cavalry-Engineer Rifle Team. In 1923 he was a member of the Cavalry Rifle Team and won the Distinguished Marksmanship Medal. In 1929 he was Captain of the Cavalry Rifle Team and Pistol Team. General Allen served in the First World War, Second World War and Korean War. He served on General MacArthur's staff, was director of intelligence, Army Ground Forces and commanded the XVI Corps and 9th Infantry Division. During his long military career he was awarded the Distinguished Service Medal, Silver Star, Legion of Merit, Bronze Star, Army Commendation Ribbon, and Distinguished Marksman."[5]

Andy Woods remembered his embarkation as a rather subdued time: "I was quiet as the men lined up to board a Liberty Ship called *Sea Porpoise*. Some of the men talked quietly about their families, their community and their young lives as high school students. There was a sense of the unknown and with it came a subliminal fear. To hide their true feelings the men forced idle chatter of girlfriends and cars and football; all ingredients of their youth which they were about to dismiss forever. There was little conversation of tanks. I was lost in memories of my own family farm in Michigan and the comfortable life I had led as the son of a successful business farmer."[6]

Charlie Fitts remembered his embarkation as something special: "Back at the barracks my buddy and I somehow had lost track of time and were late to muster. When we came into the platoon's drill area we were surprised to see soldiers in our company standing in formation with full gear. I knew we were in for it. What rotten luck to be late just when the entire division was getting ready to pull out. Captain Robert Hayner, the company commander, saw our confusion and approached. I and my delinquent pal stood at attention, expecting the worst. The captain simply told us to get our gear and get into ranks. We scrambled into the now empty barrack room and threw our belongings into our duffel bags. Not turning to look back on our temporary but commodious accommodations, we rushed to join the others boarding buses. We found seats and took the verbal jibes of our fellow travelers.

"At the pier, we were sort of nervous. For most of us this was our first time going aboard a ship of any size. The men around me were antsy and worked off their tension with exaggerated humor and storytelling. I wished I knew some really good joke to tell, but I'd never gained a flair for it. Heated discussions took place over the merits of French and English women. I listened to the banter. I had a girlfriend back in Meridian, but it was a friendship and never had gone beyond hand-holding. I was ill equipped to contribute to such a discussion, so I simply listened and learned. The men around me nervously poked and punched each other and tried to act nonchalant. I joined in and the roughness calmed my anxiety. Actually, I enjoyed the excitement of going into the unknown with young men I respected. We had gone through training together and soon would face the enemy.

"We inched our way forward along the pier in the shadow of the troopship. Someone said it was the *Empress of Australia*. Its vertical slab side was like a wall rising above us. Rows of portholes provided glimpses into its dark interior and spouts of dirty water ran from openings in the hull. I moved a few feet forward, then swung my bag to my new position. The line had an unhurried rhythm resembling a caterpillar. When at last I reached the gangway I was greeted by a sergeant and Captain Hayner. The sergeant ran a finger down a list of names on his clipboard. He put a check by my name and motioned for me to go up the gangway. Captain Hayner stopped me and ordered me to permanent KP duty while aboard ship. I took my sentence with equanimity. It seemed a fitting punishment for being late to muster.

"So I threw my bag onto my shoulder and climbed the gangway. I thought that the KP duty would give me something to do during the ocean voyage. It was likely to be boring and a little activity of any sort might be welcomed. Soldiers of the 12th Armored Division poured onto the SS *Empress of Australia* until not one square foot of space remained on the stately old ship."[7]

Elsewhere in the vast port of New York other men in other units of the division were boarding ships to make up the largest convoy of the Second World War. The 12th Armored Division boarded troopships destined for the British Isles, including the USS *General T. H. Bliss*, the USS *Marine Raven*, the USS *Sea Porpoise* and the old SS *Empress of Australia*. The holds of the ships were hot and stuffy, but the men were not allowed on the main deck until the ships had cleared New York Harbor. Once at sea, the men were permitted to leave their berthing areas, where bunks were stacked four and five high. Conditions on the *Empress of Australia* were even less attractive. For example, the British used hammocks rather than bunks. The meals served were suited to the British palate and the latrines ("heads" in Navy lingo) were scarce and difficult to find.[8]

8

Zutphen and the SS Empress of Australia, September 1944

Ernst Storch had crossed the Seine River south of Rouen on August 26, 1944. He closed his eyes as he recalled those terrible days: "I had continued walking eastward until I reached Maastricht, in the southwest of Holland. When I found what was left of my company I was given a hot meal. I looked at men sleeping in whatever posture they had assumed when ordered to halt and rest. Some of the men found shelter in houses, but the weather allowed most of the men to rest in the open. I ate some hot food and stretched out. For once, I was allowed to sleep until I awoke on my own.

"After a full day of recuperation with more hot food to raise my spirits, I was summoned by a messenger. I was told that the company commander wanted to see me. I shaved and washed as best I could, then drank a cup of black coffee. I reported to the officer and was astonished to find that I had been promoted to corporal. In addition, I was awarded the Iron Cross First Class. I saluted and returned to my unit with a sense of pride. I must have done something right, back there in that horrible Normandy business, but I couldn't think of what it might have been.

"I felt like a soldier again and marched with comparative ease the remaining miles to the Arnhem area. It was early September and the weather was comfortable. When I arrived at my destination I was billeted in a house together with several other tank personnel of my company."[1]

On September 8, 1944, Bernhard Westerhoff arrived at his new quarters in the town of Zutphen, twelve miles northeast of Arnhem, Holland. Like Ernst Storch he was dead tired. At his home in Fachingen, Germany, in 2005, he remembered the comparatively relaxed atmosphere of Holland after his near death in France: "I had walked most of the way across northern Europe and, as I removed my boots in an upstairs room of a family-owned guest house, I looked forward to a long sleep in a real bed.

"The next morning I awakened to the smell of coffee. This was extraordinary, since most 'coffee' to be found was made from roasted ground wheat mixed with chicory. I swung a leg over a kitchen chair and joined my comrades in amiable conversation. I stirred real sugar into black coffee and took a deep breath of its aroma. As we drank our mugs of coffee and spread creamery butter on slices of Dutch bread, each recounted how we had seen Harmel moving through the long column of men. One man compared him to an American cowboy who had herded the men all the way to Holland. Another commented that he hoped their fate would be better than cattle.

"The next days were occupied with writing letters to Ilse and filling out forms for the nameless people who demanded them. Germans were thorough and the bureaucrats in Bendler Strasse demanded that the exact location of each destroyed tank be recorded and attested to. It was a stupid waste of time and energy. We made up half the information. Who could remember such detail when fleeing for one's life? The men grumbled as they went about this useless business."[2]

Dr. Richard Korherr, Himmler's statistician, recorded that in 1944 there were fifteen Waffen SS divisions, a matter of perhaps 150,000 combatants. But the cumulative number in these divisions was officially listed as 368,654. The difference lay in the enormous bureaucracy of the Reich Main Office, which stretched out to the various occupied countries where they took desk roles in hidden offices.[3] The forms completed by soldiers filtered toward Berlin where the "noncombatants" put them to some mysterious use.

Despite the burden of paperwork, they had most afternoons free to spend lazing about in the autumn sunshine. Bernhard consumed much of his leisure time writing to Ilse. He was happy to tell her truthfully that he was in good health and that the Lord seemed to be taking care of both of them.

A few of the men became friends with young Dutch women. They talked about the 7,000 Reichsmark stipend for any Waffen SS member who married a girl of Aryan descent, providing she could prove the purity of her ancestry. They found the "bribe money" distasteful, but agreed that if they stayed in Holland long enough for a serious relationship to develop, none would turn the money down. Additionally, they knew that Harmel would not let ancestry stand in the way of any soldier who really wanted to get married. In reality, few of the Waffen SS regulations stemmed from Himmler or SS ideology, but rather from the leadership of individual commanders. The Reichsführer SS tended toward ceremonies and organizational problems whereas the Waffen SS focused on day to day operations. The fundamental operation of a unit was formed largely by the personality of the unit's leader.[4] Contrary to this generality, Harmel said in an interview in 1990 that he was called on the carpet twice by his superior officer, General Willi Bittrich who had received instructions directly from the Reichsführer SS to dress-down Harmel for his inattention to "racial purity" checks on Dutch women wishing to marry men in his division.[5]

The men received back pay, and with a little money in their pockets purchased small articles which they sent home to their families. Germany was impoverished by the war, and even though Holland had been looted by Germans who occupied the country for four years, it had managed to survive to this point with some possessions still intact. Bernhard continued his description of a few days of peace in Holland: "I found a music box in a shop and sent it home to Ilse. It was a useless item and for this reason all the more precious. I knew Ilse would love it and I was proud to have been able to bring my wife a little joy.

"One day as I walked around the town of Zutphen, I noticed the German hangers-on, the half-civilian, half-military bureaucrats who never saw an enemy and who exploited their puny status at every opportunity. The men called them '*Goldfasane,*' birds with gold feathers. One afternoon I was sitting at a café's sidewalk table enjoying a cup of ersatz coffee and a slice of Dutch cake. A sleazy-looking bureaucrat in a brown uniform of indistinct origin approached and asked if he could sit down at my table. His uniform had a sash with two oversized gold medallions. I was immediately repulsed by the man, but I nodded for him to sit down.

"The man had bloodshot eyes and skin that reminded me of barn mulch. The man pulled from his hip pocket a crumpled pack of cigarettes. He lighted a fresh one from the pack with the burning end of the one hanging from the corner of his mouth. A waiter approached and asked in Dutch for the man's order. 'Cognac,' the man snapped. I thought of how the Dutch hated us for treating them as this man did. I was so disgusted by the useless man that I reached in my pocket to pay the bill and get out of his proximity. At that instant the man leaned forward and looked both ways in a conspiratorial effort to gain my confidence. I was indifferent, but settled back down into my chair to hear the man out. The *Goldfasane* again looked up and down the sidewalk, then whispered that I appeared to be a man of the world, a man who could take advantage of a little good luck. Nothing could have been further from the truth, but I let him continue. He proposed a trade. If I could supply him with a little benzene, the *Goldfasane* could supply me with liquor, schnapps, cigarettes, women; items of interest to men of goodwill. The man's yellow-stained fingers tapped a cigarette and he smiled through equally stained teeth. It was clear that a transaction was in the making, and the man puffed himself up like a blowfish. He slid his chair closer to mine. His face was only inches away and his breath was a blend of rotten eggs and garlic.

"The waiter brought the cognac and the man threw some occupation money onto the table without looking up. He raised his glass in salute and downed the drink. I asked how much petrol was needed. The man's face had a creeping smile that suggested his triumph over the naive Waffen SS sergeant. Holding up two fingers he whispered that 200 liters would do. I had heard enough. I hinted that perhaps the Sicherheitsdienst or Gestapo might be interested in this conversation. The man recoiled in his chair, then caught himself and lubricated a new approach, saying that there was no need for rancor when two soldiers of the Reich had so much in common.

"I wanted to smash the man's face, but I also wanted to give him enough rope to hang himself. I threw obstacles in the *Goldfasane*'s path; the barrel would be too heavy, the amount was too much and he might get into trouble. We haggled for almost an hour; me playing and the man in dead earnest. At last the deal was made and the man left as quickly as he had appeared.

"I walked straight to the company commander's office and on the way hatched a plan. Lieutenant Hans Quandel sat behind his desk signing papers. I removed my hat as I entered the company commander's office. I saluted with outstretched arm and stood at attention as I outlined for the company commander, my experience at the sidewalk café. At first the commander was angry that I would engage in such a conversation, but after he heard that the barrel of fuel would be almost all water and that only three liters of petrol would be given away, he warmed to the idea. I emphasized that since petrol floats on water it would be difficult for the *Goldfasane* to know he was being cheated. Quandel finally acquiesced to my proposal with the caveat that if I ran afoul of the Gestapo, Harmel might not be able to extricate me.

"Two days later a willing supply sergeant named Haase filled the barrel as instructed. He sealed it and punched the official stamp onto the seal. A day later Sergeant Paul

Schröder made the exchange. He carted back to the company several crates of difficult-to-get articles that created the foundation for a resoundingly successful company party. The best liquor, cheeses, nuts, cigarettes and cigars were there for the taking. All officers were present, including Quandel who toasted the resourcefulness of those responsible for this remarkable layout of delicacies. To my thinking, the best treat was the image of the *Goldfasane* trying to run his ill-begotten auto on water. The men around me slapped their thighs with delight as I painted verbal pictures of the frustrated man when he learned that he had been out-swindled by the Waffen SS. Of course, there was nothing he could do, since to expose the deal would implicate him in a most embarrassing transaction."[6]

During the next days of September the work shifted to training the many new men arriving each day. The division was strung out around Arnhem with units in Bocholt, Elten, Lochem, Siddam and Henderloo. Bernhard moved from the *Gasthaus* in Zutphen where he had been comfortable to the town of Lochem, ten miles to the northeast. There he was billeted in a house with an accommodating farmer. It was not as pleasant as his former surroundings, but it was quite tolerable.

As Bernhard Westerhoff and Ernst Storch rested in Holland, George Hatt and Charlie Fitts were getting their sea legs. The 17th Armored Infantry Battalion was assigned to D deck of the SS *Empress of Australia*. George Hatt described his initiation to the old ship: "I pushed my bag onto a hammock. This staked out my territory for the duration of the trip. What escaped my inspection of the hammock was the nature of the beast that was to serve as my bed. I had seen movies where Errol Flynn had flung himself into a hammock on a rolling pirate ship and I tried to remember just how it was done. The first try simply flipped me onto the deck. The next left me hanging beneath it like a sloth clinging to a tree limb. I thought that perhaps it had to be mounted as one would mount a horse; from the left side, swinging the leg over the beast at its rear, but I couldn't determine the left side, or which end was the front. I again approached the hammock, this time carefully, spreading it as I rolled into it. At last, I was lying on my back and all seemed well. As the ship gently rocked alongside its New York pier, I was as stable as a nautical compass.

"My joy at having conquered the hammock was tempered by its undeniable shape. The worst cot in the Army was at least flat. This was a bag and my back began to complain. While a cot offered a certain degree of mobility, the hammock constrained its occupant to only one position, namely on the back. My choice now became clear. I could abandon the hammock or put up with the pain. For hundreds of years sailors of every nation had slept comfortably in hammocks, and I determined that if they could do it so could I. Another hour went by, and it seemed like an eternity. I rolled out of the hammock and onto the deck. I remained on hands and knees for some time as I tried to work the knot out of my spine. I slowly stood erect, leaned backward to stretch cramped muscles and looked at other soldiers who slept soundly in hammocks identical to mine. I hated to be a quitter, but enough was enough. I looked for an alternate place to sleep. Luck was with me, because I found that no one had taken advantage of the space under one of the many bolted-down tables that filled a better part of D deck berthing. Stepping over sleeping soldiers, I brought my bag which fit nicely under the table. In fact, it made a moderately comfortable pillow. The hard deck was a minor irritant compared to the obstinate hammock. It was to be my home for the duration of the voyage.

"The next morning the old *Empress* backed away from its New York berth, slowly passed the Statue of Liberty, and increased speed as it headed for the open Atlantic to join the convoy and cross the Atlantic. After a peaceful night I was hungry. I smelled food, but the smell reminded me of my old fox terrier, Patsy, back in Dallas, who, on hot days, loved to swim in stagnant ponds. The food came to D deck on hand-pushed carts. The British sailors who pushed them were of good cheer, but couldn't understand the hesitation of the soldiers. Although we had eaten lamb chops, we concluded that whatever was in those carts had been dead for a long time. The sailor said with some pride that mutton and boiled potatoes was the staple of British diet. Furthermore, it was the only food served on the ship. It would be served twice a day, the sailor said, once in the morning and once in the afternoon. At first, we tried to swallow the meat, but it was difficult to get past the odor. As a result, most of us ate only the potatoes. In a few days we longed for real food. Conversations turned more and more to the topic of the culinary art. Coney Island hot dogs, chicken with dumplings, and hamburgers with all the fixings became icons of American cuisine."[7]

It didn't take long for Charlie Fitts to recognize what a soft job he had in his KP assignment. He talked about the good luck of his punishment: "I peeled potatoes and scrubbed pans, but I had access to the deck, worked in a cool cross-breeze and had plenty of the ship's most precious commodity, space. In the ship's mess, I made note of the complaints coming from every soldier I met. Each had an overpowering desire for something other than mutton and potatoes. I had access to other foods and I developed a plan for profit. While others had to depend on the luck of a poker hand or the roll of dice, I had at my disposal the raw materials to make a small bit of change. I developed a one-item menu; an egg sandwich that consisted of one egg, fried and slapped between two slices of bread. The price for this seagoing sandwich was one dollar. It was exorbitant, but not negotiable and rank played no part in my black market venture. My own sea diet was never restricted by what I sold. I preferred baked chicken which I seasoned with dill. At the end of the trip I had over a hundred dollars in my pocket. I had no idea where or how I would spend it, but the thrill of making a little money from my KP experience had been worthwhile in itself."[8]

George Hatt told of the contest between his hunger and the repugnant mutton: "I had been hungry enough to get past the mutton smell. In order to get something into my stomach I had mistakenly assumed that anything to eat was better than nothing. An hour after eating the ship's fare, rumbling came from my viscera and I knew that it was time for some fresh air. My need was matched by that of other mutton-eating soldiers who also felt that only a shot of sea air could keep the British meal from rising. Elbowing my way through the crowd, I managed to stand on deck. I faced the cool breeze, as did all the other soldiers standing shoulder to shoulder on the deck. We looked like seagulls on a windswept beach, each nudging the other for a more favorable position into the wind.

"Finally the effect of the sea air played out and there was only the latrine left to bring comfort. I again pushed my way through the forest of standing men, pausing from time to time to get directions from those who had already visited the comfort station. While in route I discovered that the word 'latrine' had been renamed, and that 'head' was the nautical term. Whatever it was, I had to find it soon. The ship had been somewhat reconfigured to accommodate its wartime passengers. The head was a large tiled room with a stainless steel urinal running down one side and a series of open, black-seated commodes running down the other side. Occupying the two small ends were a few washbasins. The head had two doors, one of which opened onto the deck, the other on the opposite side serving an unknown, interior area of the ship. The door facing me was crisscrossed with taut barbed wire. I looked through the wire with longing. What had served the *Empress* well when transporting German prisoners westward was standing in the way of my survival. I was desperate to get into that latrine. There was no time to lose. I had to reconnoiter the passageways and find that unobstructed door. Men cursed me as I shoved passed them like a charging bull. Sanitation arrangements on the aging ship had not been first priority with the British, and the head's odor was its own advertisement. Although I couldn't see the latrine I simply followed my nose. Vaulting through the door, I made immediate use of the facility. Judging by the noises from other soldiers using the head it was clear that my mutton problem hadn't been an isolated incident. From then on I ate only crackers which were in abundance.

"I teamed up with Corporal Harold Capretta of Columbus, Ohio. We selected a gaming table that could be used for poker or blackjack. All the tables were bolted to the deck so the search was conducted with care. We found a desirable location, and the table's occupants were evicted by large and powerful gamblers who needed an honest game.

"The enterprise of Hatt and Capretta was straightforward and gained the trust of fellow soldiers. The game was continuous, because vacated seats were quickly taken by eager young men with cash in their pockets. Its operation brought the game's operators 10 percent of each pot. Were it not for the ship finally reaching its destination, the Hatt-Capretta enterprise might well have wound up owning the old *Empress*. The ship slowed and anchored in a bay until dark. We capitalized on the dead time by splitting our earnings. It had been a profitable voyage, and in spite of the early-on bout with British mutton, I look back on the trip with a measure of fondness."[9]

The *Empress of Australia* moved toward its dock in Liverpool. On Sunday, October 1, 1944, the ships came into Liverpool after 11 days at sea.[10] A sleepy band played as the men disembarked, just after midnight on October 2. Other ships made berth at other ports. The men of the 23rd Tank Battalion were off-loaded at Southampton, England. Buses took the men to Tidworth Barracks, a few miles west of Andover and a few miles east of Stonehenge.[11]

9

Operation Market Garden, September 1944

Bernhard stretched and looked out the window of his boarding house in Lochem, Holland. It was September 17, 1944, a day that would remain etched in Bernhard's memory. He described his small part in defeating General Montgomery's Operation Market Garden: "All seemed quiet and the weather was cool and cloudless. I anticipated a good Sunday noon meal served by the field kitchen near the town square. Dressing carefully, since there was no hurry on this day of rest, I sauntered out into the open air. It was noon and the sky was a pale blue. As I walked I thought I heard the noise of massed aircraft. I had heard it before when the Allies had bombed the city of Caen. I stopped and listened, expecting to hear a growing roar, but decided that my imagination was playing games. Looking ahead, I saw a few others stop and look into the sky. They were young replacements who quickly lined up for the noon meal."[1]

The Frundsberg Division had very few men, most of whom were replacements, and very little equipment in the area around Arnhem. The division was officially downgraded to the status of a Kampfgruppe. This was in part due to the September 7 order from General Field Marshal Walter Model to send Kampfgruppe Heinke south to Neerpelt. This meant that Harmel's meager force was further reduced by about one third.[2]

Walter Model, commander of Army Group B, heard the same drone of aircraft as had Bernhard, but for Model it was deafening and almost directly overhead. He had been reading reports as he and his chief of staff, Lieutenant General Hans Krebs, snacked on bread, cheese and wine at his headquarters in the Tafelberg Hotel in Oosterbeek on this leisurely September Sunday. He was startled as the noise from the aircraft quickly grew in intensity. His staff was in a state of near panic. His adjutant, Lieutenant Gustav Sedelhauser, exclaimed with some alarm that the British were landing parachutists and gliders in great numbers to the west, probably in Heelsum and Renkum Heath. Model tried to imagine what the British might be after. The only objective of any strategic value so far in advance of the British lines was his command. He decided that General Bittrich's II Waffen SS Panzer Corps headquarters in Doetinchem would be a safer location for the moment. He ordered his personal gear and classified documents to be transported to the east of Arnhem. From there he could direct whatever operation might be needed to put down this Allied attempt to capture him. Model, together with his staff and equipment, were immediately pulled out of Oosterbeek and moved east in a column of trucks and cars.[3]

The British landed the first two battalions of the 1st Airborne Division in Heelsum and Renkum Heath, west of Oosterbeek. Brigadier W. Lathbury was in command. Landing with them in a glider was Major General Roy Urquhart, who commanded the division. The 1st Glider Brigade under Brigadier Pip Hicks managed to get 359 gliders onto the ground, but much of the radio equipment and many jeeps were destroyed in the process.[4]

At 1:25 9 P.M., while the headquarters staff of the 9th Waffen SS Panzer Division, Hohenstaufen, lingered over lunch in Beekbergen, a messenger excitedly approached the table and announced that British paratroopers were landing. Colonel Walther Hartzer, commanding the division, immediately set the wheels in motion to attack the British at the landing sites.[5]

The 10th Regiment's commander, chief of staff to Harmel and temporary commander of the division, Lieutenant Colonel Otto Pätsch, called General Harmel in Bad Saarow, near Berlin, and informed him of the situation as he knew it on the first day of the landings. Harmel had been away from his command to beg for tanks and equipment from Major General Hans Jüttner, Chief of Waffen SS Operations.[6] He immediately jumped into his car and told his driver to go back to Arnhem. In Doetinchem, II Waffen SS Panzer Corps Commander Bittrich received the news that Model was on his way. By that time he knew that British XXX Corps had penetrated the German line south of Eindhoven. In addition, he was notified that the American 101st Airborne Division had landed in the area of Eindhoven and that the American 82nd Airborne Division had landed in a field south of the Maas River. He promulgated orders to his two divisions, assigning the primary responsibility for Arnhem itself to the Hohenstaufen Division and the area between Arnhem and Nijmegen (about ten miles to the south) to the Frundsberg Division. He ordered Pätsch, in Harmel's absence, to secure the bridge over the Waal River at Nijmegen and to hold the area south of the road bridge at Arnhem.[7]

As fighting might develop in specific areas, he gave both divisions the latitude to reinforce each other's forces without the need to obtain approval from his level of command.

Model, together with his chief of staff, General Krebs, arrived at Bittrich's headquarters and conferred with the corps commander. Although they couldn't be sure, they thought the British, assisted by the Americans, were trying to take the bridges over the rivers in northeastern Holland.[8]

When Bernhard was half finished with his noon meal, Captain Quandel's PKW came barreling into Lochem's central square. It stopped and the driver jumped onto his seat. He yelled, "Alarm, alarm! The Red Devils have landed!"[9]

Quandel stood beside him in the open car and hollered for his men to assemble in the town square within ten minutes. Bernhard described the ensuing action: "I grabbed my 98K short rifle and my helmet. I attached the mess kit to my belt and ran to the town square. Others were drawing hand grenades from a truck and assembling in ranks. I drew four hand grenades and took over as leader of the platoon. Soon I had the men in ranks, ready for action. It was quick work, accomplished with a sense of urgency, but without panic. I stood waiting for transportation and realized the term 'Red Devil' referred to the British 1st Airborne Division. I knew that we would be in for some heavy fighting, because these Tommies were the toughest men the Allies had.

"The company commander looked at his wristwatch as we boarded trucks that would take us to the point of action. It was just an hour past noon."[10]

By the afternoon of the first day, Lieutenant Colonel John Frost of the British 1st Airborne Division had taken his men along the Lower Rhine River and occupied houses at the north end of the Arnhem Road Bridge.[11] Lieutenant Colonel Otto Pätsch, temporarily commanding the division, ordered Major Brinkmann to cross the Arnhem Road Bridge from the south and dislodge Frost's 2nd Battalion in the houses on the bridge's north end. This adventure ended in disaster with Brinkmann being killed and his few vehicles destroyed.[12]

Lieutenant Colonel Pätsch then established Kampfgruppe Euling, which was to secure the Nijmegen Bridge and hold the northern part of the town against the U.S. 82nd Airborne Division. He also formed Kampfgruppe Reinhold to guard the southern end of the Arnhem Railroad Bridge and the southern access to the Arnhem Road Bridge. In addition, he detached a unit of about 70 men to assist units of the Hohenstaufen Division in containing and eliminating the Frost Battalion at the Road Bridge. Major Reinhold took his Kampfgruppe to Pannerden, where most of it embarked on the small ferry to cross the Lower Rhine River. On the night of September 18-19 the men marched northwest to locations in Elst while the detached unit remained in Arnhem itself.[13]

Bernhard was in command of the second platoon, which stayed in Arnhem. He took twenty men down streets toward the sound of small-arms fire. They attacked in relays. Bernhard ran into a doorway, then waited as others ran by him into a doorway closer to the British. The men dodged from one building to the next, watching across the street as their comrades did the same on the opposite side. They edged their way south, toward the great road bridge. When they encountered fire from the British they spotted its source and entered buildings to clear them of British soldiers. Some men ran across rooftops and others positioned themselves in windows from which they could observe the opponents' positions. Later in the day, they were ordered to hold their positions and to set guards so that men could rest and eat. The first day of battle had been nerve-racking, but so far, Bernhard's unit had suffered few casualties.

When an exhausted General Harmel reached his headquarters in Ruurlo his division, now called Kampfgruppe Harmel, had about 20 percent of its normal strength and had moved its headquarters.[14]

Pätsch wasted no time in briefing him. Harmel found Bittrich, who was at the south end of the Arnhem Bridge. The corps commander was enraged at the British and ordered Harmel to immediately wipe out the stronghold of paratroopers at the north end of the bridge. When Harmel asked about demolition of the bridges at Nijmegen and Arnhem he received a negative reply. He was informed that Model had specifically forbidden the bridges to be destroyed until the last moment.

Without authorization from either Bittrich or Model, Harmel ordered the Nijmegen Road Bridge to be rigged for demolition. The rail bridge to the west would also be rigged, but neither bridge would be destroyed, because of faulty rigging or partisan interference.[15]

Harmel had his hands full trying to keep the Americans and British from getting across the Nijmegen Bridge and simultaneously directing the Reinhold and Euling groups. At Pannerden Kampfgruppe, Harmel was using rubber boats, rafts and the ferry to get equipment and men into battle.[16]

Brigadier Sir John Hackett, commanding the British 4th Parachute Brigade, was wounded and was taken by jeep to St. Elizabeth Hospital in central Arnhem, which at the time was in German hands and was staffed by both British and German surgeons.

The British had taken the hospital on the first day of fighting, but had been overrun by the Hohenstaufen Division on the second day. Hackett described his impressions of seeing the Waffen SS at close range: "Now the jeep was traveling among German soldiers standing in the open, plainly to be seen in their gray-green uniforms. Helmeted heads were peering out of houses here and there. German military vehicles stood around. By the roadside one of those accursed self-propelled guns, our greatest bane, was moving into position. It was like seeing wild animals outside their cages.... German SS troops were moving in and out of houses, looting. I felt a deep and personal hatred for every one of them. When our jeep was stopped, a soldier ran his fingers over my one remaining shoulder strap. The badges of rank on it, the crown and three stars of a brigadier, clearly meant nothing to him. 'Well, well, an officer. And wounded, eh?' Yes, we wanted to get to this hospital. Slowly the under-officer pushed the British driver out and got in himself. A bigger and even more beastly blond winked at him and jerked his thumb first at the jeep and then back at himself. I could not remember a gesture I had ever found more hateful. The cocksure beast nodded, started the jeep and drove me off."[17] The driver took the general to the hospital where he met Dr. Lipmann Kessel, who assured him that he could remove the shrapnel splinter that had penetrated his intestines.[18] General Hackett said during an interview in 1989 that it took him several years before he could think of the Waffen SS with anything other than a blinding hatred.[19]

Bernhard continued his narrative. "I was sitting in a house waiting for the next order. A comrade rushed in and threw a handful of Cadbury chocolate bars into my lap. He had obtained them from the parachute supplies being dropped into Arnhem by British pilots who assumed that the city had been occupied by the British 1st Airborne Division. We munched on the chocolate. I remarked that while they were not as good as German chocolate, they were quite acceptable under the circumstances.

"John Frost surrendered at the north end of the Arnhem Bridge, and a truce was arranged for the wounded—including British, German and Dutch—to be taken to St. Elizabeth Hospital. I was there at the finish. We stepped quietly into the cellars of the houses that had been occupied by the British. It was as bad as anything I had seen. I stooped to help a man with a nasty leg wound. We ascended the stairs into the daylight. I called for a medic and soon the man was on a litter, being carried up the Lower Utrechtseweg to St. Elizabeth Hospital. As I turned around, I saw General Harmel talking with two British officers. I couldn't hear what was being said, but it was obvious that the British appreciated the humane treatment of their men."[20]

During the night of September 26, what was left of the British forces in Oosterbeek crept in a driving rain to the banks of the Rhine. By small boat, swimming and being pulled through the water by ropes, the remaining men of the British 1st Airborne Division made their escape. Like a collapsing paper bag, the Allied forces retreated south toward Belgium.

General Sir Hackett wrote, "The heavier Allied forces which were to follow us into the Arnhem Bridgehead overland were held by the enemy and could not reach us, while our own weapons, as happens with airborne forces, were too light to withstand for long those which could be brought by land against us.... In the absence of reinforcement the issue could not long remain in doubt and in the end the remnant of the 1st Airborne Division was withdrawn across the [Lower Rhine,] two thousand men out of ten [thousand], leaving the badly wounded with the enemy."[21]

10

The Salisbury Plain and St. Pölten, October 1944

The trip from Liverpool to the Salisbury Plain in south-central England was by rail. George Hatt spoke of the trip and of his impressions of wartime England: "After debarking the *Empress of Australia,* we marched in a column of soldiers to Liverpool's blacked-out train station where ladies in overcoats and hats served sandwiches and coffee. After such a miserable diet aboard ship, I was prepared to eat anything. Those sandwiches tasted superb even though they were mostly bread. Once on the train, I heaved my bag into a vestibule corner and wandered down the car's aisle. There were windows on one side and compartments with face-to-face seats on the other. Men were crammed onto the seats. I found a spot, but many men had to sit in the aisle on their bags. I wanted to see England, but it was blacked out, still fearing air raids.

"The sun came up and I saw out the train's windows the Wales countryside of green hills and rock walls. The train rattled through tiny villages, and cows looked up from their grazing to gaze at the puffing locomotive. In the afternoon the train stopped near an airfield in the area of Hungerford. I saw a B-17 Flying Fortress limping in to land at the adjoining airfield. A red flare shot into the gray sky. I thought injured men must be within this bomber, limping home to its base. My eyes remained riveted to the plane until it landed out of sight. This was my first glimpse of war's reality.

"We remained in the Hungerford area for three days. After waiting and watching combat aircraft taking off and landing, the A Company commander ordered everyone to fall out with equipment and mount big, 6-by-6 trucks for transportation to Camp R-4, Tidworth Barracks and Penning tent camp. My first introduction to Europe was the use of the word 'barracks' to mean permanent camp or base. The barracks buildings were next to Tidworth Township. They and the Penning tent camp were a part of one large facility which occupied a portion of the Salisbury Plain."[1]

Camp R-4 was near the city of Andover, southwest of London. This was the final destination for much of the 12th Armored Division during its brief stay in England. The armored infantry battalions were billeted in tents at Penning Tent Camp. Neither facility offered much luxury. Coal rationing meant living without heat and rain turned the sod roads to mud.[2]

One evening George Hatt went into Andover to a pub that was coincidentally named the Saint George. The event was engraved on his memory, "We drank half-and-half with wounded British and American soldiers. One American had been burned on his face from his own white phosphorus grenade that had exploded when struck by an enemy bullet. When speaking to the disfigured man, I made sure that I looked directly into his eyes. To have done otherwise would have been an insult to his bravery.

"I arose one morning before dawn. My company was to engage another in the same type of maneuvers we had so often conducted on the baking fields of Texas. I looked forward to this day, because I had learned to love the power of the big personnel carrier. As the sun rose, I was perched in the half-track's turret where, from its height, I could get a good view of the Salisbury Plain. It was a clear, cold, English autumn day. The centuries-old fields of grass, where ancient battles had taken place, were gray-green. Low stone walls and hedges crisscrossed the country and the half-tracks had to maneuver through their breaks. Boys on bicycles lined the Andover-Salisbury Road to watch the 12th Division's practice. My half-track deployed together with a dozen others in a line abreast. We halted and waited for a radio order to charge forward. I looked into the rising sun, coming up in the east, behind Andover. Before me were black stones rising from the earth, silhouetted by the sun. I recognized it immediately. It was Stonehenge, back-lighted against the sky. In school and in travelogues the monument had represented an ancient mystery. I was there, seeing the stones in their timeless permanence. I borrowed our squad leader's binoculars and raised them to my eyes. Through these, they looked weathered and fractured. In my excitement I pointed and told the men sitting behind me to look to the east and see one of the wonders of the world. My enthusiasm was mine alone. The drowsy men failed to take notice. I wondered how they could remain inert when such a sight was to be had for only standing and turning into the sunlight.

"The half-tracks turned and moved southwest. I looked behind me, but Stonehenge had disappeared over the horizon. The driver shifted up to high gear and swirls of chalk dust blew back from the vehicle as we thundered ahead."[3]

After leaving New York, the men of the 23rd Tank Battalion landed at Southampton, but their tanks, which were on another ship, were diverted to France where they were to reinforce General George Patton's Third Army. Upon hearing the news, Andy Woods kept an expression of concern, but inside he was elated, since an absence of tanks was likely to mean more time for exploring England. He described his stay in Britain: "We were amazed at how the sergeants could find work for us to do. We were housed in the original Tidworth Barracks. They were run-down brown buildings that must have been built at the first [days] of the war. Wood floors, lack of insulation and a single coal-burning fireplace at one end of the barrack room meant that we were perpetually cold. I tried to estimate what was worse, the heat and dust of Camp Barkeley or the cold and rain of Tidworth Barracks. My days at Texas A&M seemed like a luxurious dream.

"We were allowed to go into London six men at a time, chosen by lot. There must have been some reasoning behind this rationing system, but none of us could understand it. At any rate, I was lucky enough to be one of the first to get time out of camp. Four of the men found pubs and USO clubs, but I and another history buff spent our time looking up at the ancient buildings. Despite the bombing, England's people persisted, along with their enormous history.

"One weekend I went by myself into Salisbury and to the cathedral. It was a marvel and I went with an elderly gentleman who insisted on taking me into the highest corners of the great tower. It had a small balcony so far above the town and the surrounding

10. The Salisbury Plain and St. Poelten, October 1944

fields. The old man pointed to the north and said that in the distance, along the Avon River was where England was born. He called it Sarum. It was an experience worth remembering, and I shook the old man's hand as if he were a member of my family.

"Finally, we received M4A3 tanks. From then on, London and Salisbury were things of the past. We were up to our elbows in Cosmoline. Our job was to get our Shermans into combat readiness. They had been shipped right from the factory and it was a challenging job to get them cleaned up. We worked on them day and night."[4]

The M4A3 tanks allotted to the 12th AD had welded hulls and Ford V-8 engines with liquid-cooled 8-cylinder gasoline powered engines which produced 500 horsepower at 2,600 RPM. The blocks and crankcases were made of aluminum with steel cylinder sleeves. A few had the new 76-millimeter guns.[5] In addition, Company D of the 23rd Tank Battalion received its M5A3 Stuart light tanks.[6]

There was to be an exercise. Andy Woods described it: "We drove the tanks down to the sea, not far from where the British Tank Museum is located at Bovington. We shot about a hundred rounds at floating targets in the English Channel. It was a field day of fun. The tanks of the 23rd TB were lined up and their barrels were pumping out shells in a huge display of power. The floats didn't shoot back and I'm not sure the expenditure of all that ammo did us a lot of good, but it was fun."[7]

Ships from America had brought other supporting supplies and vehicles, including more half-tracks. Soon tanks, trucks, weapons carriers, half-tracks, towed artillery, jeeps and tons of replacement parts arrived in a steady stream at ports in southern England.[8]

On a sunny weekend in mid–October, Charlie Fitts and friends in C Company of the 66th Armored Infantry Battalion took the train from Camp Penning to London. From Meridian, Mississippi, to London, England, was a big jump and Charlie remembered it vividly. "I bought beer for all in my train compartment willing to get such an early start on British beer drinking. It was served by an obliging old man who pushed a cart through each railroad car. The beer was warm, but it went down easily as the English landscape slid by. London was a shock. This great city, the city of kings and queens, lay in ruins. We walked around Piccadilly and saw Trafalgar Square and looked up at Nelson standing so high above us. We ate USO sandwiches while sitting on the lions at the monument's base. Buckingham Palace had not a scratch. I was overcome by the eternal nature of the English. There was a kind of indefinable strength in the quiet demeanor of the people who rose above their reduced circumstances and went about their daily business with calm determination. I tried to imagine London as it had been before the war. It must have been a vibrant and historic city, but now it was scarred by bomb craters, half-destroyed buildings, sandbags in doorways and tape over windows.

"The train ride back to the Salisbury Plain was at night. The carriage's light bulbs had been removed and the soldiers were cautioned by the conductor to refrain from showing any light. Even matches had to be cupped. All that could be seen out the window were dim-out lights on automobiles stopped at railroad crossings. I caught glimpses of crossing guards: old men who held up round white signs that could be seen in the darkness."[9]

The final training of the 12th Armored Division was winding down in England, but Hitler and his staff at his Prussian headquarters were planning an offensive to take place in November or December 1944. Accordingly, the months of September and October saw comprehensive revisions in the allocation of German resources. Colonel General Alfred

Jodl of the OKW staff told Hitler that there were 96 Allied divisions on the western front, opposed by 55 German divisions. At the time, the Germans had about ten million men under arms in 327 divisions and brigades. Hitler believed that the winter months of 1944 would dampen the ability of the Allied air forces and that, with the element of surprise, the Germans could break through the Ardennes and sweep northwest to Antwerp.[10]

Supplies coming off assembly lines in Germany were diverted from both fronts and stored in designated locations throughout Germany and Austria. In 1944 German industry produced 11,000 Panzer IVs and assault guns, 1,600 tank destroyers and 5,200 heavy tanks, many of which had to be secretly hoarded for the coming operation.[11] The offensive, called Watch on the Rhine (Wacht am Rhein), was held as close to the vest as possible. No radio traffic alerted Ultra, and massive rail preparations were kept secret. Only a few Army commanders knew of the coming offensive. The locations of tank depositories were known to only a few select, high ranking officers.[12] General Wilhelm Keitel of OKW organized a railway system that was standing by to deliver tanks and equipment to 514 jumping-off points. This involved 500 trains for equipment and over 1,500 troop trains, all at a time when Allied air superiority was complete.[13] Inevitably, rumors circulated among the divisions that tanks were squirreled away in hidden places and were there for the taking, if only enterprising soldiers could find them.

On November 15, 1944, Bittrich notified Harmel that he was to move his division to Erkelenz, which lay between Linnich and Krefeld. The division moved as quickly as it could to its new destination, but the Americans made transportation difficult with heavy air cover. Because of the petrol shortage the troop-carrying trucks were delayed. They arrived in Erkelenz on November 19. On the way, Harmel received amplifying orders to engage the Americans as quickly as possible to prevent a breakthrough. He also heard of tanks hidden in Austria, but dismissed the information as meaningless rumor. Nevertheless, he ordered a quiet investigation of the matter.

To assist the division, OKW released 12 Tiger tanks and appropriate fuel to Harmel in the hopes that this meager force might turn the Americans back at Linnich. During the latter days of November, the 10th Waffen SS Panzer Division stalled American progress in the Linnich area, but it was obvious that further determined resistance was futile. In the early morning hours of November 30, the American attacks resumed after a pause in the fighting. By noon of December 2, the fighting in Linnich was house to house in close combat. At the end of the day the Americans held most of the city. The battle for Linnich was over. The 10th Waffen SS Panzer Division retired to positions in the eastern Eifel, in North Rhine–Westphalia and once again set about the business of resurrecting itself.[14]

As a result of Harmel's curiosity about the rumor of hidden tanks, Ernst Storch, who had been in Bocholt for most of the Arnhem fighting, had been asked to lead an expedition to Austria to find Panther tanks reportedly stored in the area of Linz. He had been gone for over a week when on October 28, 1944, Lieutenant Hans Quandel, commanding 6th Company, received another directive from Lieutenant Colonel Pätsch, commanding the 10th Regiment of the Frundsberg Division. Pätsch told Quandel to investigate a second rumor of Panther tanks that were supposed to be in northwest Austria. Pätsch, who was about to take most of the 10th Regiment to Erkelenz, said the tanks were about 20 in number and were reported to be stored in the St. Pölten area. He ordered Quandel to make the expedition and catch up with the division, hopefully with some tanks.

Upon receiving the order, Quandel was skeptical because he had not heard from Storch, but thought that since Harmel's trip to Bad Saarow to beg for tanks had been met with silence, the rumor might have some merit.[15] Furthermore, he knew that most of the division was in transit to Linnich to stem the tide of Americans who had taken Aachen and were heading for Düsseldorf and Cologne. Harmel had the assignment, but had no tanks until he reached Erkelenz.[16]

Bernhard related the story of the journey to find hidden tanks: "I had remained in Arnhem with a detached unit of Kampfgruppe Reinhold and had later been assigned to Bocholt.

"On October 12, 1944, the division had received a large influx of over 1,600 men, and 6th Company received its share. Each day, I had awakened early to work on the training program. Good food was once again abundant and each night I slept soundly. I had wished for a few tanks with which to train these men, but I took what weapons I had and organized a training schedule around them.

"Quandel had determined to personally lead a few men to find any tanks that could be transported to the Frundsberg Division. I never knew why Quandel thought I might be an asset on such an assignment, but I imagined it was because of my initiative in conning the *Goldfasane* in Zutphen.

"I awoke before dawn on October 29. My breakfast was interrupted by the company commanding officer. Quandel asked me if I wanted to go with him to see about getting a dozen or so new Panther tanks that were supposed to be stashed in St. Pölten, in lower Austria. I eagerly accepted. Two days later Quandel's car pulled up in front of the boardinghouse. He was in the front seat of his staff car next to his driver. Behind the open car was an Opel-Blitz truck with six other trusted tank personnel. I jumped into the rear seat of the car and the two vehicles sped off to Dülman, then headed southeast on various lesser-used roads. I kept my head turned upward, looking for Allied aircraft. The truck followed close behind as the little convoy whizzed along winding streets.

"We slowed to a crawl as we went through Cologne. The town had been bombed many times and rubble had been pushed to the sides of the road to keep the highway open. Quandel pointed to the cathedral and remarked that God must be on our side since it still stood tall and stately.

"It became evident to me that we would soon pass close to Dietz, a town that clung to the side a hill, not far from my hometown of Scheidt. Without forethought I asked Quandel if I could visit my family, which resided in the vicinity. To my surprise, the company commander agreed without hesitation. We needed to stop for a rest and this was as good a place as any. Besides, with some rest, the men could get a fresh start in the darkness of the early morning hours.

"The staff car and following truck turned off the main road and moved slowly down a winding lane through Dietz. I showed the driver how to negotiate the last few miles to the village of Scheidt and to the house of my parents. I jumped out and ran to the door. My mother answered, saw who it was and nearly fainted. I turned and waved at Quandel and the men. They cheered as the two vehicles pulled away from the house. I should have been concerned as to where the men would find lodgings, but I was consumed with the sight of Ilse, who stood in the light of the hallway. She ran to me and we clung to each other as my father closed the door.

"Ilse led me up the narrow stairs to the bedroom and to a bed which occupied a corner of the room. My son slept soundly. I stared at the child, but I couldn't comprehend the reality of where I was. After so many months of combat, the realization that Ilse and Volker were more than words in a letter was difficult to digest. The terrible reality of war twisted a soldier's mind until anything else became only a dream. Now peace was before me and I was overcome by the quiet.

"Downstairs, the neighbors had gathered to greet the hero of the hour. It was obvious that my father had done some bragging about his son in the Waffen SS. Ilse led me downstairs where I smiled, shook hands, and tried to be congenial. I was just another soldier, so I kept my composure and said very little. Beer was served and it would have turned into a party had not my mother signaled for the people to leave. She motioned for father to retire and at long last I was able to be with my wife.

"At four in the morning the car and truck parked next to the house. Quandel knocked politely on the door. Again, my mother answered. She invited the commanding officer in, then saw the smiling faces of the others who were standing next to the truck. She invited them in. The men crowded into the downstairs. They sat and stood with hats in hand. Mother rushed into the kitchen and set to work making ersatz coffee and slicing bread for the men.

"I heard the thunder of the men below and came down the stairs. I must have looked sleepy and relaxed in a nightshirt never worn by soldiers. Quandel made light of my civilian attire, but suggested that it was time to get on the move. Mother scurried from cup to cup, filling and serving. I introduced Ilse to the men I knew so well. She extended her hand to each as I said his name. She bowed her head and repeated each name. When she met Quandel she took the company commander's hand and politely asked him to take care of her husband. He smiled and nodded. As they filed out of the room, the men thanked mother for her hospitality. Quandel whispered for me to take a moment, then meet him at the car.

"Those last moments were dreadful. Still, the short visit had been a gift and I was thankful. The little convoy started engines and slowly moved away. Ilse waved until we were out of sight. We had many miles to cover to the Austro-German border and then to the small town of St. Pölten. When reaching the town we developed a search plan and followed every possible lead. Not a single soldier, civil servant or barkeeper knew of any tanks. It was a dead end, but secretly I was most grateful for the journey.[17]

11

Le Havre and Beyond, November 1944

On November 9, 1944, General Allen and his staff boarded ships that took them to Le Havre, France. During the ensuing days the division boarded troopships and LSTs bound for the same port. The ships left from Dorchester, Weymouth and Southampton. An immense amount of cargo was waiting to unload, and the officers had to wait their turn before their ship was allowed into port.[1]

James Francis rode a Sherman tank that wound its way through narrow roads to Weymouth. He wrote, "On November 11 our company drove our new tanks southwest to Southampton and Weymouth. Driving the tanks onto the waiting LSTs meant backing them into confined spaces. It took a lot of swearing GIs to get all the vehicles on board and tied down."[2]

Also on November 11, 1944, George Hatt left England to cross the English Channel with his driver and half-track on a battle-scarred LST. On its hull was painted the white number "LST 1." An LST was a landing ship tank, although many of the sailors who manned them insisted it meant "large slow target." It was designed as a large, amphibious landing craft capable of transporting heavy equipment and vehicles. The bow door was hinged and swung open laterally to allow a ramp to be deployed. This allowed vehicles, including tanks, to exit the landing craft directly onto a beach. The normal LST displaced 2,100 tons, was 328 feet in length and about 50 feet wide. The lower deck accommodated eighteen tanks while lighter vehicles were normally carried on the upper deck. In early models an elevator was used to unload from the upper deck.[3] On this English Channel crossing, *LST 1* carried 22 half-tracks, 160 troops and a huge store of ammunition and weapons.[4]

James Francis recorded the landing in France: "When reaching France, our LST went up the Seine River almost to the City of Rouen. The LST plowed into the riverbank. The tanks rolled off the LST and onto French roads. They then followed in column eastward to Auffay, where the 23rd TB camped for several days in muddy fields awaiting the last units to cross the English Channel."[5]

The division moved from the Le Havre area to Auffay where the various units organized themselves for the coming journey. Columns of tanks and half-tracks traveled the country roads. They headed for Auffay, the division's first real taste of France. The weather was hostile with drizzle and low clouds. The ground was damp and the men tried to find comfort by building temporary huts with matted straw over the ground. Many traded Army goods for French bread, cheese, eggs, apple cider and wine.[6]

George Hatt narrated his experience: "Our next movement was to Auffay, fifty miles to the east of Le Havre. The battalion made camp in and around the Château de Bosmelet, a partially bombed-out estate that had been the site of several V-1 winged-missile launchers before being taken by the Allies. After a brief respite on Thanksgiving Day the division got under way in its rolling convoy. I rode 'shotgun' in the assistant driver seat of the squad's half-track as it plowed through France on a southeasterly course through Compiègne, Reims and Nancy. Several miles from its destination, the town of Luneville, the half-tracks slowed in response to the braking of lead vehicles. The whole column had slowed as it passed through the treeless rolling hills of France's Meurth-et-Moselle area. The cause of the slowdown was a jeep that was parked alone on a barren crossroad facing the passing convoy. The jeep's driver sat rigidly while a thin, tall man in helmet stood on the passenger seat beside him.

"The assistant driver of the half-track in front jumped to attention and saluted the standing officer. Immediately, I did the same. I saw that the man was Lieutenant General Alexander M. Patch, commanding officer of the Seventh United States Army. The general was welcoming the men of the 12th Armored Division to his command. The 12th Armored Division was assigned to relieve the 4th Armored Division in southeastern France."[7]

The division was assigned to the Seventh Army under the command of Lieutenant General Patch on November 29. On December 5 it was assigned to XV Corps. The corps was made up of the 26th Infantry Division and the 12th Armored Division. The area was dotted with bunkers that made up the French Maginot Line, which had been built before the war to prevent Germany from invading France.[8]

General Patch first gained recognition in the Second World War when he led an Army division on Guadalcanal. Born at Fort Huachuca, Arizona, he came from a military family. He graduated from the U.S. Military Academy in 1913 and served as an infantry officer and instructor in machine-gun school. General George C. Marshall, who had known Patch during the First World War, promoted him to brigadier general and sent him to Fort Bragg where he supervised the training of recruits. During the early part of the Second World War, Patch organized the defense of New Caledonia. Marshall then ordered him to Europe where he took command of the Seventh Army.[9]

Andy Woods had a subscription to *Time* magazine. Copies were delivered to Andy along with other mail. The magazine was pocket-size and without advertising, having been specially published for servicemen in overseas locations. He wrote, "I was always abreast of the news. Other tank crew members asked me questions so often I finally set up a reading schedule where each crew member had the magazine for a day. It wasn't too fair since our driver had no time for leisure when we were on the road. We drove our trusty old Sherman across France without encountering any mechanical problems other than mud in the tracks."[10]

The division stopped at the French town of Luneville. There it lingered in the sodden, rain-soaked village. While at Luneville, A and B Companies were reorganized in the 23rd Tank Battalion. The battalion continued to the front, arriving in the vicinity of Rahling, France, on December 7, where it was attached to XV Corps of the Seventh Army.[11]

Like George Hatt of the 17th Armored Infantry Battalion, Charlie Fitts of the 66th AIB had been designated as assistant driver for his mortar squad's half-track. At the time

11. Le Havre and Beyond, November 1944

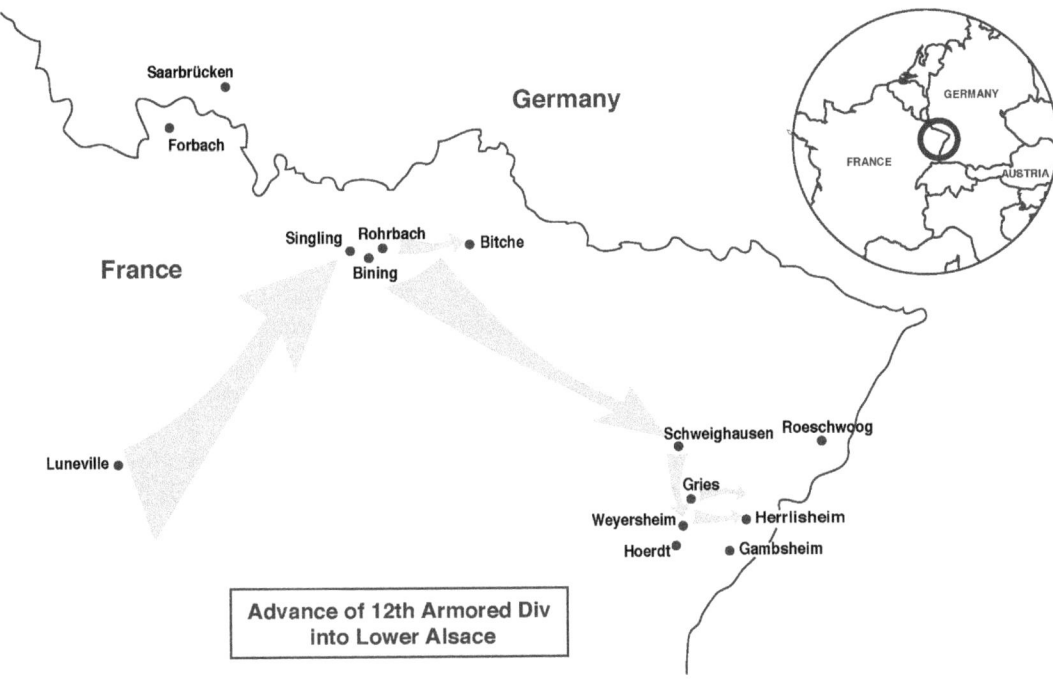

of his Camp Barkeley supplementary training the title hadn't seemed to be anything special, but it turned out to be his ticket to a comfortable November channel crossing. His designation as assistant driver gave him the run of the ship. He had lounged in his half-track most of the time, reading *Stars and Stripes* while munching candy bars.

Charlie had witnessed Le Havre as a beehive of activity with ships disgorging cargo. He described how he felt as assistant driver of a half-track plowing through the terrible weather, "When I sat in the assistant driver's seat wearing my helmet, I watched the driver wrestling the big steering wheel as the half-track inched its way off the ship. I said a silent good-bye to the LST and wished the channel had been a bit wider to have lengthened the pleasant two days at sea.

"The driver of my half-track followed other half-tracks to the assembly area at Auffay where the men of the 66th Armored Infantry Battalion were quartered in clean country homes with French people who put forth a great effort to make us Americans welcome. Wine and French cooking were the note of the day and I thought that this war wasn't so bad after all. One's memory of the outside rain and mud faded quickly under the influence of the grapes. I was quite prepared to complete my military obligation right there in front of the family's fireplace drinking the best that France had to offer. But the Army rousted its soldiers out of these delightful digs and back onto the half-tracks and the merciless French winter.

"After joining with other platoon half-tracks, we headed southeast across the French countryside, enduring an uninterrupted, cold rain. It splattered on my helmet and dripped down my raincoat in constant little streams. My squad sat quietly in the rear as the vehicle plowed along behind its counterpart in front. The giant convoy crept along in a general southeast direction in defiance of the rain which became heavier and colder as we went.

"I didn't know where we were going and didn't much care. My main concern was trying to keep the water from sneaking past my raincoat collar and into my field jacket. The men behind me tried to smoke as they stared straight ahead. They cupped their hands to protect their lighted cigarettes, but moisture extinguished them one by one, causing a flow of profanity which persisted until the most dedicated smoker surrendered to the elements. I discovered that war was largely a matter of trying to find a bit of comfort in a nasty and hostile environment.

"On November 29, C Company arrived in another town, not much different than Auffay. It was Luneville and must have had a certain attraction to the Germans, because they sent a lone Messerschmitt to strafe the place immediately after the company had settled in. Luneville lacked the charm of Auffay and the people were less enthusiastic about the Americans being in their midst. After all, Americans brought German fighters that punched out their windows with indifference.

"I stayed for the Luneville week in a small Catholic college. It was comfortable and we sat about cleaning our weapons and trying to stay warm. Sisters in habits roamed the grounds and never passed up the opportunity to politely greet their uninvited American guests. The courtyard was cold and windy the first week of December and American soldiers with hunched shoulders shuffled through it in layered shirts and jackets. The sisters, on the other hand, walked fully erect and always at a brisk pace. Their garments flowed and flapped in the wind. Whenever I encountered nuns in the cloister they were always cheerful. 'Bonjour, Monsieur,' they would say. To which I would answer, 'Mo'nin,' sister.'

"At the end of the week, I heard the half-track engines starting up. I trudged with my bag through the dark courtyard out to the street. I found the platoon's mortar squad half-track and climbed into the assistant driver's seat. There, I waited in pre-dawn discomfort as the engine idled and others climbed into the rear. One lesson I learned in my Army life was that it was best not to be impatient, since no matter how bad the present might be, the future probably would be worse. I hoped that the next little town would offer more of the excellent French wine I had found in Auffay. It wasn't that I disliked the Luneville sisters. On the contrary, they were kindly and generous, but they were Spartan and the only wine in the cloister had been part of the sacraments.

"At long last the column began to move. Each half-track trundled along behind the one in front. Rain pelted the windscreen and I leaned forward, trying to gain a little protection from it. The sun rose above a thick layer of clouds. It was another wet, gray day. I sat and stared through the rain-streaked windshield at the taillights of the half-track ahead of us. We were in the Vosges now, with low, rolling hills and tiny villages tucked into valleys. On December 7 we crept into Rahling. It was already jammed with 66th Battalion soldiers. The half-track engines had hardly a chance to cool before the word came down that we were to attack the town of Singling. This was not to be an easy takeover, the soldiers whispered. The rumor was that the Germans were in the town in some force and had given the 4th Armored Division a tough time. I only hoped that Singling would have a warm, dry room for me to thaw out.

"The pre-dawn hours of December 8, 1944, were persistently rainy and cold. The half-track took my squad to within easy marching distance of the town. We deployed to both sides of the road and carefully moved forward toward the enemy. I expected at any moment to hear the screech of shells and violent explosions. As light began to break in the east we ran in spurts down the main street. Still, there was no incoming fire. I listened to the constant hissing of rain while I strained to see through it. One squad protected an advancing squad as we had practiced so many times at Camp Barkeley. At a signal, I ran ahead, down the narrow street lined by houses with doorways that opened on a sidewalk. I slipped into one and waited for the next squad to rush by me.

"At mid-morning we were solidly in Singling with no appreciable resistance from the Germans. We still couldn't relax because a few suicidal snipers lurked in the buildings. These die-hards took pot-shots, then we'd react with a hail of automatic weapons fire at the probable location of the sniper. One by one the Germans were killed and calm finally prevailed over the little town. Then the artillery began. Shells whined overhead, but the Germans corrected their range and a mixture of mortar and artillery rounds began to burst in the street and houses. I crouched in a doorway waiting for the bombardment to end. I hoped the enemy didn't have that much ammunition. Why would the Germans want to make such a big thing about such an insignificant little town? Then I noticed snowflakes beginning to fall and, as if by magic, they silenced the German guns. At first there were only a few flakes mixed with rain, then pure snow in huge flakes blotted out visibility. I guessed that the German forward observers must have packed up and gone somewhere else. This suited me very well. I peered in a window at what looked like a dry room. I forgot Germans and politely knocked on the door of the house."[12]

John Ferguson wrote, "During the night of December 7, elements of the 17th AIB moved into the French town of Bining, relieving a battalion of the 26th Infantry Division. At that time the Americans controlled the southern half of Bining, while the Germans held the other half. The doughboys of the 17th made their approach to Bining on foot, at night, soaked to the skin after a driving rain, with mud up to their boot tops. Carrying weapons, ammunition, bedrolls and musette bags, while slogging though the mud, the men quickly became fatigued. It was a feeling with which they would become very accustomed. After making their way quietly into the town, the Hellcats crowded into houses and barns to get out of the cold weather."[13]

George Hatt's description of the 17th AIB journey to Bining continued. "The sky ahead was alight with a strange, flickering glow. It reminded me of cloudy nights back in Texas when sheet lightning illuminated the underside of dark clouds in an eerie dance of flashes. This was my first glimpse of combat artillery, perhaps American, perhaps German, perhaps both. I couldn't tell. It was a long way off, but was a premonition of things to come.

"The line of half-tracks came to a halt and the men threw down their gear. Each man grabbed his load. I heaved my assigned equipment onto my shoulder. The men formed a single-file column into ranks and we marched in route step toward the village, a few miles distant. We walked in the middle of the paved road to avoid mud that had slid onto the asphalt from the hills above. The men in front broke to their right as a column of soldiers approached from the opposite direction. They were soldiers of the 4th Armored Division. We pushed ourselves into the soft mud to make way for the oncoming soldiers, who were slogging along in a ragged column of silent depression.

"Houses appeared and I saw squads of men congregated along the street awaiting their billet assignments. I dismounted the half-track and talked with others in my squad as the men smoked and stomped feet to keep warm. Sergeant Charlie Ruma said that most of the houses on the north side of town were still held by the enemy. He pointed to a house with attached barn and nodded to me. This was to be my shelter for the rest of the night. Before I went into the barn, Sergeant Ruma called me into the house's kitchen and told me that I would be taking part in a field telephone wire patrol, but then he changed his mind and told me to go to sleep.

"The barn was made of stone. It was cold and foreboding. I entered and took hesitating steps as I groped like a blind man in the inky-black interior. I searched for a place to lie down and found a soft bale of what I thought was animal feed. It served as a pillow and I quickly went to sleep.

"I was awakened by noise coming through the kitchen door and thought that it must be time to go on patrol. Fumbling through the dark barn, I found the entrance to the kitchen. The light of the warm room caused me to squint, but I saw three fellow soldiers who had been wounded: Third Platoon Leader Lieutenant Owen Yarborough, Mortar Squad Leader Sergeant Charlie Ruma and Radioman Private First Class Dick Ault. Two were sitting, the other lying on the floor. A civilian woman nursed the men's grenade wounds. The three had left without me and had returned after encountering Germans. I leaned against the sink as I tried to overcome the shock of seeing my comrades with gaping wounds. I watched as they were evacuated by medics. I was alone in the kitchen. I stared at the bloodstained floor. Knowing not what else to do, I staggered back into the blackness of the barn and found my sack of feed. Soon I was asleep.

"In the morning, the sun beat into the barn through high windows. I looked at my pillow. It was a dead calf. I backed away from the ghastly sight and bent over, frantically brushing the back of my head to rid myself of whatever may have lingered on the carcass. I grabbed my gear and equipment and lurched out of the barn. In the daylight I took a deep breath and the creepy feeling left me.

"The rest of the day was spent cleaning and adjusting weapons, eating K rations and talking about the new environment. Evening fell and I scrambled into the house for a better place to sleep. Anything was better than that barn. I was a little late and the only available space was on the stairway. I thought that I could accordion myself into a tight fit along one step or I could stretch out lengthwise over several steps. The latter required the choice of head up or down. Head up was the only decent option, I reasoned, since blood would otherwise rush to my brain. I lasted an hour, until the stair edges became like knives, and it was necessary to slide down at intervals to relieve pressure points.

"Halfway through the night a terrible explosion down the street brought every sleeping soldier to his feet. I grabbed the banister for support as I looked at open space on the floor below. I quickly stepped down the stairs to the hallway and picked out a premium spot. Only one of the soldiers had left the comfort of the house. The rest rearranged themselves for the night's continued sleep. It was first come, first served, and we squatters were the targets of wrath, but I wasn't about to leave my spot. I pretended I was asleep. Angry voices and cuss words flowed, but those left standing were condemned to the stairway. A banging on the front door again roused the sleepy soldiers. A soldier who leaned against it yelled, 'Who's there?'

"A voice from outside the house vowed to kill the bum who had locked the door on him. The inside soldier unlocked and opened the door slightly. The angry soldier on the outside shoved the door into the bodies of men on the inside. Again, oaths and vows to kill came from the dislodged men. Cold air blew in from the outside and those in the hallway yelled to close the door. These demands were accompanied by justifiable profanity. The cold soldier slammed the door, the bodies of the affected men rolled back to their prone positions and the only one left standing was the soldier who had made the mistake of running outside in reactive panic. He stepped over bodies and ascended the staircase to my vacated space.

"A second mortar shell hit the rear of the house. This one was closer and, in the dark, lit up the interior of the house like lightning. The kitchen windows blew in and glass covered the floor. Not a single soldier gave up his spot on the floor. When the third mortar shell exploded close to the front of the house it blew through the windows with so much force that several men were slightly wounded.

"Without a word being spoken, the first floor was vacated in favor of the cellar. We crowded down the wooden stairway into a dimly lit, large, dank room. Here we found women and children huddled together in a pathetic attempt to find safety. An old woman held her rosary and repeatedly mumbled her Hail Marys while younger women tried to comfort their whimpering children.

"I felt awkward. It appeared that the rest of the soldiers also felt uneasy. We removed our helmets and tried to smile. The women recoiled from us and this provided space for some of the men to sit down. For the rest of the night the two groups shared the space as occasional mortar shells continued to fall on the town of Bining. I tried to sleep while keeping my knees pulled into my chest, but the repetition of the old lady's Hail Marys played on my nerves, and my eyes kept returning to these poor people who happened to be in the line of fire."[14]

Part II

Alsace

Introduction to Part II

On December 16, 1944, strong German forces broke through the Ardennes Forest to attack the U.S. V and VIII Corps. The news was received by SHAEF in Paris with alarm. General Eisenhower told General Bradley to move two armored divisions at once to the aid of General Middleton's VIII Corps. The 10th Division, a unit of General Patton's Third Army, was given the task. On December 19 General Eisenhower called a meeting of his top field commanders at Verdun. There he ordered General Patton to drive north into the left flank of the German advance. Patton immediately adjusted his entire Third Army to be ready for what would be needed to stop the Germans. He ordered his III Corps and XII Corps to attack northeast to restore the southern shoulder of the German salient.[1] The immediate task of the planned counterattack against the south flank of the German penetration was to reinforce the Americans in Bastogne.[2]

The Seventh Army under General Alexander M. Patch now held Patton's weakened right flank, while the French First Army, as a part of Sixth Army Group, held positions to the south from the Colmar Pocket to Strasbourg. The Third Army's 4th Armored Division had been in Alsace, forming the Third Army's most southern limb, abutting the northern units of the Seventh Army. The 4th Armored Division had been in serious fighting and was in need of refitting.[3] The generals agreed that the 12th Armored Division would relieve the 4th Armored Division, but would remain with the Seventh Army. However, both Patch and Patton knew that both the 12th Armored Division and the 14th Armored Division of Patch's Seventh Army would need additional training before they could be committed to battle.[4] By Christmas the American lines were holding and the German advance had stalled. But the divisions of the Seventh Army held 15.1 miles each on the average, versus 12.4 per division in the Third Army and 5.2 in the First Army.[5]

When it became clear to Hitler that his December 1944 Ardennes offensive was doomed to failure, he planned his final bold move: a thrust into Alsace to split the French and American forces. Hitler and OKW saw an opportunity to punch a hole in the weak Alsace front. Four converging attacks were planned initially, although improvisation became the rule once the battle was joined. The XIII Waffen SS Corps would attack south with three divisions just west of the Lower Vosges, with the Saar River as its western boundary. Its mission was to penetrate the defensive position of the Americans west of Bitche, and secure the road net at least as far as Rahling. Simultaneously, XC and LXXXIX Corps were to attack directly into the Lower Vosges, penetrating the thin American screen in the mountainous terrain. While XC Corps struck west with two divisions to complete the encirclement of the 100th Infantry Division, LXXXIX Corps would push south and east with three divisions to secure the few east-west roads through the Lower Vosges.

General Blaskowitz, commanding Army Group G, allowed discretion on the part of his corps and division commanders. He ordered the 10th Waffen SS Panzer Division to remain in reserve but to move into positions from which it could most effectively take advantage of tactical opportunities.

The XIII Waffen SS Corps, with its three divisions, was to capture the city of Bitche and secure the villages to the west, all the way to Rahling. Another corps was to attack directly west to take the area of the Lower Vosges mountains south of Saarbrücken while the 553rd Volksgrenadier Division crossed the Rhine in the Gambsheim area. This latter advance would be possible because the American troops would be forced to divert units to the north to resist the German attacks far from Gambsheim. German Army Group Oberrhein was to cross the Rhine River and move northwest from Colmar. The combined effect would clear Alsace of Allied forces and, with luck, create a rift between the French and Americans. Held in reserve would be the 10th Waffen SS Panzer Division, which would be quickly brought up to full strength.[6]

As the German high command planned its Alsace attack, General Patch's Seventh Army was stretched nearly 125 miles from roughly Saarbrücken to Strasbourg in a bent line along the west side of the Rhine River. Facing to the north and east were the 103rd, 44th, and 100th infantry divisions of XV Corps, with the 45th and 79th divisions of VI Corps in the south around the towns of Sessenheim and Drusenheim. Many of these divisions were short of men and material. In the American 45th Division the slogan had been "Win the war in '44." By early January 1945 it was "Stay alive in '45." In Alsace most territory was held by the 103rd and 44th divisions of XV Corps, while farther to the south were the 45th and 79th divisions of VI Corps. General Devers advised SHAEF that he had assembled the 36th Infantry Division and 12th Armored Division west of the Vosges in SHAEF reserve. At the same time he instructed the Seventh Army to begin to prepare an alternative main line of resistance in the Maginot Line. On December 30, a specific warning was issued to the Seventh Army from General Devers of the Sixth Army Group about a possible attack against the flank, west of Bitche.

Ultra intelligence informed General Patch that the Germans were about to hit his forces in Alsace. Operation Northwind, Hitler's designation of the German offensive, got under way on January 1 with German divisions attacking Rimling, Bitche, Wingen and Bambach. To the east and closer to the Rhine River, divisions pushed south from Wissembourg to attack Hatten and Sessenheim. On schedule, the 553rd Volksgrenadier Division ferried itself across the Rhine River and attacked Gambsheim. From there it was to turn north and take both Herrlisheim and Drusenheim.

On January 2, 1945, the 6th Waffen SS Mountain Division and the 257th, 361st and 559th Volksgrenadier Divisions attacked Wingen, which was defended by the American VI Corps. On January 4, the 17th Panzer Division was to have taken Rohrbach to the west, but, meeting stiff resistance, shifted to the south to attack Bitche. The XXXIV Panzer Corps was successful in taking Hatten. By January 7, the 553rd Volksgrenadier Division had established a bridgehead north of Gambsheim and had placed units in an obscure woods called the Steinwald.[7]

It became apparent to OKW in December that the 10th Waffen SS Panzer Division needed to be strengthened if it were to be of any use to Operation Northwind. The division received new tanks, artillery and an influx of men from Kriegsmarine and Luftwaffe sources. Meanwhile, the 12th Armored Division in Patch's Seventh Army had been steadily advancing southeast into Alsace. The American division and German division were poised to clash in the frozen fields around the towns of Herrlisheim and Weyersheim.

12

Bining, Rohrbach and Roeschwoog, December 1944

While at Luneville, A and B Companies of the American 17th Armored Infantry Battalion had been coupled with the 23rd Tank Battalion for the movement to the front. The 17th AIB arrived in the vicinity of Rahling, France, on December 7, 1944.[1] On December 9 the 17th AIB, together with tanks of the 23rd and 43rd Tank Battalions, attacked the high ground at Bining to take and occupy the concrete buildings at the top. These had been a part of the original Maginot Line and had been used as a school by the Germans.[2]

George Hatt learned that these units were going to take a hill not far from Bining. He described his experience on the Bining ridge: "I had been assigned to a squad of mortarmen who looked toward the crest of a fortified hill at Bining. There were buildings made of concrete and Germans popped up here and there at the crest. It was difficult to see through the mist, but I thought that this dismal morning would likely bring our first real combat."[3]

The 17th AIB, having met no opposition in the town of Bining, had advanced toward the nearby military installation known as the Bining Barracks. The infantrymen and the tanks of the 23rd Tank Battalion coordinated an attack on the barracks under Combat Command A. The first assignment of the 23rd TB was to support the 17th AIB in its mission to attack and take the Bining Barracks. This was a line of buildings atop a hill between Bining and Rohrbach. Unknown to the men of the 17th AIB and 23rd TB the German 11th Panzer Division had evacuated its positions in the Bining, Rohrbach, and Singling areas. The barracks were manned by a small contingent of 11th Panzer Division panzergrenadiers.[4]

A platoon of five tanks from A Company, led by First Lieutenant Robert Seymour, was to accompany the infantry while the rest of the 23rd tanks fired at the barrack buildings from an adjacent hill. Seymour's tank led the way, breaking through a low stone wall and advancing uphill directly toward the buildings. The infantry moved up the hill around Seymour's tank. The other tanks held position at Seymour's orders. Seven Sherman tanks of A and C Companies, 23rd Tank Battalion, rumbled up to the base of the hill. Private First Class James Francis, loader in Lieutenant Robert Seymour's Sherman, hung on as Seymour's tank hit a mine and was disabled, but the other tanks avoided the mines, continuing their ascent. With his head protruding from the turret, Lieutenant Wayne F. Gui-

12. Bining, Rohrbach and Roeschwoog, December 1944

Staff Sergeant Edward "Pete" Vickless, commander of the Sherman tank which, with the Detrick tank, destroyed six of the seven German Mark IV tanks at the Bruchwald/Waldgraben Canal and later destroyed a company of attacking German infantry the night of January 19-20, 1945. Photographgraph taken at Camp Barkeley by Andy Woods (Woods collection).

tteau shouted for the other C Company tanks to charge up the hill. Sergeant Edward "Pete" Vickless and Sergeant Kenneth Detrick, in two other C Company tanks, were among the first to put Guitteau's order into action.[5]

George Hatt continued his narrative. "Behind the tanks came the infantry, where I found the going tough from carrying my heavy load of mortar equipment. With head down in a crouch, I half-ran up the hill. The 23rd's tanks opened up at close range on the German positions at the crest. Germans who had been entrenched and had initially poured machine-gun fire onto the incline now scattered, with many throwing up their hands in surrender. My platoon moved up the elevation, tossing hand grenades ahead of us into suspected hiding places.

"It was over before it hardly had begun. The Germans who stood with blank faces and arms stretched into the air looked like civilians who only yesterday had put on uniforms. I volunteered to keep a watch on them. Their numbers grew and the platoon sergeant assigned more men to watch them. I slowly walked around the prisoners with my Garand at the ready. This was the first time I had seen the enemy up close and I was struck by the Germans' appearance. Their uniforms were ill-fitting, they were unshaven and their expressions were that of resignation or perhaps relief at having been made captives.

"I spotted a prisoner who stuck his hand into his pocket and pulled out a small leather folder. The movie theaters at home had played films of shifty-eyed Germans who threw hand grenades after having been captured. I leveled my rifle at the man, ready to pull the trigger. The German simply gazed at the folder. I took it from the man and looked at it more closely. It contained a small photograph of a woman and two children. I returned it to the man. The sergeant gave orders to clear the buildings and I was relieved of my guard duty so I could search the rooms for stray Germans. It was a tricky business that tested the nerves. I looked for booby traps and would have shot anything that moved. Nothing did.

"After nightfall the field kitchen brought hot food. This was a welcome interlude after our first day in combat. The word came down that we would push on to another town in the morning. I would have welcomed some sleep, but I had guard duty for my building and so forced myself to stay awake while making sure no errant Germans came back into the area held by the 17th Battalion. I was too tired to question the logic of standing guard at a blown-out window in a latrine. With rifle on safe I stood in a half stupor, crowding into a corner to stay out of the icy wind which came through the paneless window in relentless stabs. It entered every unprotected spot in my clothing. My feet slowly turned to clumps of unfeeling flesh. My field jacket, sweater, wool shirt and long underwear succumbed one by one to the elements. Minutes seemed like hours. I closed my eyes and thought of home. Then the wind bit into me, and I again stomped my feet to see if they were still under me. By the end of my two-hour guard duty I was shivering and exhausted.

"For the remainder of the squad, sleeping in the cellar, it was quiet except for the snoring and shuffling of bodies trying to stay warm. I crawled into my bedroll and slept soundly for a few hours. Before daylight, I was called outside for breakfast where the kitchen mess crew was setting up. Like a zombie, I went through the motions. Whenever I sat down, I immediately went back to sleep in spite of the freezing temperature."[6]

It was December 10 and Combat Command A had received orders to attack the town of Rohrbach, located only one kilometer north of the Bining Barracks. After clearing the town the soldiers were to continue their push north toward the Maginot Line. According to plan, the 17th attacked the high ground north of Rohrbach. Shortly after reaching the hilltop, all three companies received intense shelling and mortar fire. The remainder of the day was spent digging in. The weather turned very cold and it started to snow before midnight. The foxholes filled with slush and water, and there were many cases of frostbite and trench foot. The sufferers were evacuated the following morning.[7]

The preceding written record was augmented by George Hatt's personal description of the event: "It was the morning of December 10, 1944, and the next town to be attacked was Rohrbach, about a mile to the north of Bining. At 8:30 A.M. the company commander ordered us to move out on foot from Bining. We fanned out on both sides of the road to enter via the main street and a few side streets. My squad leader was now Corporal Harold Capretta, because Sergeant Charlie Ruma had been wounded on the wire patrol. Capretta took us down the right side behind and between the dwellings. There were numerous wire fences and I, who had been assigned as 'platoon wire cutter,' snipped holes in wire fences for the men to move from pasture to pasture. Not having encountered any Germans, we came to the opposite end of the town.

"The company commander raced from platoon to platoon giving last-minute instructions to officers and noncoms on the operation of taking the steep hill in front of us. It was clear to me that this was to be more difficult than Bining. We began the advance up the incline. A machine gun on the crest hammered the ground around the leading elements. I took what cover I could, lying down in the wet, dead grass. Bullets ricocheting off rocks ahead of me, up the hill, whistled close to my ears. I remembered the burned face of the soldier in Andover, England, and unclipped the white phosphorus hand grenade from my pack. I tossed it as far to the side as I could.

"The company commander ordered white phosphorus mortar fire to target the top of the hill. We were to advance upon dissipation of the white phosphorus smoke. I remained where I was. A few other squads who were terrain-protected managed to get into action. Then white phosphorus mortar shells landed on the hilltop, emitting smoke to cover our charge up the hill. I and Staff Sergeant Bill Ramsey followed Lieutenant Robert Ferguson, commanding officer of our platoon, to the top. Ferguson waved for the rest of us to advance. We stood and moved forward, up the hill. Machine-gun fire from the Germans had stopped, and when I reached the crest I was relieved to see the enemy positions abandoned. The wounded had been left behind.

"The top of the hill was broad and flat, with one Maginot Line concrete bunker and a few flat-bottomed sinkholes. The mortar squad was ordered to dig in and set up. We found a sinkhole and thought the natural depression would give protection for our mortar. It was afternoon and the weather hadn't improved. A drizzle started to fall, covering everything with a penetrating, damp chill. Since the depth of the sinkhole wasn't enough to insure protection from artillery, Capretta told us to dig foxholes. The drizzle turned into a rain. The temperature was just above freezing. Mud stuck to entrenching tools and each hole became a bog. I stood in my hole looking down at my boots in six inches of water.

"When darkness came, the rain turned to snow. I was wet through every layer of clothing. I refused to get into my rain-filled foxhole. I lay in the mud at its perimeter, huddled with others in misery. It was the longest night of my life. Sleep was impossible, even though I had very little from the night before. I heard moans coming from other men of the squad who shared my agony in the sinkhole. They cursed from time to time, but that required energy and after midnight the only sounds were heavy breathing. I tried to focus my mind on home. If only I could concentrate on a single pleasant thought I might make it through the night. I couldn't think of anything. I began to shiver. It was uncontrollable and worked its way up my legs until my body twitched and trembled as I fought the unrelenting cold. Misery continued through the next day and into the second night. The precipitation changed from snow to cold rain and back to snow, invading the bones and making movement painful. Around 3:00 A.M. I heard the sound of running men near the sinkhole, but could see nothing from my position. Soon the sound faded.

"When the sun rose, I was unable to think clearly. I climbed out of the sinkhole and looked around. Snow covered everything, and an illuminated mist converged with snow to veil the outside world with a curtain of dull white. I assumed the rest of the company was out there, somewhere on the hilltop. My shivering was taking from me what little vitality my body still had. Other men of the squad were in as bad a condition. Capretta was standing. He was a blur. No other soldiers could be seen. I heard no sounds, nor any men moving around on the hill. The other squad members were digging into K-ration boxes and didn't seem to be concerned.

"Below me, on the road, I thought I saw an ambulance through an opening in the mist. I started walking down the hill, possessed by an impulse to find shelter. As I stumbled along without feeling in my feet, I searched the hillside expecting to see some sign of life. Finally, I stepped onto the road in front of the ambulance. It seemed as though the road was moving under me, but I wasn't sure. I listened, but could hear nothing. I should go back up the hill and tell the others to get down to the road. I couldn't analyze my predicament. I simply stood, swaying in my numbness, trying to think. I looked down and saw that my overcoat was caked with mud. My gloves had been torn and my fingers protruded from them. As I stared at my hands, I saw my fingers moving, but couldn't feel them. The road slowly turned beneath me, as the ambulance approached. Someone came to me on foot and peered into my face. I distantly recognized him. It was Honky Harwell, a medic from Camp Barkeley. Another medic followed. They gripped my armpits and moved me along to their ambulance. The two medics talked about me. They said I had severe hypothermia. I pulled away from them and pointed to the hill. My squad was still up there and they needed help. Harwell reassured me, then told his junior medic to get up the hill and pull the others down to the road where another ambulance was on the way."[8]

At the aid station, located on the north side of Rahling, a sergeant helped George Hatt remove his clothing.[9] George continues his narrative: "The sergeant placed me on a litter and tucked blankets around me. My shivers abated and my mind began to clear. I started to get off the litter, but the sergeant pushed me back down onto it. The sergeant's voice was compassionate but authoritative, instructing me to get a little shut-eye. I stayed where I was and immediately went to sleep. For twenty-four hours I slept. When I awoke in the morning, the room was dark. I remembered where I was, but knew nothing of the room's geography. I tumbled off the Army cot and with outstretched arms, navigated around the room, then stood in place waiting for sensation to creep back into my body. After a few moments I groped forward and found a blackened window and a door. At that instant the sergeant opened it and a shaft of bright light blinded me. The sergeant again took command, pushing me back onto the cot. There was pride in the sergeant's voice as he explained how he had worked on my feet and legs through the night without waking me. My condition was serious, he said. I could have lost some toes to frostbite."[10]

While George Hatt slept in the aid station, First Lieutenant Ernest Garneau took command of the 23rd Tank Battalion's C Company tanks. On December 11 the 23rd TB was to proceed through Rohrbach and take the roads leading to Bitche. A column of tanks hadn't gone far when German anti-tank guns forced a halt. The tanks waited as American artillery shelled the suspected positions, then Colonel Meigs, commanding officer of the battalion, moved his own tank forward until he could just see over the ridge without exposing the entire tank. From there he saw a flash of fire from the direction of Bettviller and called for smoke on that position. He told the driver to back up, but the words were hardly out of his mouth when a shot from an anti-tank gun went though the open hatch cover and struck him. His body dropped to the floor of the turret. Captain Thorp was in the gunner's seat of the tank when this happened, and took command of the tank. For his bravery in action, Colonel Meigs received a posthumous Silver Star.[11]

By the time George Hatt awoke, the 11th Panzer Division had withdrawn to the east and the 44th and 87th Infantry Divisions had converged to take positions held by the 12th AD up to December 12.[12]

George Hatt continued, "On the afternoon of December 13, I opened my eyes, feeling as though I had finally regained my strength. I was escorted into a long room with stacks of equipment and was instructed to take what I needed. I selected an M-1 rifle, an ammunition belt, canteen, first aid kit and entrenching tool. I then put on my overcoat, which was dry but still mud-caked. I went out into the street, determined to find my company. Men gathered in bunches, talking and smoking. I found a field kitchen and was informed that the men of my company were in another little town called Höling, up the road and over the German-French border. I could catch a ride with them the next morning. I spotted the closest building and snuggled under a table on the upper floor. There I slept through the night in warmth and safety.

"Early in the morning I ate a bowl of hot cereal and drank a cup of coffee at the field kitchen. Then I hopped into the cab of a six-by-six truck. The gears ground and the truck lurched forward. Soon we were in Höling and I shook hands with my buddies. My squad had come down off the hill when an ambulance driver hollered at them. I spent the day talking, eating, and napping. At dusk we were ordered to get ready to move. Corporal Arlo Ward pulled the squad's half-track, known as 'Amelia,' into the yard and we loaded her up. The convoy wound along dark roads in the dead of night. My half-track followed the blackout lights of the half-track ahead of it. Arlo Ward kept the vehicle in second gear and the transmission whined as its speedometer never rose above six miles per hour. Each time we entered a village, the men in back shouted their demand to stop, but the column of half-tracks kept going. At last the column stopped in a town called Eyweiler. It was December 14.

"The men had only two concerns on their minds: where to relieve themselves and where to get warm. They stumbled into a large house at the direction of the platoon leader. Each man fell into a heap and went to sleep. I too slept. In the morning we entered the street and looked at the house of our billet. It was tall and old and needed a coat of paint, but to us it was our new home and we were prepared to make the best of it. It stood at an intersection of two muddy streets and when I examined the town with a more critical eye I saw that it was a rundown and impoverished village of farm people. One of the men occupying our house found a large tub. We boiled water and soon had the opportunity to actually get clean. I scrubbed my smelly body, shaved and put on dry underclothing. For the first time since leaving England I felt first-rate. With enough sleep and enough food, I felt like I could lick the whole German Army.

"Eyweiler turned out to be a home away from home. We sat around in our house, complaining about the Army, the war and life in general. I thought it wasn't half bad, at least in comparison to the top of that hill at Rohrbach. Each day was full of sleep and good conversation. We slogged our way down the muddy street to the field kitchen three times a day. Between meals we looked forward to the next meal. All in all, I was quite content. The days were spent cleaning weapons. As assistant driver, I squeezed grease into the suspension's zerks and oiled moving parts in the engine. Most of the time, we played cards, wrote letters, read mail over and over, and talked about home. Woven into each relaxing endeavor were jokes and jibes. We laughed at mundane stories of high school antics and adolescent attempts to attract girls. On December 20, we ate breakfast and assembled to move to the next town. As it turned out we headed back to Bining and the old concrete buildings on top of the ridge along the town. It was like going home, except that Eyweiler, with all its ramshackle houses, had begun to grow on us."[13]

While the men of the 17th AIB had relaxed in Eyweiler, CCB had advanced across the border to Utweiler, but then had pulled back to consolidate positions. The division now faced the 257th Volksgrenadier Division which had taken over positions formerly held by the 11th Panzer Division.[14]

The evening of December 24, Christmas Eve, was special in every unit of the 12th Armored Division. In C Company of the 66th Armored infantry Battalion, the cooks were preparing the next day's meal. Weston Lewis Emery described it as follows: "Staff Sergeant Nello Lazzari was a huge-framed soldier who was also the company cook. He was known in the platoon as 'Tiny.' On Christmas Day he and his men prepared a special dinner. One of the helpers was PFC John Nemeth, who described Christmas as follows: 'I helped Tiny Lazzari, the mess sergeant, deliver the hot turkey dinner on Christmas Day. Some men caught two swine pigs and took them to the rear in Sergeant William Houghton's half track. Tiny served everyone pork barbecue.' That was our Christmas."[15]

The 23rd Tank Battalion received packages from home. Around Christmas the 23rd TB also received its winter clothing. This was a three-piece fleece lined coverall with suspenders, a jacket with zipper front and knit cuffs and collar, and a cloth helmet-liner that covered the ears and back of the neck. A wool knit cap was issued also. At about this same time the 12th AD was placed under SHAEF reserve command. This resulted in the division being moved around the Upper Alsace from village to village with only occasional skirmishes.[16]

In Bining the men of the 17th AIB had mixed feelings. It started with men who thought of home and languished in a dream world of Christmases gone by. Each man was isolated from his buddies by a barrier of personal thoughts. Then a man in George Hatt's barrack room started to hum a Christmas carol. Another joined in with words. Soon, nearly every man in the room was singing familiar songs of the Christmas season.

George remembered, "An informal parade of shuffling, off-key serenaders strolled around the hill overlooking the town of Bining, singing time-honored melodies. As the men left each room, the listeners became vocal and they added their strains to the growing magnitude. The Bining Barracks, one-time part of the Maginot Line, and one-time German military school, was transformed on this night [by] musical strains that echoed against the hills on the far side of the small town.

"I opened my eyes the following morning to a sunlit room. This was enough to draw me outside into the cold. Above me in the blue sky were countless white contrails of bombers heading for Germany. It was a bittersweet sight. The Americans were pounding the

Germans. That was good, but it was Christmas Day, and somehow, I wished the war could be suspended on just this one day. After morning roll call, some of the men opened packages from home that they had kept until Christmas. In the afternoon, I and my pals in the mortar squad walked down the hill to the field kitchen. We got at the end of the line for Christmas dinner. Those who had already eaten leaned against houses and belched. Others trudged back up the hill with full mess kits, risking the prospect of cold food for the comforts of their bedrolls.

"When I passed my mess kit over the steaming trays of food, the cooks slopped mashed potatoes, peas, corn, slices of turkey and a wedge of apple pie onto the tin. The pie pressed against the mashed potatoes which oozed over the side. I had only my fork and spoon, but I wasn't about to lose a single bit of this meal. As I walked up the hill, I finger-scooped the overflowing mashed potatoes from the edge of the tin and savored their delicious taste. Strolling at a leisurely pace, I dug around the pie wedge to expose the peas and carrots. By the time I had reached my billet, only the turkey and pie were left. These, I had saved for last. Stabbing a slice of turkey, I nibbled at the corners and chewed with patient enjoyment. At last the apple pie stood by itself on the tin. I looked at it while I contemplated the option of saving it for later. But in these times, I had learned that later often meant never. My fork neatly severed the tip of the slice and I chewed the pie without haste. Before swallowing, I allowed the flavor to linger on my tongue. While it may not have been as good as mother's pies, it was a bit of home. I closed my eyes and tried to imagine sitting at the Hatts' dinner table. I could almost hear the sounds of the house. Leaning back, I shut my eyes and took a nap."[17]

For Charlie Fitts and Robert Arrasmith the holiday season was just so many more days spent in a foxhole. Charlie explained, "The men of the 66th Armored Infantry Battalion had relaxed for a few days in Singling, but at 11:45 A.M., December 22, I and the others of my squad took over foxholes that had been dug by their prior owners. Our orders were to hold the line and this we did. Complying with this order meant living in a hole during the worst winter to hit Europe in a century. It was cramped, backbreaking torture. I never knew if my legs were asleep or frostbitten. I had the freedom to get out of my foxhole, but I never knew where the Germans were. It would have been just my luck to get caught out in the open. On the rare occasions when this was necessary, I stretched my limbs with trepidation. When the blood did its work and life returned to my body's extensions, I sighed with relief.

"When nature called, there was no retreat. A soldier gritted his teeth, exited the hole and removed himself a suitable distance. It was agony to remove clothing in the bitter cold. Each man hurried this natural function, but a man's body, having been so confined, was not about to be hurried. The result was a contest between the man's persistence and the winter's attack on his vitals. This was something they had not told me about, back in Camp Barkeley.

"I had lost track of time. Each day was like the last. The gray sky of Christmas Day took on a luminescence from a winter sun that was afraid to show itself. I ate some and drank some. I exited the hole as little as possible. I tried to visit my buddies, but their foxholes, like mine, were too narrow for more than one man. This meant I had to lie in snowy slush if I wanted to converse. It wasn't worth it. My buddy George O'Bryan, in the next foxhole, 50 feet away, hollered, 'Hey, Charlie! You know it's Christmas?'

"Then I thought, of course, it's December 25th. A forlorn feeling of homesickness engulfed me as I sat huddled in my bulky winter clothing with helmet pulled low over my eyes. I thought of all the Christmases back home. I dug into my pocket and got out the last letter from my parents. My mother did most of the writing. Dad just penned in a few lines at the end of each letter. I read it again. This time I dissected each sentence, making up in my mind, what must be behind each vignette of life back home.

"My daydreams of home were interrupted by the sound of trucks coming from town. For some reason I pictured infiltrating Germans dressed in GI uniforms. I grabbed my rifle and started down the hill. Kettles on portable tables steamed in the cold air and delicious smells advertised their contents. I and George O'Bryan lined up and dug our mess kits from our gear. A mess sergeant said to each man as he came up to the first tray of food, 'Compliments of Tiny Lazzari. Sorry, no napkins or finger bowls. Just good old-fashioned, down-home cooking.' My mess kit overflowed with food. I passed it under my nose and smelled the aroma. I closed my eyes and said a blessing for the folks back home and the men, who, through some miracle, had obtained the fixings for this wonderful meal. How they had managed to prepare it in the face of freezing temperatures and isolation was a mystery. I sat down on my helmet and watched O'Bryan shoveling food into his mouth. 'Merry Christmas,' he said between gulps.

"I wondered what the people in Meridian were eating this Christmas Day. Turkeys were in short supply, but I knew that whatever it was, mother would serve a perfect meal. I also wondered what the Germans, out there in the hills, were eating on this special day. My job was to kill them, but on this day I couldn't bring himself to think ill of them. After the last bite, I pushed my finger around the edges of the mess tin to get every last vestige of flavor. O'Bryan lit a cigarette and blew smoke into the air. We walked back up the hill in silence as we thought of home."[18]

On a hill overlooking Utweiler, Robert Arrasmith of the 56th Armored Infantry Battalion sat in another foxhole identical to the one occupied by Charlie Fitts. His battalion had engaged the Germans in the town and since then German artillery fire had become a daily nuisance. Baker Company had been one of the first into the town, and it had been Robert's initiation to combat.[19] It was Christmas and he endured the relentless weather as did the others of the 12th Armored Division. He spoke of the unrelenting cold: "I tried to deal with frostbite by removing my shoes and massaging my feet. In the quiet of Christmas Day, while trying to keep bundled up on my snow-covered hillside I heard voices singing Christmas carols. It was strange because I had heard the same songs before, sung by my German prisoners in America. Now the singing came from an enemy, and the thought was troubling. I heard English words from the voices of men around me who sang the same songs, but in a familiar language. I listened, and the music in two languages seemed a contradiction to our war. Then I thought that these Germans would kill me if they got the chance. After an hour the voices stopped and again the woods were quiet. A few snowflakes came through the trees and I took off my shoes to again rub my feet."[20]

In the early hours of the following morning, all three armored infantry battalions were assembled for another move. Charlie Fitts related his resignation at the prospect of again fighting the winter in his half-track: "The engines roared and off we went again, but it seemed as though we were moving southwest. The driver was only a shape in the darkness, but I watched him wrestling with the steering wheel and gears. It was no easy job to keep these things on the road and keep on station behind the slit of red taillight that dimly glowed from the half-track ahead. I asked our driver where we were going. Benestroff was the answer."[21]

By December 26 and 27 the Hellcat Division had withdrawn into a reserve area about 25 miles southwest of Rohrbach and stretching as far south as Schweighausen.[22]

During the same time period, the Frundsberg Division had also been assigned as a reserve division. The division was spread from town to town in the Eifel. The 6th Company was encamped in Irlenbusch, south of Rheinbach, in early December. After Ernst Storch had chased after rumored tanks during most of November, he and two other Frundsbergers returned from the area of Linz. Ernst described his return to the division: "The men were off-loading a trainload of Panther and Panzer IVs. After reporting the dismal failure of my mission, I pitched in to help with the conditioning of the new tanks. I was amazed that after having scoured the Linz area for an elusive few tanks, my company was now the recipient of a trainload of factory-fresh tracked vehicles.

"I asked questions [about how] our luck had changed, but received scant information, other than it seemed something big was in the wind. Even though the work was hard, I was glad to be back among my comrades. When my trusted fellow crew members slapped my back, I knew they had missed me. I realized that I had missed them too. I was told that I was now the gunner in Second Lieutenant Helmut Stratmann's new 611 tank. Over the next week we fine-tuned the procedures and rehearsed a series of emergency drills.

"Stratmann ordered us to stand down. The driver lit a cigarette and the loader leaned back to relax. I pushed myself out the commander's hatch so that half my body was in the cold December air. Stratmann squatted on the engine cover, talking to Bernhard Westerhoff who looked up and recognized me. We exchanged mutual condolences on the failures of our two wild-goose-chase missions. I didn't tell either of the two in conversation that I had secretly stolen three days from our search to visit my parents in Vienna."[23]

The two divisions of the II Waffen SS Panzer Corps had been separated. The 9th Waffen SS Panzer Division, Hohenstaufen, was to take part in the Ardennes Offensive while the 10th Waffen SS Panzer Division, Frundsberg was held back and outfitted with replacement personnel and equipment, including an ample supply of tanks.[24]

By the middle of December 1944 the Frundsberg Division was brought up to full strength. It grew to 13,000 men, had between 80 and 90 tanks and was ready for any role given it in the coming great offensive.[25]

Bernhard Westerhoff was relieved of duties to become the company's new sergeant major. He was now directly under its commanding officer, Hans Quandel. Bernhard's new duties included responsibility for assignment of new equipment and personnel to the platoons. His job was to insure that each unit was ready for combat.[26]

The strengthened Frundsberg Division was to be held in reserve and used as necessary in a new offensive, one that was intended to split the American Seventh Army from its French units to the south of the American positions in Alsace. It was code-named Operation Northwind and would take advantage of the feeble American front north of Strasbourg. The bulk of the division, called the 1st Detachment, would cross the Rhine River from west to east. From there it would move south to Freistett and Bühl, on the east side of the Rhine River and across from the French towns of Gambsheim and Offendorf. Only two companies, called the 2nd Detachment, would be left on the west side of the Rhine River, the 6th and 7th Companies. These two would strike south at the appointed time to attack the Americans from the north.[27]

Heinz Harmel's original orders from General Blaskowitz read, "The 10th Waffen SS Panzer Division will be committed east of the Haguenau Forest and contact will be established as soon as possible with the bridgehead of the XIV SS Corps." This was the Oberrhein Force, which was to be commanded by Himmler himself.[28]

In the eastern Eifel, soldiers of 6th Company were able to take a break from their work as they waited for the 1st Detachment to cross the Rhine River and move south. Bernhard Westerhoff remembered the few days of relaxation: "As Christmas approached, we sang folk songs and played skat in the evening. Sometimes during the evening, we listened to the news from Berlin. Dr. Goebbels spoke of mysterious secret weapons and reminded the people of Germany that it was always darkest before the dawn. We talked about what the secret weapons might be and concluded that they were just wishful thinking. Goebbels may have been spinning lies, but it made no difference to us.

"Christmas was celebrated in a hall. Traditional hot Glüwein was served in punch glasses. Its taste was a reminder of home. The men told a few jokes and talked of times past, but it was a subdued affair, unlike the raucous time of a year before in France. For most, it was a time of reflection and thanks.

"Harmel appeared at the door. Punch glasses fell to the floor as I yelled for the men to stand at attention. The division commander held up a jovial hand and ordered us to resume our conversations. He moved from one man to the next, shaking hands, asking questions about families and complimenting the men on their readiness. As Harmel moved around the room, going from one man to the next, I watched his infectious grin. Then *der Alte* left as suddenly as he had appeared, at the end waving his hand and wishing us all a Merry Christmas.

"Two days later, Christmas had come and gone as we continued our work. At the end of a trying day, I dumped myself into a comfortable chair. I knew that whatever was in store for the company, it surely would take the lives of many of those around me, perhaps even me.

"I was ordered to company headquarters where officers explained in detail Operation Northwind, the coming great offensive in Alsace. They said the division was approaching full strength and 6th Company would soon move to Limburgerhof, to arrive on January 4. This was a small city just south of Ludwigshafen, a few miles to the west of the Rhine River. Some of the trip would be by rail, but there would be many miles to cover on foot.

"In Limburgerhof the work continued, because several more Panzer IV tanks were being delivered by rail. I had to inspect those assigned to the 6th Company and allocate them to the other senior sergeants. Each tank had to be readied for battle. Numbers were painted on each tank to designate the company and tank within the company. Additionally, I obtained whitewash paint and the men slopped the white chalky liquid on their tanks with mops. It might have been an enjoyable job had it not been for the bitter cold.

"I scurried to find enough winter weather clothing for my men. Each day seemed to be colder than the last and I warned the young replacements that keeping their feet dry might mean the difference in surviving this winter. I knew that these would be the last days of preparation before we were called upon to fight the Americans. We had time for a little relaxation. We played skat, listened to each other's worn-out jokes and wrote letters.

"One evening a corporal brought two bottles of schnapps to the billet. He refused to tell us how he had come to own such a marvelous wealth and he steadfastly denied that he had stolen the bottle. We sergeants were not inclined to search too deeply into the circumstances of the find. We preferred to relieve the corporal of his cargo. It was logical, we said, that the schnapps should be quickly consumed. Otherwise it might fall into the hands of the young Luftwaffe replacements that were not of age for such powerful alcohol. We also agreed that it was better to drink it this very night for fear that Quandel would use it as petrol for the new panzers. Thus persuaded, the corporal relinquished the two bottles. They were objects of admiration. Not only were they schnapps, but they were *Goldwasser* schnapps. Since then, whenever I drink Goldwasser, I think of that night when the little particles of gold looked so out of place in our world of war.

"Two men threw their skat cards onto the table and grabbed wineglasses while a third slit the first bottle's seal with his pocketknife. I was the most senior man present, and it was my duty to sample the Goldwasser before any of my men risked being poisoned. I swirled it to let it breathe. I had seen that done in a movie. I emulated the suave character in the movie by slowly tilting the glass to my lips and pretending to savor the schnapps. It tasted fine, but it could have been petrol and I would have approved. I gestured grandly for all glasses to be filled. The unopened bottle of schnapps remained untapped, perhaps for a future round of skat. It was snowing and only the sounds of breathing could be heard in the smoke-filled room. We fell asleep where we sat."[29]

Sixth Company consisted of 11 Panzer IVs, and would be supported by a small contingent of infantry from the 21st Panzergrenadier Regiment. The tanks moved south through Limburgerhof and Hexheim.[30] Tank commander Stratmann described the journey: "Our transport pulled out of Limburgerhof. Then we followed the road through Schifferstadt, Landau and Hayna, where we camped in the cover of a forest. Most of the time we traveled by night to avoid Allied aircraft. Eventually we reached the Leutenheim-Roeschwoog area where we spent a few days."[31] As dusk fell on January 3, 1945, 6th Company reached Roeschwoog. The men rushed their weapons and tanks under cover before Allied planes could find them. Vehicles were backed into barns and under trees. Bernhard related, "I was lucky enough to find a favorable accommodation in the house of a middle-aged lady. Before daybreak, my driver backed our Panzer IV into the driveway of the house. In doing so he demolished an arbor and vine which in summer must have been a point of pride for the lady. Both the driver and I apologized with genuine regret. She took the accident in stride, and as I continued to talk to the lady we became friends.

"By midmorning the area looked calm and peaceful. The tanks were hidden and it seemed as though we were invisible, not counting the damage to the arbor. Leopold Franke returned to the division, but in view of the advanced state of planning, Quandel remained as 6th Company commander. Franke was temporarily assigned to the 1st Detachment on the east side of the Rhine.

"During daylight hours I remained in the house, out of sight of Allied planes. I and the lady, Frau Schneider, spent the day in relaxing conversation. She was fearful of the war and I did my best to reassure her that no further harm would come to her or her house.

"A young lady named Manda entered the parlor and found me with Frau Schneider taking tea as though the war didn't exist. In a few minutes, Manda brought from the kitchen a tray of pastries, passed to me a torte-laden dish and joined in the conversation. She explained that the pastry had come from a shop in the town's center. It belonged to

Frau Schneider, her aunt. Although such delicacies were seldom to be found, Frau Schneider knew the back doors to many of the area's bakers and farmers.

"Manda invited me to the shop, which was a small pastry café, and although I promised I would try to come, I didn't think it would be possible. The next day I was told that Quandel would remain in Roeschwoog for a few days. Since I had a bit of time, I managed to find the café. Inside, I was greeted by Frau Schneider and Manda. The two women treated me with special kindness. I found their hospitality overwhelming, because Alsace civilian population was often hostile to the Germans and particularly to the Waffen SS.

"Steaming pork, red cabbage and potatoes on a blue oval platter were placed before me. After I had stuffed myself, the two women sat down at the table and poured tea. They talked of the war. Frau Schneider had a son in the Wehrmacht. Soldiers had come and had forcibly taken him away. He was only a boy and she lived in daily fear that he would be killed. She hated the Nazis and told me of her hatred. I was thankful that she was able to separate me from the reputation of the Nazis and the Waffen SS. In doing so, she somehow bridged my uniform to see the man under it. I explained to her that few men of the Waffen SS were Nazis in spite of our being a part of the Nazi government. I was not a party member and had no interest in politics. I was just a soldier, like her son. She asked me who was going to win the war. We three were alone in the café. I said that victory seemed improbable. Goebbels said that victory was in sight, but the maps told a different story. She asked why I kept on fighting. I told her that I had no choice. I had a wife and son and had to do my best to protect them.

"I think Frau Schneider and Manda understood. There was nothing more to be said about the war, but Frau Schneider described her inability to get a letter to her son. She knew not where he was or even if he were still alive. I proposed a solution. I would use my military postal number. Frau Schneider could write a letter to her son and I would mail the letter myself. Frau Schneider grabbed my hand and squeezed it. I was embarrassed. She disappeared into a back room and emerged with paper and pen. For a half hour she wrote at a table in the corner while Manda and I talked of life in better times."[32]

13

Schweighausen and La Breymuhl, January 1945

The 12th Armored Division had its battalions in various towns of the lower Alsace during the latter days of December 1944. Private First Class Charlie Fitts was in Bettviller with the 66th AIB on December 19, 1944. Later he wrote, "We went to the front and recaptured Bettviler, which had fallen while we were at Hirschland. While we held that town against continual counterattack shelling, Lieutenant James Kramer joined us from 66th Battalion headquarters and took Lieutenant Joseph's place as platoon leader. Lieutenant Joseph had replaced Captain Hayner after he was wounded."[1]

The 17th Armored Infantry Battalion was commanded by Major James W. Logan. Able Company was commanded by Captain Carl J. Helton, B Company by First Lieutenant Michael J. Muska, and C Company by Captain Steven M. Gombos.[2] The experience of the 17th Armored Infantry Battalion in the Bining and Rohrbach areas revealed to company commanders a problem that would plague the 12th Armored Division in the coming days of January. The problem lay not in battalion-level leadership, but in equipment and to some extent in the inexperience of the soldiers. George Hatt wrote, "The Battalion failed to establish communications between the three rifle companies and the Battalion CP. This failure presented an outstanding deficiency in 17th operations during December. Failure was caused by lack of batteries, and refusal of some units to turn on their radios for fear of revealing their positions to the Germans. Poor coordination of frequencies and lack of experience with the equipment led to poor communication. Furthermore there was no effort to lay wire for telephone communication."[3]

In the latter part of December 1944, the 17th AIB had moved to Inswiller. The division was still under SHAEF reserve status and the men spent their time training and cleaning equipment. Having some time on their hands, a few enthusiastic tank crew members of C Company, 23rd Tank Battalion, decided to enlighten the 17th Armored Infantry Battalion rifle carriers on the comforts of life in a tank. Pete Vickless and Ken Detrick had been with their infantry counterpart at Bining and drove to Inswiller for a day of orientation. This venture received approval since the 23rd Tank Battalion would be working hand in hand with the 17th AIB in the future.

Vickless and Detrick brought up their two Shermans and invited the men to take an orientation ride. The infantrymen gathered around the tanks and were waved aboard the Shermans in a gesture of hospitality. The men wore heavy clothing since it was cold, snowy and icy. Detrick commanded the first tank, which roared to life and thundered down the road. Men rode in and on the tank. Their winter gear flapped in the wind. It returned and the next tank, commanded by Pete Vickless, was ready. The bow gunner, loader and gunner climbed down from the tank to make room for the curious infantrymen.

George Hatt described his experience in the Sherman: "I approached the gunner, Corporal Frank Conway, and rhetorically asked if the Sherman was safe. His answer was reassuring. Two men climbed up on the engine deck. The first awkwardly threw his legs into the tank commander's hatch. He disappeared into the tank. The second squeezed himself into the oval hatch of the loader. I watched him as the infantryman's body slowly descended below the hatch rim. When his shoulders reached the rim, Conway shouted instructions as to how to fold his arms. At last the man was inside and now it was my turn. Conway told me to go around to the front of the tank and get into the bow gunner's position by a hatch that opened onto the front armor. He told me where to place my feet and how to slide into the hatch without skinning my arms. Finally, I managed to descend into the bowels of the machine. It was very tight and I had a twinge of claustrophobia. Vickless, who had taken his place in the turret with torso and head exposed, waved at those standing below him on the ground, inviting them to mount the engine deck. He seemed to enjoy showing off his machine to the infantrymen. The driver told me to reach up and pull the hatch cover shut. I did so and dogged the hatch. The interior was eggshell white, which reflected the dim interior lights. Daylight [seeping through] hatches provided a flickering second luminescence. A shaft of hatch daylight silhouetted the driver's body as he pushed and pulled the track-control levers. The engine started and revved. It was deafening. The tank leaped forward and immediately descended a steep, ice-covered hill. I knew things weren't as they should be when the driver pulled on both control sticks. The tank slid to one side as it continued down the hill, and I was thrown against the tank's right side armor. I tried to brace myself by holding onto the bow gunner's machine-gun butt, which whipped from side to side. I glanced at the driver whose legs were stiff and whose arms had a vise-grip on both track control levers.

"I imagined my gullible buddies riding on top must have been flying off like rag dolls. Suddenly the tank stopped and tipped violently to one side, balancing on its right track. It teetered there for a moment, then bounced back onto both its tracks. I looked at the driver pushing the start button to bring the stalled engine back to life. I attempted to rise, but bumped my head. The other two infantrymen in the tank demanded to exit and the tank commander opened the turret hatch to let one out. The other pushed himself up and out of the loader's hatch. Sergeant Vickless sat on the turret and beckoned for the men who had fallen off in the near-disaster to come aboard for the ride back up the hill. The infantrymen began their climb while shaking their heads in refusal of the tank sergeant's offer. Pete Vickless seemed truly disappointed by their lack of trust. I was the only infantryman to make the round trip. The tank roared back up the hill and onto the road. As I emerged from the tank, my buddies watched with a sense of admiration."[4]

On January 7, the platoon sergeant stuck his head in the door of the squad's billet and yelled for the men to saddle up. Curses and moans came from the lounging soldiers. Again, the half-tracks rumbled and squeaked through the valleys of Alsace. Again, the men huddled in the dark of the open half-track as it followed in line down endless little roads. Again, the half-tracks braked to a stop in a town with quaint houses lining the street. It was Schweighausen.

13. Schweighausen and La Breymuhl, January 1945

Sherman tanks of the 714th Tank Battalion, 12th Armored Division, on a sortie from Rohrweiler as part of Task Force Power which was to strike La Breymuhl and Herrlisheim on January 8 and 9, 1945 (National Archives).

The men moved into houses more comfortable than those of Inswiller. The elderly man and wife who lived in the house occupied by George Hatt and his fellow mortar squad team members were most hospitable.

On the day following their arrival George Hatt's mortar squad was stationed on the side of a road leading southeast out of Schweighausen. He looked down the empty road to make sure no Germans were coming. He described his attention to duty in the following terms: "As I peered down the road, I heard cackling. I was close to a chicken coop. I decided that the Germans must be somewhere else and entered the coop without hesitation. I wrung the necks of two plump hens. After being relieved of sentry duty, I took the limp bodies to my billet house in the center of town. When entering the house I held the birds high over my head, pronouncing them as legitimate booties of war. My buddies whistled and praised the return of the warrior. I presented the game to the old man of the house who clapped his hands with joy. He said that he and his wife would prepare the game for the table.

"Two hours later an aroma drifted from the kitchen to the squad's room where the perpetually tired soldiers lounged on the floor. The old man knocked and entered the room with a white towel over his arm. His wife followed in an apron as she held a large tray of food. The men cleared a small table and the couple laid before them chicken with potatoes and vegetables. Rich brown bread and butter accompanied the entrée. My experience in France at that point could be marked by the occasional but outstanding meals I had eaten: the wines of Auffay, Christmas dinner in Bining and now this in Schweighausen.

"Two days later I and Adrian Mariluch asked Sergeant Capretta if we could visit Ray Collier, Bill Little and Jack Jensen who were in a billet a couple of blocks away. Permission was granted and I pulled on my field jacket and pile liner for the walk through the slushy streets. Upon arriving, I and Adrian were greeted with the hospitality of long-lost friends. The fact that only days had passed since we'd talked didn't matter. Any break in the monotony of waiting was cause for celebration. The men of the billet produced a bottle of dark red wine which they said had been set aside for just such an occasion.

"Collier explained with great flourish that this particular wine was best served warm. He opened the bottle and placed it on a wood-burning stove. After a bit of conversation the bottle was removed from the stove and allowed to stand. Then Collier poured a goblet full to the brim. He handed it to me and I sipped the warm wine. After my first few swallows my feet began to respond by showing signs of life. By the time the goblet had been emptied, my feet had been transmuted from warmth, through comfort to complete lack of sensation. I felt as though I could tackle anything, but not at the moment.

"Sergeant Capretta burst into the room and ordered all men to fall out for mortar practice. We assembled in the cold afternoon air and marched out of town to a nearby field. I was a lowly ammunition carrier for the mortar squad. I had no responsibilities pertaining to the intricacies of the mortar. Capretta suspected that I wasn't paying attention to the drill. In spite of our former business relationship on the *Empress of Australia* he ordered me to set up the mortar single-handedly. I saluted and went to work, telling my feet how to proceed. The ground was covered with a thin film of ice, and each time I set the bipod legs and barrel in position, all three did a split like a can-can dancer at the Folies Bergère. My concentration was distracted by Sergeant Capretta's laughter. Finally, I sat on the ice and in my warm wine-glow simply shrugged my shoulders. That was the end of the mortar drill."[5]

As the Germans began their offensive in Alsace during the first week of January, the Americans in the area of Gambsheim-Drusenheim-Weyersheim responded as well as they could with the limited resources at hand. On January 1, 1945, the commanding general of the Seventh Army received permission from the Sixth Army Group's Lieutenant General Jacob L. Devers to release from SHAEF reserve the 36th Infantry Division and the 12th Armored Division if necessary. As enemy pressure grew, it was directed that the 12th Armored Division would establish a reconnaissance screen west of the Saar River and south of the Maginot Line.[6]

On January 5, the 232nd Infantry Regiment was assigned the task of hitting the Germans at Gambsheim. Lieutenant Colonel William Zeller, executive officer of the regiment, took his two battalions toward Gambsheim from the Weyersheim area. Radio communication was poor and coordinating the two task groups was difficult. One battalion ran into heavy machine-gun fire coming from a wooded area to the northwest of Gambsheim called the Steinwald. The other force crossed the Landgraben Canal and continued eastward but, lacking a clear order, returned to the canal. At nightfall on January 6, the Americans remained in position. Key officers of the two groups returned to Weyersheim for more specific instructions. Zeller assumed direct command of the effort. He brought the lagging group across the Zorn River and then pushed the men over the Landgraben. Six supporting tanks approached the Steinwald and were turned back by fire from Panzerfausts. American artillery silenced the Germans who were attempting to defend the woods, and the U.S. forces were able to move through and around the wooded area. Led by Lieutenant Colonel Zeller, the force reached the Gambsheim railroad bed. Still without radio communication and without wire telephone, coordinating the two groups was impossible. Zeller found a company of men awaiting orders at the Landgraben Canal. He was told by a sergeant that the company was returning to Hoerdt on orders received over the tank radio net. He rushed back to his trailing units and deployed them along both sides of the Weyersheim-Gambsheim road for the advance. Meanwhile, the other group was at the Gambsheim railway station. The plan had called for one group to attack Gambsheim from the south through Kilstett and the other to attack it from the north along the railroad line, but without communication such a coordinated attack was impossible. The group attacking from the north saw tanks in the town and believed them to be Shermans. When the tanks opened fire on the group it was apparent that the Germans were in Gambsheim in sufficient force to overcome an American attack. The northern group disengaged quickly without great loss and returned to Weyersheim. The group approaching from the south never made it to Gambsheim. The men returning from the aborted attack arrived in the Weyersheim area in a state of shock, some speaking incoherently. Despite this, it was estimated that German strength in the Steinwald was minimal.[7]

German divisions attacked on January 1 from northeast to southwest against a 25-mile front. The 44th and 100th Infantry Divisions were able to blunt the advance of the Germans to the north, but the 45th Infantry Division was driven back in several sectors. In the south, German forces held an area around Colmar south of Strasbourg. A strong German force crossed the Rhine River and quickly overwhelmed the Americans in the Gambsheim area. It was apparent to American intelligence that the German crossing of the Rhine River between Offendorf and Gambsheim was intended to create a bridgehead from which a pincer movement could retake Strasbourg from north and south simultaneously. As the situation developed, the 12th AD was thrown into the lower Alsace to thwart the anticipated German movement. Unfortunately, American intelligence had drastically underestimated the German forces. It was determined at Seventh Army Headquarters that a quick attack could take Herrlisheim, a pivotal town in the area.[8]

Colonel Charles V. Bromley, CCB's commanding officer, drew up a plan whereby a force would move out of the Bischweiler area on January 7, march through Rohrweiler, then continue east to the village of La Breymuhl, where it would turn south to take Herrlisheim from the north. The hasty plan was in response to pressure from VI Corps headquarters and was based on faulty assumptions of German strength.[9] A German prisoner had reported that only a company of 553rd Panzergrenadiers was in Herrlisheim and the Waterworks.[10] Bromley's intention was to take Herrlisheim simultaneously from the north using the 56th AIB and 714th TB while other American forces would attack it from the south.[11] He had been offered the opportunity to attack only from the south through French lines with the Rhine on its right flank; however, he decided upon a direct attack which would use the Bischweiler-Rohrweiler route still held by the 79th Infantry Division.[12]

Colonel Bromley's 56th Armored Infantry Battalion, 714th Tank Battalion, 49th Armored Field Artillery Battalion, and B Company of the 119th Armored Engineer Battalion made up the force that was attached to the 79th Infantry Division of VI Corps. At the same time, on January 7, Bromley moved his headquarters to Hochfelden, which added an element of confusion in a demanding situation. He ordered his force to attack the town of Herrlisheim on January 8. Early that morning, the 56th AIB and the 714th

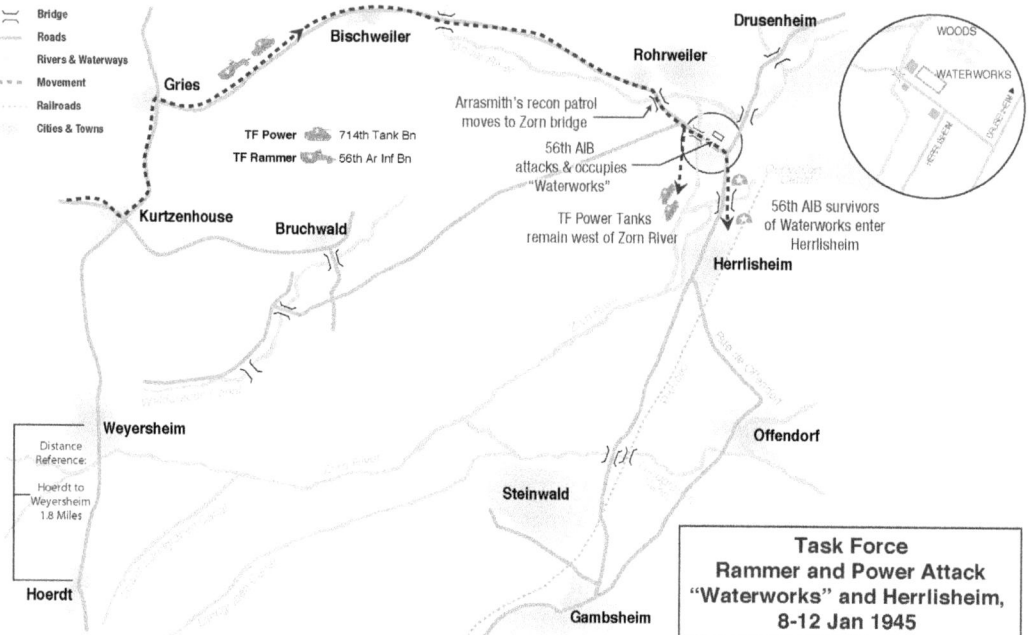

Task Force Rammer and Power Attack "Waterworks" and Herrlisheim, 8-12 Jan 1945

TB moved through Kurtzenhouse and into Rohrweiler, which would be their jumping-off point. The 56th AIB was to move eastwards about a mile, cross a river, then swing south and attack Herrlisheim from the north.[13] Destroyed bridges over the Zorn Canal and Moder River prevented the 714th tanks from supporting the infantry of the 56th AIB; however, Colonel Bromley was under the impression that both the Zorn Bridge at La Breymuhl and the Moder Bridge were intact.[14] Few provisions were made for radio communication between the tank crewmen and the infantry. The result was that the 56th AIB moved into an unknown situation entirely on its own.[15]

While most of the 12th Armored Division was still performing drills and reconnaissance, Robert Arrasmith in the 56th Armored Infantry Battalion was taking his first steps toward what was to be his worst nightmare. The battalion was preparing to engage the Germans. He simply obeyed whatever orders came to him, but he had little understanding of what he was facing. Rumors were tossed around as Robert and his fellow soldiers in B Company moved in half-tracks from one location to the next. He overheard sergeants talking about Task Force Rammer and assumed that he was somehow a part of that group.

Before sunrise Task Force Rammer in Combat Command B pushed off from the town of Kurtzenhouse along with Task Force Power, the 714th Tank Battalion. Robert rode in a half-track along with other soldiers who vaguely knew that they were going to occupy a couple of towns. He wasn't concerned because he had been told that most of the Germans had already moved out and crossed the Rhine River to the east. The sun had not yet risen on January 7, 1945, as Robert's half-track headed toward Bischweiler. From there it would go on to Rohrweiler.

On January 8 most of the division's headquarters staff was located in Hochfelden, but two days later it moved again, this time to Weyersheim. This produced further communication problems at a critical time of attack.[16]

13. Schweighausen and La Breymuhl, January 1945

The Moder River formed Rohrweiler's southern perimeter; dense woods were to the east and north of the town. Colonel Bromley, commanding Task Force Rammer, could not be assured that Germans might not be lurking in the woods between Rohrweiler and Drusenheim even though both of the towns were in American hands. Drusenheim was occupied by the 3rd Battalion of the 314th Regiment, reinforced by A Company of the 232nd Infantry.[17]

Robert Arrasmith told of his naive introduction to combat: "My half-track halted just east of Bischweiler on the Bischweiler-Rohrweiler road paralleling the Moder River. I followed other men in my company as we leaped down from our half-track and crept along the road expecting the enemy to jump out from every bush. A sergeant at the head of the column signaled for us to scatter into the field north of the road. I ran into the field and looked to the east in the direction others were moving. It was a bitterly cold morning and the area was shrouded in dull-gray fog. At the edge of the field was a shadowy, dark line of dense trees. To the right of the trees was the town of Rohrweiler. The roofs of its houses were dark silhouettes as the sun rose behind them.

"Tanks of the 714th Battalion had kept to the road, and as they approached from the west, B Company emerged from the field to accompany the tanks entering the town. All seemed in order, and thus far, I hadn't seen a single German soldier.

"Captain Beach, our company commander, wanted to know just how far away the Germans were. At noon, I and nine other men were assigned to a reconnaissance patrol to investigate the road that crossed the Moder River and then ran southeast toward the village of La Breymuhl. We crept along both sides of the Rohrweiler-Drusenheim Road. We took every step with caution and tried to stay off the road itself even though walking in the snow-covered field was difficult. We spotted a small bridge ahead, and instinctively dove to the ground. I lay on my stomach and my ammunition pouches bit into my thigh. The weight of my hatchet which I carried on my leg was becoming a burden, but it had been with me since basic training and I refused to let it go. I rose slightly and scanned down the road to the bridge. On the other side was an undefined massive red brick building. I thought I could hear German commands being given and could see movement among the buildings. Then mortar rounds burst all around us while machine-gun fire dug up the field.

"I didn't need to be told to get out of the area. I ran back to the road toward Rohrweiler expecting at any moment to be killed by flying bullets. After I had run out of machine-gun range I looked around and found that I was alone. The poor visibility prevented me from seeing beyond fifty yards, but I thought the other men of the patrol had made their escape by keeping to the woods. Then I heard heavy boots of men running toward me and knew that the Germans were in hot pursuit. I ran until I saw an abandoned car beside the road. It had been blown up and its rusting body was sitting upside down with tireless wheels jutting skyward. It offered a hopeful hiding place. I jumped behind it and grabbed my hatchet. Digging furiously I managed to excavate a hole in the frozen earth beneath the car. I slid into the hole and pushed snow and dirt to cover the excavation. My heart thumped in my chest as I knew that if the Germans looked closely they would see the fresh dirt on the snow.

"The sound of boots came nearer and stopped. I peeked out of a gap between the car's down-turned roof and lip of the hole. All I could see were black boots caked with mud. The Germans were breathing hard from the chase, and they talked in excited tones.

Drusenheim on January 6, 1945, as the U.S. 314th Infantry Regiment (79th Infantry Division) takes up defensive positions in the northwest quadrant of the town. The buildings are shown intact, but many were destroyed in the subsequent German attack of January 16 (National Archives).

I tried to remember the German I had learned from my prisoners, but I could only understand a few words. I remained motionless as the Germans walked up and down the road, each time passing the abandoned car. My breathing was so loud I thought the Germans must surely hear it.

"I was terrified and shivered from fear and the unremitting cold. At last the voices seemed to fade. I again looked through the gap, saw nothing, but couldn't be certain the Germans had gone. I remained quiet for another ten minutes, then dug my way out of the self-made tomb. I jogged to Rohrweiler, not looking back to see who might be chasing me. Upon reaching the town I hollered the password to the sentries along the road and found my way back to my squad. Buddies wanted to know what had happened to me and I gave them a blow-by-blow description of my escape. It would have been a better story if three men on patrol hadn't been killed. I repeated my story to the company commander, who insisted that I show him exactly where the firing had come from. I pointed to the spot on the map where I thought the action had taken place. The captain called it 'the waterworks.'

"Around noon, my squad again headed southeast out of Rohrweiler. We walked along the road advancing slowly to the southeast. Each man was ready to dash into the fields if the Germans started shooting. As I passed the abandoned car I wondered how the Germans could have missed me. I knew the La Breymuhl Waterworks were not far ahead and from what I had seen earlier I expected the Germans to open up at any moment. We had to get by the Waterworks if we were to get into Herrlisheim.

"Heavy machine guns and mortar rounds began dropping around us. I dove for cover just north of the La Breymuhl Bridge. Here I was momentarily safe from machine-gun fire, but I had to get my squad up and moving in the face of intense fire coming from behind the brick walls of the Waterworks. Suddenly, the fire lifted. I looked to the west and saw the tanks of 714th Battalion along the Zorn Canal's west bank. They were pounding the old buildings with fire and the Germans responded by shifting their fire away from the infantry and onto the tanks. Taking advantage of the situation, I and the others of my squad ran to a utility building on the opposite side of the road from the brick Waterworks buildings. The next moment an explosion came from behind. I saw pieces of bridge descending in the midst of billowing smoke. They were the remains of the Zorn Canal Bridge on the road leading east from Rohrweiler. It was an insignificant bridge, one of hundreds that dotted Alsace landscape, but it stopped our tanks from supporting us at the Waterworks.

"Infantry pushed its way across the road and into the shrubbery surrounding the half-demolished walls of the Waterworks. As each man ran across the road he fired his weapon from the hip. Covering fire from American infantry came from both sides of the road, but German sharpshooters hit a lot of us. They shot from behind walls and broken machinery. Soon, bodies littered the road. Mortar rounds mixed with small arms fire and each strike took the lives of more infantrymen. It was treacherous and intense combat of the worst kind.

The brickyard, west of the waterworks at La Breymuhl, lay adjacent to the Moder River and Zorn River/Canal (National Archives).

"We began jumping over the half-demolished brick walls. We ran headlong into German positions, firing as we went. It became soldier against soldier in hand-to-hand combat. Men were killed with knives, some even strangled. My mind and body fought savagely with no regard for my own preservation. I killed, leaped forward then killed again. Gradually, the Germans withdrew from the roofless remains and ran to the east, leaving their dead behind. I stood in a pile of red brick rubble. I looked around and saw only Americans who also stood quietly with rifles ready. Realizing that the noise of battle had ended, I sat down where I was. As the adrenaline ebbed in my muscles they began to shake. I trembled and didn't understand why my legs should be shaking. Exhaustion overcame me and I lay on the bricks, looking skyward. My breathing slowed and the shaking stopped. Raising myself on an elbow I looked at my comrades who were sprinkled on the bricks and dirt like brown leaves on a fall day.

"After five minutes of rest, sergeants began hollering for their men to keep after the Germans. I rose, gripped my rifle and began stumbling over the loose bricks toward the north and east end of the structure. I mounted a wall and from there fired at movement along an orchard's edge. The orchard was to the east of the Waterworks with its southern border along the north side of the Drusenheim Road. Meanwhile other infantrymen pushed farther northeast, enduring heavy mortar fire and taking casualties as they went.

"My squad pulled out of the building's skeleton and took shelter in a barn at the southeast corner of the La Breymuhl and Herrlisheim Road intersection. My body sagged under the strain of the day's almost continuous fighting. My stomach reminded me that I hadn't eaten since long before daylight. Opening a box of C rations, I ate the crackers, but couldn't summon the energy to pry the lid off a can of franks and beans. I fell back where I was and closed my eyes to sleep for only an hour when I was ordered to help defend the Waterworks from a possible counterattack. I staggered out of the barn and back to the killing ground of the brick buildings. I crouched among the rubble as mortar shells exploded around me.

"Germans came from the orchard, running hard to retake the red brick walls. They pinned themselves to the east walls and lobbed concussion grenades into the interior. The grenades failed to cause damage and we lobbed our own grenades over the walls into the laps of the Germans. It grew dark and two German tanks came up the road from Herrlisheim trying to bring down the brick walls with their cannons. They couldn't depress their guns adequately and so inflicted almost no damage. Private Robert L. Scott grabbed a bazooka and rushed to within six feet of the lead tank. The tube failed to fire when the trigger was pulled. Scott ran back, grabbed another bazooka and returned to the tank. He fired at point-blank range and succeeded in blowing off a track. He was knocked over by the blast, but lurched back to safety. The crew of the second tank heaved cables onto the crippled tank's towing clevis and pulled it back to Herrlisheim."[18]

By now the entire force of the 56th Battalion's three companies had been committed to the fighting in the waterworks. It was an ugly and savage engagement, with each side pushing in more and more men. Germans and Americans were dying in equal numbers. In the early morning hours of the next day, American light tanks raced back and forth between Rohrweiler and the destroyed Zorn Bridge. They carried the wounded out and replacements in. Each tank was pummeled with mortar and artillery fire as it negotiated the short distance along what came to be called "Purple Heart Lane."

At sunrise, the Germans began to surrender in large numbers. Staff Sergeant Charles

"Purple Heart Lane" east of Rohrweiler with fields on both sides of the elevated road. Tanks were forced to avoid the fields because beneath a frozen layer of soil was soft mulch, which made traction impossible (National Archives).

Peischl of B Company left his protected position and told the surrendering Germans in their language that American medics would attend to their wounded.

Tanks of Task Force Power followed the west side of the Zorn river toward Herrlisheim. They took stations along the road to the west of the town and shot a few ranging shots at the town's Central Church steeple. The ground was crusted with ice beneath which was soft earth. The roads were built up higher than the surrounding fields which gave the defending Germans excellent opportunity to harass the tanks of the 714th TB. Entering the fields was an invitation to getting stuck in the unfavorable ground, so the 714th tanks did their best under difficult conditions.[19]

The fighting at the waterworks had reduced the strength of the 56th AIB. It had not only taken many lives and wounded many others; it had taken the energy from the those that had survived. Despite exhaustion and little sleep during the previous night, the men of the battalion were ordered to take Herrlisheim. Ferguson described the condition of the battalion: "Running into heavy German resistance, the 56th fought for hours in the Waterworks plant just outside of Herrlisheim and remained in the Waterworks overnight. Resuming the offensive the next morning, the infantrymen of the 56th ran into stiff machine gun and mortar fire, which slowed their advance and inflicted heavy casualties."[20]

Because the bridge over the Zorn Canal at La Breymuhl had been destroyed by the

One of the two temporarily repaired bridges over the Moder River at the southeast approach to Rohrweiler. The road running east from this bridge to the bridge over the Zorn Canal at La Breymuhl was called "Purple Heart Lane" by the soldiers of the 56th Armored Infantry Battalion, who suffered great loses at the Battle of the Waterworks on January 8, 1945 (National Archives).

Germans, the 56th AIB had lost the support of the 714th TB. Those tanks had remained on the west side of the bridge and now were restricted in movement as they waited for the engineers to bring a Bailey bridge from sources that were far in the rear. The 56th AIB was effectively cut off as it prepared to enter Herrlisheim.[21]

Robert Arrasmith described his advance into Herrlisheim and his two harrowing days in the town: "I and my squad members went to work with trenching tools, digging where Platoon Sergeant Charles Peischl pointed. We dug furiously in the ice-hard clay. Then the sergeant heard something. He whispered for us to stop digging and to shut up. We grabbed our rifles and stood motionless, breathing hard with white vapor coming from our open mouths. It was afternoon, but the fog hung low in patches.

"I saw the Germans as approaching silhouettes in relief against the blazing houses of Herrlisheim that had been hit by 714th tanks lined up on the other side of the Zorn. I looked from the unsuspecting Germans to Peischl, who stood as still as a tree trunk with his Thompson ready to fire. The Germans sensed danger and halted in the mist, close to us. Then Peischl sent a stream of bullets cutting into the Germans. We followed, and many Germans were killed by Americans they never saw. Peischl forgot the need for foxholes and the squad skirted around the dead Germans as we continued along the road to Herrlisheim. We stopped again, this time to listen to artillery shelling the town in front of us. It was a softening-up enterprise for the major event to take place that day. The revised plan of attack called for A and B Companies of the 56th Armored Infantry Battalion to continue south into Herrlisheim, but just how many of us were a part of the effort I didn't know.

"We stayed together and kept off the road, paralleling it as we had been taught in basic training. There was sporadic small arms fire coming from the houses that I could see ahead. I began to think that this mission might be a pushover after the beating at the Waterworks. The squad came to a concrete-lined canal that was about thirty feet wide and quite deep. The steep slope of the canal's slippery sides was an invitation to drowning. I looked to see what the other squads were doing. They seemed to be paralleling the canal to the west. I signaled for the others to follow and we too turned west. I saw men scrambling across a narrow footbridge and followed them. Soon we were on the south side of the canal, heading into Herrlisheim from the northwest. American artillery fire had stopped. We would now mop up any Germans left after the artillery had done its job.

"Our tanks redeployed farther south along the bank of the Zorn to the west of the town and fired blindly, but well ahead of our advance. Then [the shelling from our tanks faded] as I approached houses. Bullets hammered stone dwellings and ricocheted near me. Each tumbling bullet whined and the noise seemed to come from all directions.

"The northern outskirts of Herrlisheim were bristling with German machine guns. I thought this wasn't going to be the easy occupation that the higher-ups said it would be. The job was to occupy the town, house by house, but from the start I knew we were outnumbered and outgunned. Losses were mounting and I could hear behind me cries for a medic. Still, we pushed forward along Rue de Bischweiler and Rue de Village. By evening, the radios failed. Our platoons had lost radio contact with each other and with the company command post. None of us knew what to do. As the sun set, we had penetrated to the Rue de l'Argile, occupying a total of about forty houses. German guns in the northeast sector of Herrlisheim effectively sealed off the approaches to the town from all directions. We didn't know it then, but we were trapped. I could feel the German presence at every dark corner and every abandoned house.

"Herrlisheim had been deserted by most of its inhabitants and the buildings were hollow structures with dark, glassless windows. Most had their roofs shot away and gables stood like skeletal ribs. German shelling from Offendorf had been well spotted by German observers in the steeples of churches, but that, too, had ceased. Now the houses of northern Herrlisheim looked empty, but we hid in the houses, sometimes alone, sometimes with a buddy. We waited for the Germans to come while praying for rescue by our division comrades. I was alone in the remnants of a house on the Rue de l'Argile. It was a typical two-story Alsace dwelling that had once had a fine slate roof. It had shattered and most of the tiles had fallen to the ground. The upper story with its furniture and carpets was soggy from melted snow. Only its fruit cellar remained intact without damage.

"I blindly descended steps into the cellar. It was dark and I felt my way into a corner. Here I sat and removed my boots. I had to attend to my feet, which now were numb from the cold. When I slid my socks from my feet I worked my toes. There was no feeling when I rubbed my feet. I pushed downward on my legs and massaged my feet, trying to get blood into the extremities. A slight tingling sensation signaled that perhaps my toes were not beyond help. I was thus occupied when I heard voices in German at the entrance to the house. I quickly pulled on my moist socks and boots, then ascended the stairs as quietly as I could. I still heard the harsh voices and so retreated up the main stairs to the upper floor. Entering a bedroom I looked around the darkness for a place to hide. The front door banged open and blustering German soldiers entered. Before I could formulate any kind of plan for hiding, I heard shouting and heavy footsteps on the stairway. Looking up, I thought I saw the sky. Part of the roof above the bedroom had been shot away. It was large enough for a person to go through, and I quickly mounted a dresser. From there I pulled myself up through the hole and slid out onto the steeply slanting roof.

"The remaining slate shingles were covered with ice and snow. I slid on my back down the slope and flew off the roof of the house into the pitch-black night. I landed in a deep snowdrift that cushioned my fall. I had survived the fall, but expected at any moment to be shot by the inquisitive Germans who must have heard the racket above them. I bounced out of the drift and ran through frozen gardens to the rear of a house on Rue de Village. A shell hole, the size of a car, provided a convenient entrance. Its walls provided cover from the marauding Germans and its cellar offered protection from the bitter cold. Again I removed my boots and soggy socks. I rubbed my feet with the little energy I had left. My feet were painful and my toes were numb. This was a sign of frostbite. I was also hungry and I was in imminent danger, but most of all, I was tired. It had been three days since I had slept. My body had reached the end of its endurance and I lay in the cellar only half-conscious. With desperate deliberation I managed to retrieve from my kit my last pair of dry socks. I pulled these over my feet and laced up my boots. Then I gave in to fatigue and slept."[22]

During the night of January 10, German tanks roamed the streets of Herrlisheim, shooting into buildings at random. The isolated infantry companies of the 56th Battalion spent a lonely, anxious night. On January 11 all was quiet in Herrlisheim. Those few who got out were safely behind American lines in Rohrweiler. Those left in the town were either killed or captured. A very few still remained in the houses. They were hounded by German patrols.[23]

In La Breymuhl, the waterworks remained in American hands and Bailey bridge building materials had arrived. The engineers went to work as more 714th tanks awaited orders back in Rohrweiler. The bridge was completed in the afternoon of January 11. Battalion headquarters ordered that a reconnaissance platoon with powerful radios be sent into Herrlisheim so that Combat Command B could determine the status of the infantrymen in the town. Six tanks started down the Rohrweiler-Herrlisheim Road, but when they drew near Herrlisheim, they encountered fleeing American soldiers who shouted that the Germans had surrounded the remaining Americans and were in the process of killing them one by one. The officer in charge of the unit turned his tanks around and returned to Rohrweiler, where he explained what he had encountered at the northern outskirts of Herrlisheim.[24]

The same six light tanks responded when Colonel Bromley again ordered them to enter Herrlisheim and get the men out. The tanks were under way and again preparing to cross the Bailey bridge at La Breymuhl when a radio message from Bromley's Combat Command B told them to return to Rohrweiler. He had again changed his mind. The men in Herrlisheim were to fight off the Germans by themselves. Bromley's vacillating orders were a product of his subordinate officers who pressed him for a rescue mission and the persistence of those at corps headquarters who still believed the German forces were weak. The soldiers in Herrlisheim waited for rescue when the decision had been made to abandon them. In fact, a few tanks did manage to get into Herrlisheim, but the well-spotted artillery in Offendorf soon turned them around. The German commander of the town's forces, Captain Charles von Lüttichau, ordered his men to mop up the remaining Americans.

Robert continued, "I was jolted by the stepped-up shelling as I ascended the cellar stairs. I looked out a window to see German Panthers creeping along the Rue de Village shooting at houses for no apparent reason. I remained in the cellar on the Rue de Village into the night. Shelling came in waves. As I tried to sleep, German tanks roamed the streets of the town shooting at anything resembling an enemy. One nearby blast awakened me, but I quickly went back to sleep. It was only a matter of time before the Germans found me. In the meantime I would sleep. I awakened in the afternoon of January 11. I removed my boots and again massaged my feet. After putting my boots back on I celebrated the fact that I was still alive by opening my last C ration pack.

"With darkness came a deepening depression. I had no food and no hope. At around midnight, someone entered the house. I vaguely heard the sound of boots on the main floor above. There were voices. I listened. They were American. I instinctively started yelling that I was down in the cellar. Footsteps thumped on the stairs, then a flashlight beam blinded me. I raised my hand to shield my eyes from the brightness and squinted to see who was there. An American with an Alabama accent hollered for others to help him get a frozen soldier up the stairs. I could only manage a hoarse whisper. I tried to convey the condition of my feet which were numb. The burly corporal from Alabama hoisted me onto my feet. He supported me up the stairs. Blood began to flow in my half-frozen limbs and I took a deep breath. I could walk on my own. We went out by the front entrance, which I had never seen. On the Rue de Village stood a light tank with its engine running. Men clung to the back of the tank. Someone shouted for the guys to shake a leg. The krauts were closing in. I squeezed between the other equally exhausted soldiers, and the tank crept up the road that would take us to Rohrweiler and safety.

"I looked at the other men as the tank headed north. They were wrecks. I must have looked the same. My eyes closed for what seemed to me to be only seconds. Then the tank halted and we swayed to the deceleration. The sergeant jumped down from the turret and ran forward. He quickly returned with bad news. The bridge over the derivation canal was down again. The tank was now trapped on the south side of the derivation canal, although it was to the east of the Zorn Canal. The tank commander gave the soldiers a choice. They could stick with the tank and risk death that way or try to make it north on foot and risk death that way.

"We climbed down. Better to risk it on foot. The tank sped off down a side street. I and the four unknown men looked down at the canal. It was dark, but I could see that it had the same steep concrete sides I had seen a few days before. We agreed that to try swimming across would be suicidal. I thought of the footbridge I had crossed when entering Herrlisheim. To retrace those steps would be to walk into a hidden firing squad. I wasn't in charge of anything or anybody, but I ordered the men to look for something to make a raft. The men searched to the east along the south side of the canal. I ran over to a man who had stumbled upon a stack of loose lumber. Heavy planks looked like railroad ties. Spools of thin cable and spikes were partially covered in snow. The others remained where they were as I went to work with my hatchet. It had helped me survive once before. Perhaps it would do so again. I and two others lashed the planks together. After an hour, a heavy, crude semblance of a raft was pulled over to the edge of the canal. I motioned for the other two to help me push the monster down the slope. It slid into the water and I held it by a length of cable. I jumped in after it. The water was near freezing and it jolted my body. The unstable craft would never remain upright without someone to hold it. The cold water gripped me like a vise. I sucked in air and managed to hang on to the raft with one hand. Two soldiers on shore took my jacket sleeve and haltingly lowered themselves onto the flat boards. They barely supported the weight. I descended the slanted sides until the canal's bottom left my feet. Using a sidestroke, I pulled the raft the short distance until my feet again touched the opposite sloping side. I held the raft as best I could, as the men scrambled up the bank. Then, I dragged the raft back to the south bank where the other two men slid onto it. I pulled the raft across. As I tried to climb the last few feet of the canal's side, my body succumbed to fatigue and cold. Water poured from my clothing and I shivered violently. I reached out for help, then slipped and began to slide back into the water. That was my last memory of Herrlisheim.

"Seven hours later I was awakened by a medic. When I opened my eyes everything was white. A doctor came to my side. I had come close to not making it, but with the exception of my feet I was recovering. It took a month for my frostbitten feet to recover. It was a slow and painful process."[25]

The partial success in liberating some of the trapped men in Herrlisheim has been attributed to the accurate American artillery fire which kept the Germans from overwhelming the small retrieval force.[26]

While Robert Arrasmith had gone through torment in Herrlisheim, most soldiers of the 12th Armored Division had yet to face Germans in strength. In battalion-sized units, they edged closer to a confrontation with the enemy, converging on towns in the area of Weyersheim.

14

Althussheim, January 1945

Private First Class Wilhelm Balbach of the 13th Heavy Artillery Company, 10th Artillery Regiment, 10th Waffen SS Panzer Division, was only 19 years old. He had been drafted into the military and after basic training had been assigned to the Frundsberg Division over his protests. As a result he had little enthusiasm for his job as an observer for artillery. His only comrade was Corporal Ludwig Scheffler, with whom he liked to discuss the merits of Beethoven, Bach and the other masters.

On January 7, 1945, he lounged on a cot during an hour off duty. It was to be his last relaxation for the duration of the war. He explained his sudden reversal of fortune: "Scheffler disturbed me by announcing that he had good news. He said that we were to take a Kübel and reconnoiter the roads to Freistett and Bühl. When I showed a lack of interest, he explained to me that the division's artillery would be transported over specific roads and that it was important that no obstructions prevented the guns from reaching their destination. I wasn't impressed. Scheffler shook my shoulder, demanding a respect for his rank that was not in my nature. I contemplated Scheffler's plan and a few half-hearted questions prompted Scheffler to embellish his explanation with promises of promotion and medals.

"I rose from my cot and acquiesced to Scheffler's optimistic future. We arranged ourselves for proper presentation to the company commander. The officer's pep talk followed the same strain as Scheffler's. The artillery regiment was an important element of the Frundsberg Division. Its movement to the south was crucial to its mission. The officer outlined the forthcoming move of the regiment to the Rhine River west of Bühl and Freistett. His finger slid along the map and we made mental notes of each town along the way. We were both artillery observers and knew what was needed for clearances and road widths. The lieutenant emphasized that his 88s were delicate and he didn't want them banged up going around sharp turns between brick buildings. At the end of his exhortation he glared at us and demanded our oath that no mistakes would be made.

"We saluted and trotted back to the billet to stuff our personal gear into travel bags. We picked up a Volkswagen Kübel and the relevant maps. Scheffler took the wheel and I sat beside him with maps on my lap. As he started the engine I guessed that the lieutenant had given us this responsible assignment because we were the most trustworthy of the Frundsberg observers. That conjecture made me feel a little better.

"The Kübel had a canvas top that snapped into a retractable wooden frame, but its sides were open. We zipped down the road like carefree vacationers. Scheffler gripped the wheel with three fingers, two of which also manipulated a lighted cigarette. He was the essence of confidence. His left arm poked through the canvas flap into the cold air which penetrated the interior like an arctic storm. It was clear to me that this adventure was going to be a test of my patience. Scheffler pulled off the road and started digging through his gear for gloves. I followed the example. I knew they would hinder my map reading, but it would be better than frozen fingers. Scheffler pulled his coat collar as high as possible, then steered the Kübel back onto the street. Soon we were speeding along unfamiliar roads as I penciled onto my map each potential hazard to a convoy of trucks and guns that would follow in two days.

"Each time the little car came to a village, Scheffler downshifted to keep the engine at a high RPM. I noticed that each shift was producing ominous grinding sounds. I mentioned this to the determined Scheffler, who ignored any mechanical problems. We pressed on until he too had his doubts about the transmission. He was forcing the gearshift handle and he knew that a Volkswagen's transmission should be smooth and light to the touch. When we entered Althussheim, Scheffler braked for a sharp corner and tried to downshift. A loud bang came from the transmission and the gearshift lever sat limp in its housing. The Volkswagen glided to a stop in the center of the village.

"It was getting dark and I looked up and down the streets for signs of life. They seemed deserted. The likelihood of finding a mechanic was remote. They had long since been inducted into the Wehrmacht. We strolled along the winding, narrow streets of the town until we came upon a house with a slit of light shining from behind blackout curtains. It looked inviting and Scheffler knocked. An old man came to the door. He was only a

Private First Class Wilhelm Balbach, observer for the 13th Heavy Artillery Battalion of the 10th Waffen SS Panzer Division, who called down the barrage that destroyed at least 12 Sherman tanks on January 16, 1945, in the fields between the Steinwald Woods and the town of Herrlisheim (Balbach collection).

shadow in the dimly lit hallway. Scheffler asked him for a night's lodging. The old man tried to complain, but it was the law. Citizens were required to provide a space for soldiers who asked for a billet. As he stammered, his wife came to the door. She opened it wide and waved for us to enter.

"I heard the old man whisper to his wife. He wasn't thrilled to have soldiers with dusty boots sleeping in one of his beds. I looked down at my boots. They seemed surprisingly polished and I wondered why the old man took such offense at our presence. The lady of the house apologized for her husband. She said that he had not adjusted well to the war. Their son was on the eastern front and they hadn't heard from him in over a month. Scheffler mumbled something and I said that I was sorry for the inconvenience. The four of us entered the living room, closing a heavy curtain. There was a fire and the room was cozy. Two overstuffed chairs and a divan made up the furniture, and the lady gestured for Scheffler and me to sit. I stepped to the mantel above the fireplace. I looked at a small photograph of a young man in Wehrmacht uniform. The couple's son had the appearance of every other young man. He was my age, but already looked tired. The old lady was proud. She said his name was Gunther. He had been in the Hitler Youth and couldn't wait to get into the Army. When she admitted that he was fighting the Russians her voice showed the strain of uncertainty.

"The old lady was looking at me with a faint interest and I gave her my own brief biography including living on a ten-hectare farm with the obligations that went with it. The land was rich and my father worked from sunrise to sunset. My older brother Hermann and I had gone to school in Groningen, then to Gymnasium in Crailsheim. Upon graduation I went to work for the city of Würtemberg, then did my service with the Reich Labor Service, building bunkers in Marseilles, France. I was drafted into the Waffen SS. That was in September 1943.

"The next day Scheffler and I tried to find a mechanic. It quickly became apparent that this effort was futile. Our only hope for continuing the assignment was to flag down a passing vehicle. In the afternoon we stood on the street and waited for a Wehrmacht or Waffen SS truck. None came by. Not a single vehicle of any kind came through the town. It was as if we were stranded on an island without a ship in sight. In the late afternoon we gave up and returned to the house. Again apologizing for the second day of lodging, I assured the old woman that the next day would bring more success.

"The second evening with the old couple was pleasant. Having young men at the table reminded the old couple of better days when their son had brought his schoolmates home for dinner. We engaged in nonpolitical conversation that dwelled on the foods of the world, music and film. After the evening meal we four sat and enjoyed a glass of wine that emerged from the old man's cellar. He winked as he poured his hoarded prize.

"We slept soundly and arose long after sunrise. We stretched and tried to summon an interest in finding transportation. When we walked back to the Volkswagen, we found it surrounded by several elderly men who had been collected in an attempt to fix the transmission. The old man addressed his colleagues with a plea for innovative ideas. None had any, but they peered into the engine compartment with fierce enthusiasm.

"As we discussed our plight, a flotilla of trucks came barreling down the road. The gray-haired men cheered and we waved in frantic appeal for a ride. Each truck followed the other in tight convoy and they roared by us as though we were invisible. They disappeared as quickly as they had materialized. The old men dispersed, having rendered their individual opinions about the hopeless transmission. We stayed by our derelict Volkswagen for the rest of the day. Scheffler smoked and swore, but his ranting brought us no closer to a source of transportation. As dusk settled on the town, I pondered our return to the house. We couldn't impose ourselves on these good folks for another night. We had already drunk the last bottle of the old man's wine. As if reading my thoughts, Scheffler offered his opinion that the elderly couple enjoyed every minute of our imposition. It was our duty to return and grace the couple's dinner table with our mighty appetites.

"The third night was spent in song. We four sang in doubtful harmony every folk tune in the German arsenal of music. The old man produced another bottle of wine and I thought that he must have a cache of wine to last for the war's duration. The next morning was January 14 and we said our tentative good-byes, not knowing what the day might bring. We were tardy in getting to the Volkswagen and as we did so, the leading trucks of the detachment were passing the stricken car at the side of the road. Engineers in trucks with assault boats went by us without stopping. We waved our arms but the drivers didn't slow. At last an Opel staff car with two officers stopped and asked what we were up to. Scheffler explained our predicament and the officer halted the next truck. The canvas flap at the truck's rear was raised and we climbed in.

"Two benches were crowded with soldiers in overcoats and white camouflage capes. I stared at imaginary spots on the opposite side of the truck-bed's interior. There was little conversation. Each man's gaze was occasionally broken by a cough or the need to light another cigarette. The engineers asked no questions of their new arrivals. I tried to make out the faces of those closest to me, but the canvas kept the interior so dark the men were only dim figures. During the four-hour ride, sitting in a squat position on the bed of the truck, I rested my head on my knees. Then the truck slowed, turned and started bouncing across rough terrain. The jostling floor of the truck caused me to raise my head, but I kept my eyes closed and tried not to think of my aching legs. When the truck eventually came to a stop and the rear flap was raised by a shouting sergeant, the dull morning light was welcomed. We had been the last men to enter the truck, and so were the first ones to exit. I crumpled to the ground when I was pushed out by those behind me. Two men with strong arms lifted me to my feet. The Good Samaritans marched off with the other soldiers before I could thank them.

"Scheffler was beside me. Neither of us had any idea where we were. We looked around at the field, watching the soldiers hurrying to form into platoons and the variety of vehicles that were turning to leave. We contemplated how to find our artillery regiment. A nearby voice mentioned the town of Freistett."[1]

The crossing of the Rhine River by the 1st Detachment began on January 10. However, it took several nights to complete the transfer of men and equipment. At the time of the crossing the Detachment had 7 Pak 88-millimeter antiaircraft guns which had been modified for ground use, 34 Panzer IV tanks, some of which were in the 2nd Detachment's 6th and 7th companies, and 25 Panther Mark V tanks, all of which were in the 1st Detachment. The Paks and Panthers had to be transferred across the river.[2] The engineers of the 10th Regiment crossed the Rhine on January 15, 1945.[3]

Wilhelm continued his account. "Scheffler pointed in what he thought was a westerly direction. Four heavy half-tracks pulling 88-millimeter guns hauled into view. They were moving slowly on a dirt road, heading west toward the Rhine River. We instinctively started running toward what we knew must be our company. We ran diagonally toward the lead half-track. When we caught up with the line of vehicles we recognized our fellow artillerymen. We jumped up onto the forward-facing seats and squeezed ourselves between comrades. An artilleryman told me that they were going to cross the Rhine, and it was a part of a big operation.

"Before dawn on January 15, the men began the laborious and dangerous job of getting the guns across the river. The current was swift, the banks muddy and the ferry barge was hardly large enough to do the job. Men worked and swore. Vehicles and men pulled and pushed their loads onto the ferry that resembled a motorized raft. The boatmen struggled to tie down the vehicles and guns for the crossing. I sweated along with the others, pushing the caissons and guns onto the ferry. My boots were muddy, my helmet was heavy and the freezing mist penetrated my clothing. It was miserable and exhausting work.

"I was ordered onto the ferry. It struggled against the current and soon slid up onto a slippery bank. The boatmen clamored for the soldiers to get their equipment off as quickly as possible. The west bank of the Rhine River was worse than the east side. The mud extended in an ugly bog from the river bank westward a hundred yards into the gray mist. Tall reeds had already been trampled by previous Frundsberg arrivals. Furrows in the mud signaled the effort made by other soldiers as they had coaxed their guns through the mire.

"Over the shouts of men and sloshing of boots in muddy water, I could hear sporadic artillery and small arms fire coming from the southwest. I paid no attention as I concentrated on heaving a two-wheeled caisson up the bank. The engineers had rigged a long cable from higher ground to the landing site. A crew attached the cable and waved to a man with a portable radio. The cable tightened and the caisson began inching its way out of the mud as men pushed from behind.

"Scheffler and I followed in the wake of the caisson as it moved to firmer ground on the river's west bank. On a north-south road that was full of Frundsberg traffic we walked south until we met a military policeman. He told us that the command post of the 13th Heavy Artillery Company was in Offendorf, to the north. Scheffler thanked the man, then swore under his breath that we would now have to retrace our footsteps. At this point in the operation, we were both weary and would have been happy to be in Althussheim drinking wine with the old couple. We had been working in mud and our feet were raw from wet socks inside wet boots. By the time we entered Offendorf we felt in need of a rest, but knew that would be unlikely.

"The little town had not much to offer in accommodations for so large a force. Regimental command was in the town hall. We reported to the first officer we met. Scheffler and I tracked mud into the busy building. We approached a youthful lieutenant, saluted and inquired as to the whereabouts of the 13th Artillery Company. It turned out to be in the adjacent house.

"Our company commanding officer didn't mention our absence. He had too many other pressing demands. He ordered us to get cleaned up and to report back to him for assignments. A sergeant pointed to a house and we entered a spacious, but crowded, living area. After having been assigned a room with three other soldiers we were able to remove our wet clothing, take a short sponge shower and put on clean dry socks. We dug the caked mud from our boot cleats and scraped the soles clean. Hating to put the damp boots back on, I pulled on a second pair of dry socks. I felt presentable although not comfortable.

"When we returned to the command post, Scheffler and I received different orders. We shook hands and split up. I was to be an observer under Technical Sergeant Schmidt. My job would be to direct fire for the company's 88s on the west side of the Rhine River and heavy artillery located on the east side of the river. Of course, I would do so under orders of the technical sergeant. He and I were escorted by an officer to regimental headquarters. The same youthful lieutenant I had met earlier now stood in front of the sergeant and me. On a wall was a map. He pointed to Offendorf, Herrlisheim and the position the two observers were to take in the field south of Herrlisheim. The officer let us study the map before continuing. Schmidt hardly looked at it, but I tried to memorize as much of the detail as possible. The officer then pointed to two positions along the Offendorf-Gambsheim railroad. He instructed us to establish communications with two antitank gun positions. Each of these had two 88-millimeter guns. One was located just south of Offendorf and the other just north of Gambsheim. The officer added that we would be assigned a wireman who would string the telephone land wire and hook up the telephone.

"I again peered at the map and saw the two 88-millimeter gun emplacements, one only a mile south of Offendorf and the other near the town of Gambsheim. I tried to visualize the spot in an open field where Schmidt and I would set up the observation post. The officer's finger swept over an area that looked like flat land on the map. I asked the officer what the dark area was to the southwest. He said it was a wooded area called the Steinwald and was held by the 553rd Volksgrenadier Division. The Americans were to the west, northwest of Weyersheim. The officer cut his instructions short by telling us that Lieutenant Colonel Ernst Tetsch and General Harmel would be counting on us. He turned away as Schmidt and I saluted. Shortly thereafter, I met an energetic young man who would be the communication cable layer for the observation post. His job as wireman was not enviable. The reels of wire were heavy and the telephone pack was even heavier. He introduced himself as Jens.

"Schmidt was eager to get going. He was the senior rank and assigned me to carry two extra reels of wire. It was clear to me that Jens and I were in for a long and freezing walk. I was glad I had worn my second pair of socks. It took Jens an hour to install the telephone equipment at the 13th Company command post. He then reported to Schmidt that he was ready. As we walked off the road and headed across open fields, the whirring of the cable reel could be heard as it unwound from Jens' side.

"As we trudged westward in the afternoon of January 15, I tried to size up the technical sergeant who would be my leader for this assignment. Schmidt initially seemed like a no-nonsense professional who lacked any personality of his own. Whether or not the man had actually been an observer remained to be seen.

"The brightest daylight had never risen above a dull, gray haze and now the sky was becoming dark. The town of Herrlisheim was only a horizontal dark smudge in an indistinct field of dirty white snow. It was over our right shoulder as we walked west. I kept my eyes on the irregular ground. The last thing I wanted was to step into a snow-covered hole and twist an ankle. When Schmidt stopped in front of me, I plowed into the sergeant's back. Nothing was said except the order to start digging. What now befell Jens and me was the hateful task of trying to penetrate the frost layer of the field. He and I

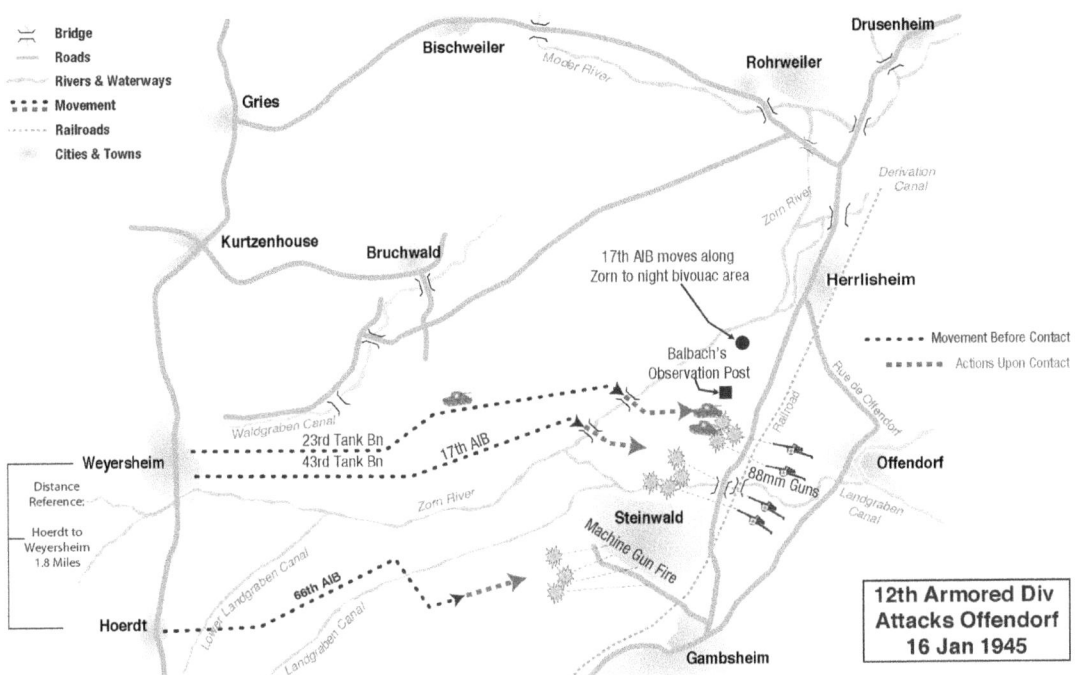

dug out rocks while Schmidt watched and gave moral encouragement by alternately praising and cursing his two underlings.

"It was dark, but the work continued. The sergeant wasn't satisfied with the depth or length of his hole. He kept up his verbal assaults, demanding more gusto. I was tired, but I did my best. At last Schmidt jumped down into the pit and inspected the straightness of the sides and quality of the flat bottom. At that point I knew poor Jens and I were in for a terrible time. I collapsed into the excavation. Even though it was unlikely that any Americans would attack in the night, Schmidt demanded that Jens immediately assemble his equipment and test it before relaxing. Schmidt had patience. He had no place to go and watched the young man fumbling with wires in the dark.

"When first light on January 16, 1945, began to appear in the east, Schmidt seemed to be nervous about the location of the observation post. Mortar and small arms fire was coming from the southwest. He complained that perhaps they had not gone far enough west. Jens commented that they were at the end of their three reels of wire. I knew that Jens was no more enthusiastic about digging another hole than I. I suggested that the sergeant may wish to leave the two observers where we were and return to Offendorf for clarification. This idea somehow struck a resonant chord with Schmidt. He ordered his two men to remain where they were; he would go back for clarifying instructions. It came from him as though it were his original thought. His parting salvo was to remind us that he was counting on us. With that he jumped out of the hole and sauntered east.

"I sarcastically added a few names of people who would also be counting on us, including Tetsch, Harmel and the Führer himself. Perhaps Schmidt would get lost or twist an ankle in the snow. Jens was intimidated by the sergeant, but I saw him as just another swine who pushed his rank as far as he could.

"Jens said nothing. He tested his equipment by checking in with company and with each battery. All was working well. We relaxed and ate part of a sausage and bread that served as field rations. We were exchanging views of the world when we heard heavy machine-gun fire coming from the southwest. It sounded like the zipper-chatter of the new German 42 heavy machine guns. I turned my red pencil light onto the map. It was coming from the wooded area called the Steinwald."[4]

15

The Steinwald, January 1945

Despite the disaster at the waterworks and Herrlisheim in early January 1945, General Allen, commanding the 12th Armored Division, continued to receive pressure from Corps to push on ahead to the Rhine River. At midday on January 14, 1945, 66th Armored Infantry Battalion Field Order #3 was issued orally to company commanders. It was the order to attack the Steinwald woods, but it was quickly countermanded by Field Order #4. Then at 5:00 P.M. of the same day, a patrol mission order was received by the 66th AIB from CCA. The attack on the Steinwald Woods was postponed. Company commanders tried to make sense of the stream of orders coming from Battalion. Those at the battalion level tried to keep up with those coming from Division, and the common soldier simply waited for it all to get sorted out. Charlie Fitts sensed the confusion. He wrote in 1984, "When in Niederscheffolsheim, I was lucky enough to get the last pair of Sno-Pac winter shoes. I wore them on a six-man patrol that went out the night of January 14, 1945. We saw nothing and heard nothing."[1]

Because of the American attack on Gambsheim on January 5–6, the Germans had strengthened its defenses in the Steinwald. The German force organized under the command of Captain Charles von Lüttichau contained an infantry battalion, an antitank battalion and an assault gun battalion. This force was in addition to the 88-millimeter guns which were being mounted behind the eastern rise of the Gambsheim-Offendorf railroad bed. Von Lüttichau's force, a part of the 553rd Volksgrenadier Division, took up position in the Steinwald.[2]

The official divisional history compiled in late January of 1945 stated, "On January 15 a new field order, Number 5, was issued to the effect that 66th AIB was to attack 16 January and seize woods described as Le Stainwald (Steinwald) and advance through the woods in direction of Offendorf, 43rd TB to cross Zorn River and move rapidly and directly to take Offendorf, the 17 AIB to follow 43rd TB and mop up and secure Offendorf."[3]

The Annuaire de la Société d'Histoire et d'Archéologie du Ried-Nord estimated the 553rd Volksgrenadier Division's official strength to be 12,000 men.[4] Lise Pommois listed its actual assets as follows: "The division had about 3,500 soldiers as of January 19, 1945. The Hölscher Regiment controlled the Second Waffen SS Police Regiment which occupied positions north of Herrlisheim on January 16, 1945. The Marbach Regiment, also known as the 3rd Oberrhein Regiment, held positions north of Herrlisheim and in the Steinwald. The 3rd and 4th companies held the Steinwald. These two companies had a weapon inventory of six 80-millimeter mortars, three 75-millimeter guns, fifteen panzerfausts, four 75-millimeter guns and many machine guns. The command post of the Third Company was in the southwest edge of the woods. There were about 250 men defending the woods."[5]

The specific objectives of CCA were to clear the enemy from the Steinwald Woods, Offendorf, Herrlisheim and Drusenheim. To accomplish this, General Riley P. Ennis assigned the 66th AIB, supported by a platoon of five tanks from the 43rd TB, to take the G-2-reported, lightly held woods area to the northwest of Gambsheim called the Steinwald. He assigned the 17th AIB, supported by the remaining tanks of the 43rd TB and C Company of the 119th Engineers acting as infantry, to attack and take Offendorf. Ennis' staff believed that after having taken Offendorf, it should not be difficult to take Herrlisheim, which lay a few miles to the northwest.[6]

Little notice was taken at CCA and Battalion of the many canals to the west of the Steinwald that would make tank support nearly impossible. Perny commented, "The Germans could send out patrols with impunity due to the inexperience of the Americans. In addition, multiple canals and water courses were not very favorable to tanks."[7]

Ferguson described the weather conditions that dramatically affected the fighting of January 16: "There was a deep snow, and many of the men wore white sheets or cheesecloth as camouflage."[8] The snow was actually about a foot deep, but it covered a sheet of ice that was punctured by outcroppings of grass clumps and low bushes. Patchy fog shrouded the fields to the west of the Steinwald, but on that morning there was no rain.

Private First Class Charlie Fitts described the day. "With my new winter Sno-Pac boots, I felt like I had a good chance of not getting frostbitten in whatever the 66th Armored Infantry Battalion might have in store for me. On January 15th the company commander called a meeting of his officers and noncoms. He told them that the company was going into action. It wouldn't be just another town to occupy. This time the company was going to be a part of a huge sweep to the east where the division would spearhead a general advance all the way to the Rhine River.

"The job of the 66th would be to flush out some Germans from a wooded area called the Steinwald. Intelligence had reported that only a weakened unit of a Volksgrenadier division held the woods. Since everyone knew that a Volksgrenadier division was made up of old men dragged from their homes at the point of a gun, the job of the 66th shouldn't be that tough. In the early morning hours of January 16, the 66th Armored Infantry Battalion left its village with the unpronounceable name and again headed southeast. This time the men were alert and adjusted their equipment as the half-tracks followed one another to the town of Hoerdt, a few miles southeast of Weyersheim. We arrived at 3:15 A.M. and were bitterly cold from riding in the open half-tracks. Twelve inches of snow covered everything. I thought that at least the freezing temperature had brought an end to the mud. Now the ground was frozen. I thought that setting up my mortar in the snow shouldn't present any particular problems.

"We assembled beside our half-track. There was no talking and none of the joviality that had marked most of the earlier Alsace movements. Platoon sergeants handed out large sheets of white cheesecloth. We draped the cheesecloth over our coats like rain ponchos. Then the sergeant gave orders in muffled tones and we fell into a four-abreast column. We started route-step marching to our deployment area. I tried to step in the footprints of the men in front of me. It was dark and cold as the string of infantrymen

15. The Steinwald, January 1945

trudged east along the snowbound road from the village of Hoerdt. My Sno-Pacs were a real blessing. My feet were warm and my socks were dry. One thing I had learned in the infantry, a man's feet were his best friends. Keep them happy and they'll take you for many miles without complaining. We left the road and with hunched shoulders trod across white, smooth fields. It was tough going because patches of slippery ice lay hidden under the snow. A man could lose his footing and fall. I walked over a bridge in the darkness. I traversed the Zorn River, although I didn't know its name at the time. I next crossed another small ditch on a narrow footbridge. It must have been an irrigation canal. I tried to remember the briefing, but nothing seemed to fit the map I had studied. I tried to see the ground where I was stepping, but it was just a dim white surface under my feet. The snow was deep enough in spots to cover the top of my Sno-Pacs. A fog lay heavily on the field and I could feel its moist swirls about me. I wondered how we were going to shoot at something we couldn't see. The men around me were only noises, like invisible moving shadows. The mist muffled the sound of the men ahead and behind.

"I tried to keep a mental picture of where we were in relation to the other companies. Another company was supposed to be on our left on the other side of the ditch we had crossed. The two companies were supposed to attack the woods side by side and would take care of the Germans in the wooded area. The battalion would have surprise on its side. No softening artillery fire had been dished out this morning to tip off the Germans that an attack was coming. Suddenly, the man in front of me stopped in his tracks. I almost bumped into him before halting. My buddies on either side of me did the same. We waited where we were for something to happen. I took off my helmet and set it upside down on the ground. I squatted and sat on it to wait for whatever might happen next. The column of fours had broken into a jagged length of infantry. Each man stood or squatted in the quiet of the darkness. There were only occasional whispers as each man waited patiently. I was uneasy. I visualized that if the fog suddenly cleared at dawn we could get caught out in the open with no cover. I stood up and looked into the mist in what I thought was an easterly direction. I saw nothing.

"Ahead there seemed to be confusion. Sergeants came by, waving their arms for the men to flank right, to move southeast. I followed the rest as I tried to put together in my mind what was happening. We came to another ditch. At its bottom was a coating of slick ice over what must have been a stream. We selected the spots to cross that presented the least chance of slipping. None of us wanted to get wet feet just before going into combat. I had been one of the few who had been issued Sno-Pacs, but even I avoided any chance of slipping into the iced-over water. I followed several men who had spotted some black rocks at the bottom of the ditch. Those ahead of me were getting good traction on those rocks. I leaped from one to another, then to the bank on the opposite side. Scrambling up the steep slope of the ditch, I tried to orient myself to the situation. We stopped and whispered to each other. We tried to imagine what was happening, because a mortar squad was only as effective as its knowledge of terrain. We concluded that we had been on the wrong side of the canal and had had to cross it so as not to get in the way of A Company.

"I could see a faint glow through the mist in the east. Soon it would be dawn and we would be able to get to work with the mortar. Word was whispered down the line: deploy for assault. As we began to spread out, the hammering of a heavy machine gun came from ahead of us. I fell to the ground, as did the other men around me. Then another machine gun to the southeast opened up. The earth around us ruptured in small but deadly bursts of bullets. Their smack, as they passed overhead, was mixed with screams coming from those hit by them."[9]

Ferguson described the scene: "A scant 70 yards separated the prone GIs from the German machine guns just inside the tree line, and any movement from the Americans brought an immediate burst of German automatic fire. Anyone trying to rise immediately fell back down, riddled with bullets."[10]

Charlie Fitts recalled the ensuing hours: "As the sun rose and the mist lifted, German snipers replaced the machine guns. It was deadly quiet except for screams and moans from the injured lying in the field. Three or four times a minute, Germans aimed at anything moving. Those in panic who jumped to their feet to escape were shot. I lay as flat as I could, but still felt as though I were the only target. George O'Bryan was on my left. He was out there about fifteen yards lying flat on the ground. He appeared only as a dark clump in the white snow. Paul Rice was on my other side about the same distance. Dale Matheny was a short distance farther out. These were the only men I could see. A few other men jumped to their feet to run, but were cut down by rifle fire. I tried to understand the situation. Men were hollering for medics, but no one could traverse the killing ground. The wounded slowly died from the cold and their injuries. I raised my head to see what was happening and received a volley of shots that dug up the soil around me. Gradually I slid my body rearward. My helmet stayed put and this allowed me to swivel my head without turning my helmet. I strained to see what was happening, but the snow on the ground was a white barrier to all but my closest companions. I decided that if I were to live, I would have to lie still until nightfall."[11]

Dale Matheny was a squad leader in the First Platoon and described his capture. He remembered that while lying prone in front of the Steinwald, he and Nick Vertucci, squad leader in the Second Platoon, carried on a whispered conversation with Charlie Fitts to find out if the men around him were OK. He wrote, "As the day wore on, Charlie and I kept talking and I began to think that our only chance would be to hang on through the day and try after dark. Charlie agreed."[12]

Charlie Fitts continued, "O'Bryan's loud whisper attracted my attention and I slowly turned my head within my helmet to see. O'Bryan wanted to know what was happening, as if I had any idea. Lieutenant Joseph had yelled for the men to charge the woods, but he had been cut down as he spoke the words. I and my buddies simply lay where we were and remained motionless. In the prone position, the warm boots did me little good. The snow melted under me. I was chilled, then the cold gripped me like approaching death. Hours went by. I had to urinate. I thought of the coffee I had drunk last night in Niederschaeffolsheim and cursed myself for being so stupid. More hours went by. I urinated where I lay. The warm liquid felt good, then froze against my body. I wondered how long this misery could last. I had to hang on until dark when I would have a chance of getting away. My legs were numb and trying to move them was useless. The sun must have been higher in the sky. I estimated that it must be noon already. I couldn't tell. Heavy clouds kept the sky a blanket of gray. Time stood still. The rifle fire grew infrequent. Sometimes a bullet would strike close to me, but most of the shots were distant. Sometimes only a single shot was fired, sometimes there were three or four in a volley. Otherwise the field was as quiet as a cemetery. Time passed — another minute or perhaps an hour. Again, I urinated. I knew my legs must be frostbitten, but there was nothing I could do about it. The realization that I would be dead from exposure before the fall of darkness was terrifying. My legs were lifeless and if I tried to run now I would only fall and be shot. To be killed quickly by the enemy may be better than a slow death at the hands of nature, I thought.

"I heard noises. They were voices, or so I thought. Then the ground shook. Someone was trying to drag me. I could feel tugging at my feet. I rolled over onto my back and looked at a German soldier who was trying to remove my Sno-Pac boots. The soldier jumped back and pointed his gun at me."[13]

In 1984 Charlie Fitts wrote of his capture, "George O'Bryan and I were close to each other and started to make a run, but about that time a burst hit somebody that did try to make it out. We thought we could make it until dark, but Jerry started looting the bodies and discovered that all of them were not dead. I had on a pair of the new Sno-Pacs the Germans wanted. He turned me over to take them off and saw that I wasn't dead. It scared him and he pulled his pistol. I'll never know why he didn't shoot. He told me to rouse and saw that I couldn't move too well, and he helped me up. My feet and legs were frostbitten because I guess I had peed in my clothes at least three times during the day. We went to a bunker several hundred yards away and someone, a medic I guess, rubbed my feet and legs with something that smelled like horse liniment. I helped and when I came out of the bunker, a shell hit a tank that exploded and the tanker came out, followed by a ball of fire that hit his back. In ten minutes the smell was horrible and he had no eyelids. I smelled human flesh burning the first time when Ollie Brown was hit directly with a white phosphorus shell. Nothing but one hand and his arm was identifiable."[14]

Perny described C Company's commanding officer, Lieutenant Joseph's, reaction to the situation. "The company was almost entirely decimated. The men had been told that 160 Germans and 6 armored vehicles occupied the woods. German machine guns opposite the drainage ditch opened up. The GIs didn't even have holes for shelter. It was impossible for the GIs to move at all. They managed to get two machine guns into action, but both were quickly destroyed. Most of the men died between the drainage ditch and the Kleingraben Canal. At least 68 bodies were recovered in the weeks that followed."[15]

Charlie Fitts remembered the Steinwald bunker: "The medical orderly took me into the bunker. There were a number of other Americans lying on cots. A doctor came over and the orderly removed my pants. While struggling to the bunker with the German for support, I had performed some sleight-of-hand by removing my wristwatch and stuffing it into my pocket. I now worried that a German would find it and confiscate it. The removal of my long johns and trousers to medicate my frostbite might have been welcomed except for my worry about the watch. My legs felt like they were on fire. The doctor rubbed a strong-smelling liniment onto my legs. This made them hurt all the more, but I knew that whatever the Germans were doing for me was what they would do for one of their own. When the doctor moved on to another patient he motioned for me to keep rubbing the liniment onto my legs. Finally, they came back to life, tingling and throbbing, then with full feeling. I kept my eye on the orderly, who moved from cot to cot administering to each wound. I pulled my long underwear and pants up as high as I could, then deftly slipped the watch out of my trouser pocket. I pushed it into my groin, then finished pulling my pants up tight. I tried standing and was wobbly, but managed to remain erect. I looked down to see myself as a filthy, foul-smelling wreck. Still, I was alive and in one piece. I flexed my knees just to be sure. I felt my watch rubbing between my legs, patted my prayer book in my jacket and saw beneath me my Sno-Pac boots. All in all, I had survived to this point better than most of my compatriots. I stood for a moment and said a silent prayer of thanks.

"An orderly escorted me into the open. I looked around, and saw fellow soldiers standing in a tight group. A German motioned for me to join it. I had a feeling of relief at having survived my ordeal, but it was accompanied by shame at having been captured. I had not fired a single shot. My mortar lay unused, scattered pieces in Alsace snow. But the sight of comrades I admired who were also prisoners gave me a certain sense of comfort. It didn't take me long to spot Paul Rice and George O'Bryan. They were standing with Dale Matheny and talking in whispers. I elbowed my way into the group. I greeted Luther Scott, George Rich, Bob Hoeweller and Tom Wood. It was good in this bleak situation to be with men I trusted. We tried to estimate our fate, but had little idea what was in store for us. As the last of the prisoners joined our growing group, the guards started shoving us around. It was obvious that they were organizing us for a march to the rear. I transferred my watch back to my pocket and got into line. A few old Germans with rifles shouted in German and pointed. We understood and started to move. As we walked I thought that the war would end soon and my stay at the hands of the Germans wouldn't be too long. When we passed through Gambsheim I was amazed at what I saw. The town was a beehive of activity. The Germans had equipment, weapons and vehicles in substantial quantity. They trotted in small groups and sergeants shouted orders. It was clear to me that my captivity might be longer than I thought."[16]

Forty-nine soldiers from the 66th AIB were taken prisoner on January 16 in front of the Steinwald.[17]

16

East of the Zorn River, January 1945

Communication between companies within a battalion and to the battalion was not normally shared with other battalions. Like spokes in a wheel, avenues of communication moved from the ground up through a particular spoke to battalion level and then to division headquarters. Intelligence from battalion to battalion was only shared when Division thought it necessary, and even then it was filtered by Division before being disseminated. A case in point was the action of Lieutenant Francis Perkins, commanding officer of B Company, 23rd Tank Battalion. On January 14 he was ordered to take five tanks and head east from Weyersheim to probe the area on the east side of the Zorn River all the way to Offendorf. James Francis described the outcome: "On January 14, Second Lieutenant Francis Perkins, commanding officer of B Company, 23rd TB took five tanks into no-man's-land between the Steinwald and the town of Herrlisheim. It was a probing mission intended to affirm the intelligence reports of weak enemy forces. His tiny unit hadn't gone far before an unknown anti-tank gun blew the track off Perkins' Sherman. The men bailed out, then a second shell dislodged the turret from the hull. On the ground, Perkins yelled for the remaining four tanks to withdraw. He made his report to Battalion, but no attempt was made to locate and remove the anti-tank gun or guns. On January 15th Perkins was ordered to repeat the mission. This time he was more cautious and observed German tanks in the outskirts of Herrlisheim. Again, making his report, Perkins' observations resulted in no action."[1]

Hard information existed as to the probable strength of German artillery close to Offendorf, but it only got as far as the 23rd Tank Battalion headquarters. Whether this information was ever received by Division is unknown; however, the 66th AIB, the 43rd TB and the 17th AIB had no inkling of what lay ahead of them on January 16.

In the first days of January 1945, C Company of the 23rd Tank Battalion had left Rohrbach to move toward an unknown destination. The next stop for the tanks had been the village of Uhlweiler. Upon arriving, a tank was stationed at each end of the two-lane road entering the town. The rest of the sixteen tanks were dispersed into side yards and along side streets. Private First Class Andrew F. Woods, loader for the lead tank commanded by Lieutenant Wayne Guitteau, was too late to bed down in the schoolhouse, where most of the tank crews found a warm place. He and a fellow latecomer, a medic named Brad Dressler, found a house owned by the Berbach family.[2] Woods and Guitteau were taking the first steps toward the combat that was to rage in and around Herrlisheim.

The night of January 15 had been troubling for George Hatt in the 17th Armored Infantry Battalion. Sergeant Capretta had held a briefing for his men, and George had tried to memorize the geography of the coming day's attack. Through the night he had gone over in his mind the locations of the villages: Weyersheim, then east to Offendorf. Herrlisheim on the left. The Steinwald on the right. Capretta had said the attack would be a cinch, but George couldn't get rid of the idea that the Germans might not want to give up Offendorf without a fight.

In 2005 he referred to his written notes as he described the events of January 16, 1945. "At 2:00 A.M. we assembled in the street to mount our half-track. As I sat in my perch at the front of the half-track, I inventoried my eighty pounds of fighting equipment including mortar rounds, bazooka, three rockets, rifle, bayonet, rifle ammunition belt, two bandoliers of rifle ammunition, gas mask, two fragmentation grenades, white phosphorus grenade, wire cutters, first aid kit, water canteen, C rations and pack of morphine.

"After an hour of bouncing and rocking, the half-track slowed and stopped. Capretta's voice ordered us to dismount. As each engine was shut down the convoy became quiet. We worked at the side of our vehicle, assembling gear and heaving the loads onto our backs. Capretta checked each man in our squad. Those up ahead began to move and Capretta waved for us to get going. The drivers stayed with the vehicles, and as we walked off toward Geudertheim, they waved.

"I looked at the houses lining the street. The sun had yet to rise, but the snow gave off a luminescence and I could see the dark shapes on either side of the march. We entered Weyersheim. It was larger than Geudertheim. The cobblestone streets were lined with houses and in the center of town was a fountain. The city hall was across from the fountain and a church was opposite it.

"I wore cotton undershirt and shorts, woolen long underwear, wool shirt and pants, wool sweater, wool cap, helmet and scarf, a pile-lined inner jacket, wool-lined outer jacket, wool gloves, two pair of socks and Sno-Pac boots with felt inner soles. I was still cold. With the layered clothing and equipment I breathed heavily as I kept up with the man in front of me. The road was icy and slick. I heard a soldier behind me fall. The man swore as he got back onto his feet.

"I heard our tanks coming from behind us. It was probably the 23rd's Shermans, but I couldn't be sure. They were heading east, just as we were. As we continued to march in route step I heard small arms fire up ahead and to my right. Picturing the map, I assumed it was the 66th cleaning up the Germans in that forested area."[3]

The tanks that passed George Hatt were most likely those of the 43rd TB, which was to lead the way toward Offendorf. The 17th AIB with the 43rd TB on its left had the mission of getting to the railroad tracks and then moving to the southeast across the tracks and attacking Offendorf from the south.[4]

The tanks of the 23rd TB were to follow close behind those of the 43rd. Private First Class Andy Woods explained, "In the predawn hours of January 16th, the 23rd Tank Battalion wound its way through the narrow streets of Weyersheim. We stopped in column behind the 43rd tanks at the Zorn Canal to wait for the construction of a bridge by the 119th Engineers. Two hours later, after crossing the bridge to the east side of the

Zorn Canal, our tanks came to a stop while those of the 43rd went on ahead. The holdup at the Zorn provided us with a dull light as the sun came up in the east. I was loader in the Guitteau tank, and although I stood high out of the loader's hatch I could see nothing to the east because of the haze. Lieutenant Wayne Guitteau, our platoon commander, kept a running verbal account of what was happening from tank radio communication.

"I heard artillery shells streaking overhead. German bombardment, coming from across the Rhine, was concentrated on Weyersheim, to the west of us, while American artillery concentrated on Offendorf, to the east of us. We were under it, sitting in an open frozen field. It was a strange feeling. I crawled out of the tank and listened to the whistling shells. Little could be seen in the heavy mist and dull light, but I was glad I was not in Weyersheim.

"We got the order to move ahead. Guitteau got back into our tank, as did I. We pulled through C Company's tanks to park randomly, farther to the east. I watched A Company tanks start up, move through us and fade into the eastern mist. I waited at my tank, which was named *Cleopatra*. The 23rd Tank Battalion had been commanded by Lieutenant Colonel M. C. Meigs, but he had been killed in December. His replacement, Major William Edwards, conferred with Lieutenant Guitteau and several enlisted men. I saw the long faces and watched the battalion commander deposit his personal effects into the custody of his jeep driver who would remain behind in the coming operation. I said nothing of what I saw to *Cleopatra*'s driver, Frenchy Dubois, or to our gunner, George Cox. Charlie Company tanks which had remained at the bridge were thus far unscathed."[5]

George Hatt described his perspective of the events of January 16 in a paper written in 1993. "After a kilometer of quiet hiking from Weyersheim, Captain Helton halted the company. The order was given to spread out and dig in. Designated partners got together and started the task of hacking two-man foxholes in the hard frozen ground. Visions of mortar shells coming into the company's position made us all dig vigorously. The excavation was becoming a lot easier, because we had dug energetically and managed to penetrate the 18 inches of hard, icy ground that covered the soft earth below the frost line. Then the word came to move out. It was passed back along the line. We again lifted our loads and began walking east.

"The morning sun was glistening on the white ground. We sensed something new. From the direction in which we were marching we could hear the unquestionable sound of a German burp gun, which seemed to be answered by what sounded like the slower sound of an American light machine gun. Intermingled were explosions, perhaps bazookas. Maybe tanks or mortar shells. American and German fire sounded the same to me and it was some distance away. No one knew what it was, but everyone was troubled by the thought of that gunfire. We thought of the 66th Battalion and its assignment to clear the Steinwald and thought that must be the source of the sound.

"Our column then turned left off the road toward the north, and one at a time we ran across the Zorn River that had [paralleled] the road from outside Weyersheim. We crossed the river on an old footbridge probably put up for the local farmers so they could get to their fields. Each soldier anticipated that the first shell would inevitably come in when he was in the middle of the bridge. However, the river was quite narrow and the bridge was only about 50 feet long. So each man crossed quickly. All was quiet when our last man in the company stepped onto solid ground on the far bank. Then, moving in a northerly direction, we broke out of the riverside trees into an open field. The company commander passed orders back to keep 30 yards between each man. That's how much margin was kept by each man from those about him. The word from our leaders was that one shell should not hit more than one man. After a short time we wheeled to the right to move eastwardly, the direction of the Rhine River. The sun was well up with some haze when we came upon a second bridge. It was at a level a few feet below the general terrain and among heavy brush and trees. This bridge, a treadway, had been built by our division's 119th Armored Engineer Battalion to allow us and vehicles which would come later to go back cross the Zorn River. This time we crossed to the east because the Zorn had made a sharp turn to flow north. Then our force moved up onto a very flat, open plain. A bit of scrub and brush was growing here and there. The steeple of a church could be seen ahead. We thought it might be our objective, Offendorf, still quite a distance away.

"Soon, we in the 3rd Platoon heard a few scattered small arms shots at the head of the company and everyone became more cautious of everything around us. Every bush was observed carefully; every mound of dirt was expected to be a parapet. Strange men began to straggle back, in different uniforms; Germans with hands clasped overhead. They looked frightened and pale. On the left flank, white-painted American light and medium tanks passed us moving parallel to us toward the enemy lines. One tank could be seen stopped where it had broken through the ice into a marsh. Another was trying to pull it out.

"A canal that ran east to west (later identified as the Landgraben Canal) was on our right flank. Shells were falling regularly on the other side of that canal, in an open field west of the Steinwald. I wondered if it could be our artillery. A few men among us fell, not many. One of our staff sergeants, named James M. Caplinger, was knocked down when a bullet or shrapnel struck him in the hand and swung him around violently. He was evacuated, recovered, and returned to be killed later in the Rhineland.

"All of us moved to the east over the plain. After a few minutes we saw in the distance other buildings in addition to the church steeple. It was Offendorf, all right. Now something new was harassing both those of us in the infantry and the tanks. It was enemy projectiles that came with a deep, loud crack as they struck the snowy ground and went off with whining flutters. They struck as fast as lightning bolts and were gone. Everyone knew that this was the sound of high velocity armor-piercing shells. One came every fifteen to thirty seconds and skipped down the white, frozen field kicking up snow dust every hundred yards, so fast that all the dust clouds appeared to rise at once. No one bothered to duck when he heard the shattering sound. Each knew that if he heard it, it was gone; if it hit him he wouldn't hear it. So the infantry troops all moved forward in an upright posture.

"Raymond O. Collier, Jr., of El Paso, Texas, who was then a 60-millimeter mortar gunner in the 2nd Platoon, told me in recent years that U.S. fighter-bombers came from the west and dropped bombs in the vicinity of Offendorf. Even though I personally don't recall the bombing I'm sure it happened. A few mortar shells came in and burst with sudden shock. A light tank a hundred yards to our left moved to the rear with someone lying on its rear deck, red with blood. A stretcher bearer, Private First Class Marvin Tishcoff of South Bend, Indiana, passed the word to me after sundown that the wounded man was my very close buddy, Private First Class Raymond Collier, who later was to suffer amputation of his right arm. During the next several days I wasn't able to learn anything about the extent of the injury and it troubled me terribly.

"As our troops moved on toward Offendorf, more and more German soldiers came across the field to surrender. With hands high and white surrender-rags, some came several hundred yards through the open field before reaching the forward elements of our company. Our mortar squad's gunner, Private First Class Edward Ostrach, was grinning and remarking, 'The Krauts are giving in without our platoon firing a shot!' These Germans were all wearing long overcoats and looked like fresh troops. Everything became rather easy and all was quiet in the Steinwald, which now was about 600 yards to the right front of our tank force, which was on our left to the north. I was feeling pretty good about how we were winning this battle. Orders had been given not to fire into the woods because the 66th was there. Yet some of us looked at the winter-stripped forest with doubt. Privates Fuchs and Schumaker, two of our 1st Platoon machine gunners, shot into it, but were ordered to cease firing. They claimed they saw German soldiers.

"We drifted to the right into the Landgraben Canal dikes and men in our platoon were walking in as low a bent-over posture as possible. Sergeant Capretta had us strung out behind him as we passed the Steinwald. Private First Class Adrian Mariluch and I stayed close together as we raised our heads and looked over the far bank of the canal and saw that we had come within a few hundred yards of the Steinwald woods. The platoon stopped a few minutes. Then we were ordered to turn north into the field away from the canal."[6]

At the same time, Wilhelm Balbach crouched in his observation post foxhole not more than a quarter mile northeast of George Hatt. Wilhelm told of the approaching Americans: "I heard the squeaking of tank tracks. I listened intently, then shook Jens into action. The young wire-puller listened and nodded in agreement, then grabbed his telephone. Without Schmidt to order us around, I knew what to do. I had no binoculars, but continued to peer through the mist. I could see nothing. The noise of the tanks was now supplemented by shouts from American infantry and occasional small arms fire.

"Gradually, I could see dark, lumpy shapes. They moved slowly as infantry darted around them. The map was on my lap. I picked off the coordinates and ordered Jens to report lead tanks at coordinates G-12-J-22. I estimated the number of tanks and added a count of 22 Shermans with many infantry. Estimated range from Offendorf Battery, 1,200 meters, from Gambsheim Battery, 2,000 meters.

"Not more than a minute elapsed before one of the Gambsheim 88s opened on the south tangent tanks. The Shermans had passed our observation hole and we were now in the target area of our own guns. Explosions flashed not far from us. We pushed ourselves deeper into our hole. Pieces of tanks flew into the air, crashing down close by. It was a harrowing barrage, and I thought the Americans must be taking a terrible pounding. I stuck my head above ground. My view of the destruction was from the north tangent of the second wave. The lead Shermans were now being subjected to a remorseless bludgeoning from both batteries along the railroad embankment. The four 88s were in rapid fire. Expert Luftwaffe crews had been together a long time, and they worked with precision as they trained from target to target in rhythm with the loaders. Artillery in Freistett was now responding to my firing coordinates. Phosphorus shells began exploding over the American infantry. I watched from my foxhole as Americans dropped from the awful shelling."[7]

George Hatt continued his perspective. "I instinctively ducked as artillery shells began landing to my left. Bullets began chipping ice and dirt around the advancing men. I saw Staff Sergeant James Caplinger spin around and fall from a bullet or shrapnel. From ahead and close to the northeast edge of the Steinwald woods came a flash followed by a swish across our front and a dull clang of an 88-millimeter shell smashing into one of the 43rd tanks on our left. Then there was another flash, swish, and another clang. After that the explosions came one after another. The tanks backed away with their guns still pointing toward the enemy and then moved forward to new positions and fired in return. Their shells exploded on a long railroad bank running north from behind the woods. This exchange of shells seemed to go on for half an hour. After a tank was struck the crew would egress, jump to the ground, run a few feet, then lie down for protection. Crewmen came out of the turret and out of the front hatches. Some were trying to help injured crew members to get out. When firing ceased between the two opponents, eight 43rd Tank Battalion tanks lay crippled or burning. Shortly following the time when a tank was struck, a little smoke began to rise from the turret hatches. The smoke became heavier and some flames appeared. Then the munitions inside started exploding, blowing smoke straight up out of the turret hatch. This occurred numerous times within several burning tanks. It was curious to see a large smoke ring blown hundreds of feet into the air.

"Everything and everyone stopped, and defensive positions were formed. We started hacking that frozen ground for the second time that day when an 88 shell came slamming into two A Company men. It was Fuchs and Schumaker, the machine gunners. The shell got them and their Browning 30-caliber light machine gun. It left two torn corpses and a destroyed gun. This machine gun section was perhaps the nearest of our troops to Steinwald.

"Digging got harder with each swing of the shovel. The day was getting long and we were tiring. Adrian Mariluch and I finished a hole four feet deep. Looking around we could see that a large proportion of our men dug a little bit then stopped. Others decided not to dig at all. My thinking at the time was that they weren't dealing with reality. They just did not believe that anything was going to hit us and they were just too tired or lazy or frightened to dig. However, German artillery shells began to hit in our area. Down deep in our hole Adrian and I pulled our heads as low as we could and prayed there wouldn't be a direct hit on us. A shell would detonate when it struck the earth and then there was the sound of spinning shrapnel pieces buzzing and whining until we heard them thump into the ground all around our hole. I don't remember if any of our troops were struck by those artillery shells. Adrian and I felt relatively safe in our foxhole.

"Request was sent to the Army Air Corps to help with the large guns thought to be in the Steinwald, and four beautiful bomb-laden P-47s soon circled overhead while an artillery shell pointed one finger of red smoke, then one of white, at the enemy weapons. The P-47s dived in. One at a time the bombs were released and sped downward. These were large bombs, 500-pounders. Each explosion blew a dozen huge, whole trees in the Steinwald toward the sky. The bombs hit close to the American lines. Company A men in advanced positions were only a few hundred yards from the impact of the bombs, and the ground seemed to them to jump with joy. One bomb hit in the field 50 yards north of the woods. Also a white phosphorus bomb hit at the edge of the woods and made a great white cloud.

"Artillery shells from across the Rhine River were coming into the company's positions one and two at a time when orders were given to fall back. Everyone hurried, a few were carried, and time-burst shells exploded harassingly overhead. Word came across the field to fall back. I saw men moving to the rear. I grabbed my equipment and started running to the west. Mariluch had run on ahead and we became separated. As I ran with my equipment thumping on my back, a soldier beckoned. The man pleaded for me to help save his buddy. Stopping by the two men I sat my equipment down and together with the uninjured soldier figured out how to carry the man to safety. I knew that I couldn't carry both the eighty pounds of equipment and the injured man, [so I abandoned] my mortar rounds and bazooka. I and the uninjured soldier fitted a rifle under the man and lifted him between us. The injured soldier balanced himself by holding onto our shoulders. We ran side-by-side to the west with him between us. I wasn't sure exactly where we were, but I saw three medics attending to a soldier. We carried the wounded man to them and carefully sat him down. The medics went to work on him. I made a quick farewell and began looking for my platoon. It was my responsibility to find my unit as quickly as possible. Men had streamed westward and now were strewn out along the east side of the Zorn Canal. Most were walking north. I followed them. The sun was setting and I suddenly realized just how tired I was. Although my burden was lighter, I trudged along wishing I had slept better the night before.

"The shooting had stopped. All was quiet. I saw familiar faces and there was Sergeant Capretta talking calmly to a soldier as if today had been just another workday. Men tried to find warmth by pushing into small bundles of bodies. Some dug foxholes. Some were nervous and just walked around keeping some sort of guard. We were all in desperate need of rest."[8]

Andy Woods listened toward the east where nasty cracks of tank and antitank guns mingled with violent explosions. They came from the east, but he still couldn't see through the haze. He described his reaction. "I nervously paced beside *Cleopatra* while wanting to ask someone what was happening. It was clear that neither Guitteau nor Major William Edwards, the battalion's commanding officer, knew any more about the tank battle being fought in the fields to the east than did I. I saw one A Company tank that had not moved with the other tanks. It had bogged down in a soft spot and two of its crew were examining its tracks. They seemed unconcerned about the noise of battle ahead of them. The cannon fire died away, and in its place was only the scream of tank engines. Time seemed to stand still. Then two A Company tank crew members ran out of the mist toward C Company. They waved their arms and shouted that all the tanks had been destroyed. I could hardly believe it. A Company had sixteen tanks. Most of them, together with their crews, had been destroyed at the hands of German 88s. Wayne Guitteau also was shaken by the news."[9]

The 12th Armored Division had suffered a terrible loss on January 16, 1945, in the fields between Herrlisheim and the Steinwald. North of the fields and northeast of Herrlisheim lay the town of Drusenheim. It had been occupied by the 314th Infantry on January 7, 1945. It had subsequently been reinforced by A Company of the 202nd Infantry. The area from Drusenheim through La Breymuhl, the forest between Drusenheim and Rohrweiler, and Rohrweiler itself had been thinly held by this combination of units. These men had been ordered to hold fast on January 16 and to support the 12th Armored CCB attack against Offendorf and Herrlisheim.[10]

Lieutenant Colonel Huff, commanding the 2nd Battalion of the Drusenheim forces, sensed that the greatest threat was from the northeast, and he concentrated his automatic weapons and antitank weapons in that section of town. He also moved a platoon of the 314th from the Drusenheim woods southwest of the town to a position in the farthest northeast zone of his battalion's defenses of Drusenheim.[11] The anxiety of Lieutenant Colonel Huff was well founded, although his intelligence was vague on the morning of the 16th.

The German 2nd Detachment comprised two panzer companies, the 6th and 7th of the 10th Waffen SS Panzer Division. It had driven south that morning from Roeschwoog to attack Drusenheim. Engler wrote of the route taken by the 7th Company, "The roads through Roeschwoog, Auenheim, Stattmatten, Dengelsheim and Dalhunden offered a secure route for the Germans to move south along the west bank of the Rhine."[12] The 7th Company would attack the town from the northwest while the 6th Company would attack from the southeast. The latter company traveled south along the Rhine River Road through Old Fort Louis, then pivoted to the northwest. Bernhard Westerhoff rode in his Panzer IV as 6th Company lined up to attack Drusenheim. Company commander Hans Quandel was in the lead tank.[13]

Bernhard's memory of the day was vivid. "Before dawn the company readied itself to move out of Roeschwoog. The night was black at 3:00 A.M. on January 16 as tank engines came to life and men assembled in the streets. The column began moving south. Supply and administrative units remained in Roeschwoog. The column of eleven Panzer IV tanks passed through Old Fort Louis, which lay on the west bank of the Rhine. The lead tanks had to keep a steady pace and this was difficult in the dark. The column moved slowly, paralleling the river southward to a point southeast of Drusenheim.

"Only a mile or so from Drusenheim, near the Rhine River, I shut down the engine of my tank and told the crew to get a bite to eat. I watched Quandel from my turret hatch. He stood beside his command tank talking to an officer of the 21st Panzergrenadier Regiment. About 120 of the infantrymen were in company with our tanks attacking the town. After two hours Quandel waved his arm for the tank commanders to start their engines.

"In the early morning we attacked. It was well coordinated with 7th Company tanks attacking the town on its northern border. Sixth Company's tanks pumped a barrage into the city. There was no returning fire."[14]

Engler wrote, "Much of the 10th Waffen SS Panzer Division was already engaged in battles south of Drusenheim when the Americans holding the town felt that pressures were enveloping them from three sides. There was to be no escape for most of the 314th 2nd Battalion. From the surrounded battalion command post, a report went out by radio to Regiment at 8:10 P.M. telling of the extent of the enemy's occupation of Drusenheim. The panzers were moving unopposed from house to house firing into the basements."[15]

The attack by the eleven-tank Quandel force against the town's southeast sector met with little resistance. Bernhard continued his narrative: "After our barrage we slowly entered the town. It seemed empty. We thought that the Americans must be in the process of evacuating the town. We drove into three side streets to the town's center and fired only a few shots. The Americans had built two Bailey bridges on the south edge of the town. As the Americans ran across the bridges I gave the order to hold fire. I could see no reason to shoot men in the back. The other tanks were silent as the last American soldier ran across the bridge.

"It was full daylight and Allied planes could be expected at any moment. Once again the tanks were stashed where they couldn't be seen from the air.

"The Americans had retreated so quickly that they had abandoned their stores. The men of 6th Company gathered small arms, ammunition, clothing and food. K and C rations were stowed in every cranny of every tank. While I ate cold franks and beans from a can, my gunner approached, wearing a new American winter jacket. He was proud of his find, but I reminded him that his own men might shoot him by mistake. Other men took advantage of the booty by smoking Chesterfield and Camel cigarettes.

"In the absence of a German field kitchen, which had not yet arrived, Stratmann took over an American field kitchen. He and his crew, including Ernst Storch, pumped the kerosene cylinders and the stove sprung to life. Hot meat loaf and beans were served to the ever-hungry Frundsberger tankers and grenadiers.

"The men of 6th Company slept in houses, schools, offices, and a few in their tanks. I suppose those in 7th Company did the same in the parts of town to the north of us. January 16 ended for us in the comfort of captured material. We were unaware that a battle had been fought that same day to the south."[16]

The fields between Herrlisheim and the Steinwald still smoldered from the wreckage of Sherman tanks during the night of January 16. Wilhelm Balbach and his wirepuller Jens had sat in their foxhole for the rest of the afternoon. At dusk they had eaten the remainder of the sausage and bread, then dozed as they tried to keep warm. When night came the temperature dropped. It no longer was a struggle to get comfortable. Now it was a fight to keep from freezing. They were captives of their hole.[17]

In Drusenheim, January 17 dawned as another gray, overcast day. Bernhard continued, "My 612 tank was in front of Stratmann's as the column moved out of town heading south on the two lane road to La Breymuhl. Quandel turned right to head west and the column followed. I slowed to look ahead into a hamlet of houses and brick skeletal walls of the Zorn-Moder Water Regulating Plant. All seemed quiet. I remained standing in the turret and, with binoculars, searched the dark ruins of the once-stout buildings for signs of the enemy. I spotted a hidden antitank gun behind a brick wall. Quandel's tank began shelling the structure. He must have also seen the gun. The crack of cannon and smashing explosions was matched by return fire that exploded around my tank. I slid down into the protection of the turret.

"Our infantry dove into ditches and behind rocks. They quickly set up their machine guns and kept up a blistering fire on the American infantry behind the walls. The Americans were fighting back with anti-tank guns and machine guns well positioned to inflict serious damage. I yelled for the driver to head for a ditch to the left of the road. From the partial protection of the gully, I hollered azimuth orders to the gunner. He trained our gun quickly and we fired at the walls of the brick structure. Whenever an antitank gun fired, I kept my eye on the point of flash and directed the gunner to the exact spot. I saw one of our tanks take a crippling hit. Crew members bailed out and dove into ditches to join the infantrymen.

"I watched the action through my ports, but as firing from the walls of the water regulating plant diminished I threw open the hatch and rose above the turret. With binoculars I scanned the area ahead. Smoke and dust were carried away in the afternoon breeze. The Americans had abandoned the brick structure and it seemed safe to move on."[18]

Stratmann later added his impression of the fighting at the Waterworks: "We rapidly deployed to positions that would allow us to take the two bridges over the Moder and Zorn. We attacked against strong American infantry positions that were manned by troops normally held in Rohrweiler. As always I rode behind Quandel. I wasn't sure of what our company commander had in mind, but in a short time the Americans abandoned their positions and disappeared into the forest."[19]

Bernhard continued, "Quandel radioed his tanks to get back on the road, but to keep guns trained on the brick structure. Stratmann's tank followed mine and I waved my appreciation for the luck of us surviving the skirmish. We cautiously moved toward the next town of Rohrweiler. The Americans had built a Bailey bridge over the Zorn River just west of the La Breymuhl water plant. The tracks of the Panzer IV were wider than the Sherman's and extreme caution had to be taken in crossing the river. As my tank crept over the bridge the tracks hung over both sides. I glanced down into the water and saw a Sherman which had slipped off the bridge and flipped over onto its back in the dark, cold water. The same fate was only inches away and my driver swore as he responded to my constant corrections. Once over the bridge we picked up speed, dispersed and prepared to shell Rohrweiler, a mile west of the bridge at La Breymuhl. Most of the tanks stayed to the north of the road, seeking protection in trees and brush to the northeast of the town. Our infantry moved on both sides of the road and they charged ahead, running from one position to the next. The Americans pulled back into the town well ahead of us.

"It was never in Quandel's mind to actually attack Rohrweiler. Our mission was of far greater importance. After we had pumped about twenty shots into the town, Quandel got his tanks back onto the road. Before dusk, we moved our tanks up a narrow dirt road into the forested area east of Rohrweiler. It was a safe area for the night. We spent the night of January 17 in and around our tanks. We listened to the sounds of battle in Herrlisheim, less than two miles to the southeast. We tried to estimate what combat was going on there, but assumed our forces were giving the Americans some serious thought about a war that was not yet over. Then with full stomachs we slept soundly."[20]

17

Herrlisheim, January 1945

For George Hatt, January 17 started as an extension of the previous day. While the men of the 17th Armored Infantry Battalion tried to sleep on the icy ground close to the Zorn Canal south of Herrlisheim, Major James Logan, its commanding officer, received orders from Combat Command A, General Riley P. Ennis, commanding, to forget Offendorf and instead to attack the town of Herrlisheim. James Francis described the order: "All three components from CCA and CCR which had attacked from Weyersheim on the morning of January 16th were now given new assignments. The 66th AIB was ordered to take Offendorf while the 17th AIB would take Herrlisheim. The town would be attacked from the southeastern entrance (the Offendorf-Herrlisheim Road) by the 43rd Tank Battalion, while the 17th AIB attacked from the southwestern entrance (the Gambsheim-Herrlisheim Road). To support the 17th AIB, tanks of the 23rd Tank Battalion were initially to support the 66th AIB's attack on Offendorf, then were reassigned to support the 17th AIB attack on Herrlisheim. These three components of a coordinated attack lacked proper planning and radio communication."[1] Incredibly, 12th Division Headquarters in Brumath believed that all was going according to plan, including the occupation of the Steinwald by the 66th AIB.[2]

The town lay only a mile from where George Hatt was resting. Major Logan ordered the two commanders of A and B Companies to take their men into Herrlisheim and occupy houses in the center of town. The commanding officer of A Company, Captain Helton, then assigned Private First Class William Funke as one of two runners to assist Major Logan in his communications while in Herrlisheim.[3]

What Funke and his fellow soldiers didn't know was that waiting for them in eastern Herrlisheim were a battalion of German soldiers of the 553rd Volksgrenadier Division equipped with mortars and antitank guns. Furthermore, by coincidence, units of the 10th Waffen SS Panzer Division had just entered the town from Offendorf. By the morning of January 17, 1945, Major Logan faced a strong enemy determined to wipe out the Americans as it had done earlier in January when men of the 56th AIB had tried to take the town from Rohrweiler and La Breymuhl.[4]

Early in the morning Sergeant Capretta started kicking the boots of sleeping men. George Hatt was jarred awake, and when he opened his eyes it was still dark. He described his circumstances: "At about 3:30 in the morning on January 17, squad leaders left their men in the cold darkness and gathered about their platoon sergeants for new orders. Sergeant Capretta came back and told us to get ready to attack again before sunup toward

Herrlisheim 1945

a town that had been on our left the day before. In an hour we in the company once again shouldered our burdens and formed into a column of movement. As our column turned left and stretched forward toward the Zorn River, cold weariness groaned in my body and mind as I knew it must have for everyone else. At this place the Zorn ran to the north-northwest and was bordered by tall, dark, ghostly trees. After traveling a mile along the evenly spaced trees we turned right, toward the southeast, away from the river. Here I was surprised to find that our path crossed that of clattering gray Sherman tanks moving directly from our right to our left. I later found out that the tanks were of the 23rd TB, taking up positions on the southwest tangent of Herrlisheim.

"Our infantry column moved quietly another mile and turned confusingly to head toward the area that lay between the two German-held towns of Herrlisheim and Offendorf. Everything seemed easy, as it had during the early part of the preceding day. No resistance had been met as the individual men slipped quietly over a raised highway that joined Herrlisheim with Gambsheim. As we crossed the narrow two-lane highway, Sergeant Capretta said, 'Hatt! You stay close to me. You are my bodyguard.' I thought of the impossibility of protecting his body if German machine guns opened up on us. Anyway, I was with him at the head of the squad.

"I saw Captain Helton in the predawn gloom walking back and forth rapidly, waving his arms and pointing as he directed Able Company platoon leaders to turn left, to the north. Our platoon, the third, was placed along the right-hand side of the highway with the Second Platoon farther to our right. I could see men stretched forward fifty or sixty yards and others spread to our right-hand side. First Platoon, under Lieutenant Marvin R. Drum of Garland, Texas, followed in reserve position in the middle and behind the Second and Third Platoons. Our squad could see about 200 yards away, a town, our objective. As our attacking group moved forward, dawn began to lighten the horizon, illuminating the church steeple, treetops, and house roofs. Sergeant Capretta and I were near Captain Helton and could hear him giving orders to an artillery observer assigned to Able Company. The observer called loudly and persistently on his radio for pre-attack artillery barrages. Seconds later, 105-millimeter shells came crashing into the quiet, sleeping little town. Then the shelling stopped. The captain shouted for us to move out. There was a brilliant flash on the edge of town burning through the dimness as one of our rifle squad members tossed a white phosphorus incendiary grenade into a trench of groggy, frightened German soldiers, members of the 553rd Volksgrenadier Division. A lot of these Germans came out with hands up. We counted 129 of them. They were freshly shaven and moved quickly into American territory, eager to leave the fighting lines for prisoner cages.

"I saw what appeared to be a platoon of GIs across the highway on the west side, carrying a 30-caliber heavy machine gun toward town. I perceived this to be 17th Armored Infantry Battalion Headquarters Company personnel because one of that company's weapons was the heavy machine gun. Also our company leaders informed us that B Company was on the left side of the road. Morning light appeared as A Company's Third Platoon, led by Lieutenant Owen, entered town on the main street. The Second Platoon continued forward through the field to the right, and the First Platoon followed in its reserve position."[5]

While George Hatt's company entered Herrlisheim, Andy Woods' Sherman tank cut through the column of the 17th Armored Infantry. Charlie Company's 16 tanks moved cautiously to the west, then north along the east bank of the Zorn, which at that point ran roughly north and south. The order of battle for C Company was: Company Commander, First Lieutenant Ernest Garneau; First Platoon Commander, Second Lieutenant Reitano; Second Platoon Commander, Lieutenant Wayne Guitteau; and Third Platoon Commander, Second Lieutenant James Sadler. Lieutenant Guitteau ordered his five tanks to flank right and stop. This brought the tanks' guns to bear on the southern part of the town. Here they waited for orders that were to define the timing of attack with the tanks of the 43rd TB entering Herrlisheim from the southeast on the Herrlisheim-Offendorf Road. Lieutenant Owsley Costlow, Third Platoon leader of A Company, later wrote, "Radio silence was in effect. The code word to begin the attack was 'Zippo.' Daylight arrived; all shadows disappeared. We were in a large field. We were ready, but no 'Zippo.' It became midmorning, with us just sitting there exposed. I ran back to the company commander's tank. Captain Lange said he was waiting on Battalion. Surely all the elements of surprise were gone now, so if anyone was out there in front of us they most certainly knew we were there. The silence was shattered by 'Zippo,' move out at your own speed."[6]

In a post-action review of the Herrlisheim fighting on January 17, 1945, Lieutenant Wayne F. Guitteau and several other platoon commanders were interviewed by a board of review on January 26, 1945. Guitteau said:

"We moved our tanks along with three tanks from A Company, led by Lieutenant Watson (to Herrlisheim). Upon reaching Herrlisheim, the 1st platoon of C Company, under Lieutenant Reitano, moved into the liberated section of town, southernmost section. I took one section of my platoon into town. About that time my own tank was knocked out by an enemy tank which came up a side street 100 yards away from us in the liberated section of town. Heavy artillery started falling on the town about this time and my company commander, Lieutenant Garneau, and Lieutenant Reitano were wounded by this fire."[7]

Major Logan set up his 17th Armored Infantry Battalion command post in a house on the east side of Rue de Gambsheim. After a few hours in the house, falling mortar rounds made it clear that a more substantial location had to be found. He relocated his command post in a house and barn, across the street at number 32, adjacent to an alley which bordered the property's north side. Across the alley to the north was the residence of the Gries family at number 36.

It was only a short distance from the southern edge of town. Bill Funke was at Major Logan's side as he and his staff entered the yard of the Zilliox family. Funke looked around as he entered the work yard of the residence. In front of him was the barn, to his right was the house and to his left was a long, covered shed that contained stacked hay. From inside the shed a dog barked. Funke wondered how the dog had survived the shelling and random bullets. Charles Zilliox and his fourteen-year-old son Fernand ran from the door of the house and beckoned for the Americans to go into the barn. There he ushered the men down a flight of steps into a long, narrow cellar. Without speaking a word of English, Mr. Zilliox pointed around him, then gestured that the cellar was safe from the explosions in the street. Major Logan nodded and thanked the man, who retreated back into the house.[8]

One of the staff officers guessed that many civilians were probably hiding in cellars. His observation was true. The Zilliox family occupied a second cellar under the kitchen of the main house. The barn cellar was entered by about six wooden steps from a heavy door in the barn. Major Logan confirmed that the ten-by-thirty-foot, dirt-floored cellar would be adequate. His men went to work setting up the radios, maps and chairs that would be needed to coordinate the Herrlisheim attack.[9]

On the eastern side of the town two companies of 43rd TB tanks were entering Herrlisheim via the Offendorf-Herrlisheim Road. The official division history written on February 1, 1945, reported the events surrounding the destruction of the 43rd TB: "On 17 January the 43rd TB with 1st Platoon, of Company C, 119th Engineers attached, was ordered to follow the 17th AIB to its attack position south of Herrlisheim and thence to move to an attack position east of the town and to attack at 0700 to seize the town. The 17th AIB was to attack to the north and the 43rd TB was to attack to the west. The commanders of the two battalions were directed to coordinate their actions. The 43rd TB with a total of 26 tanks reached its attack position east of Herrlisheim at 0745. As the town was approached, fire was received from the rear and at least two tanks were destroyed. At 0849 the battalion S-3 reported that the battalion was in town, that it was confronted by at least one enemy self-propelled gun and an unknown number of anti-tank guns and that the battalion was proceeding slowly. The 17th AIB had its last contact with the 43rd TB at 1000. At 1030 a platoon sergeant radioed that they were in Herrlisheim and virtually surrounded. Lieutenant Colonel Novosel stated by radio that 'yesterday was a circus compared to what it is today.' He gave his location as the southeastern part of town. When asked by the 43rd TB rear Command Post if more tanks could be brought into town to relieve the situation he replied that it could not be done because of the intense anti-tank fire."[10]

Ferguson wrote, "The 43rd Tank Battalion, advancing separately from the infantry, entered the eastern edge of Herrlisheim, where the tankers quickly received heavy fire from German tanks and anti-tank guns. In very heavy and confused fighting during the day, the infantrymen took up defensive positions in the town, while the 43rd TB separated from the infantry, seemingly disappeared. During the terrible fighting of January 17, the German forces destroyed or captured 29 American tanks, plus the 12 tanks destroyed on the previous day. The 43rd TB lost every tank in its task force, as well as the battalion commander, Lieutenant Colonel Nicholas Novosel."[11]

Nicholas Novosel told his own story of January 17 in the following words: "On 16 January the 43rd Tank Battalion and the 17th AIB attacked toward Offendorf. Between German AT guns and tanks in the Steinwald Woods we took quite a shellacking. Finally, at dusk we pulled back behind the 17th AIB. At about midnight we received orders to hit Herrlisheim again.

"Early on January 17 the remaining 23 tanks (in contradiction to the post-action report above) of the 43rd Tank Battalion took off for Herrlisheim. Our support was one platoon of engineers and the artillery forward observers. We made it without incident into what appeared to be an orchard-type area. This was soon after daybreak. All of a sudden all hell broke loose. There was a low haze, low enough to obscure visibility for our gunners, but high enough for enemy anti-tank gunners to see us. It was like shooting fish in a rain barrel for the enemy. I had two tanks shot out from under me before we made it into the town itself. We set up in a house across from the cemetery. A few other men and I went to the railroad crossing and helped some of our men cross with smoke grenades. The Germans were shooting at anything that crossed their tracks.

"After I was hit, I ran into a building and was taken care of by my people. I did not recall much until I woke up in a German aid station. The Germans took some fragments out of me. The next time I came to I was in what appeared to be a schoolhouse. It appeared to be set up as a hospital in Germany."[12]

Perny reported the following: "A complete battalion was thus destroyed, either before reaching Herrlisheim or immediately after. Five destroyed tanks were in the area, to the east of the crossing with Rue de Offendorf. The shells of eight others, including that of Colonel Novosel, were found in an orchard. Another tank was covered with bricks and debris. The honor of capturing 60 men and 12 Shermans and destroying seven others went to Captain Erwin Bachmann."[13]

In summary, Lieutenant Colonel Novosel attempted to get his tanks into positions within the town that would best protect the advancing infantry. Ten of the 43rd's tanks remained in the south of Herrlisheim in an orchard, while another 14 Shermans moved to the north-central part of the town and parked in a column on the east-west Rue de Capitaine Reibel (now Rue de Général Reibel), there to await further orders. The tally of 43rd TB tanks destroyed and captured on January 17 was: 2 destroyed on the Herrlisheim-Offendorf Road; 10 destroyed in the orchard opposite the south cemetery; 2 destroyed by German Panther tanks; and 12 captured by Erwin Bachmann. This accounting is consistent with Bachmann's description and the 12th AD official history.[14]

The Rue de Offendorf, looking south at the southern section of the town. Photograph was taken in March 1945 and includes destroyed tanks of the 43rd Tank Battalion which were under the command of Colonel Nicholas Novosel. The entire battalion was destroyed on January 16 and 17, 1945, and Colonel Novosel was wounded and taken prisoner by the Germans (National Archives).

17. Herrlisheim, January 1945

In 1946, George Hatt wrote about the house-to-house advance into Herrlisheim. "We saw that Herrlisheim was made up primarily of homes. We saw no commercial buildings. We were to find out that the town church and city administration building were at town's center and that a few merchant buildings were near the administration building. Side-by-side houses lined each street. Between the houses were small yards, some of which had concrete manure pits. In many cases, in the back of a yard was a barn. The town appeared to be dedicated to agriculture. We saw no civilians anywhere. Our company was walking past all of the houses without taking the time to be sure they were cleared of enemy troops. This made me quite apprehensive. I thought perhaps we should toss grenades into each building as we went by. However, that was not practical. So I tossed stones the size of hand grenades into each house I passed thinking that it might scare any hiding German soldier into exiting the building. However, it appeared that none was in the houses since none came out.

"Soon I heard small arms fire at the head of our platoon. Private Tom Smith hobbled by us, struggling to the rear, using his rifle as a support. He said with an apologetic grin, 'They shot me in the leg.' A bullet had gone through his calf. When we were a hundred yards or so from Herrlisheim's center, we saw up ahead a German burp-gun squad run across the street from left to right. Then some heavy explosions began farther down the street. We had met strong resistance and the leading elements were stalled. At this point, Private First Class Irving Worden ran up to me and asked if I would help him with

Rue de Offendorf looking north at the intersection of Rue de Château. In March, muddy, unpaved streets, destroyed tanks and houses mark the end of the Battle of Herrlisheim (National Archives).

Staff Sergeant Bill Ramsay of New York State, because he couldn't get anyone else to assist. I agreed and followed him forward and to the right off the main street, along which we were advancing. I do not recall asking my squad leader, Sergeant Capretta, for permission to go with Worden. I don't remember seeing the sergeant at that time. The two of us went in between two closely built houses and came to a hedge where one of the other members of Worden's squad was positioned with his rifle, observing through the hedge. Worden led me by way of a gate inside the hedge into a small barnyard abutting a two-story barn. As we started in, a German Jagdpanzer fired into the upper loft of the barn. The concussion was devastating.

"Worden told me that Ramsay had been wounded. So we rushed to Ramsay, who was lying on his back in the middle of the barnyard. The German tank crew could not see us because the tank was on the opposite side of a high fence. Nevertheless, every few seconds the tank would fire into the upper part of the barn with a high-explosive shell, and shrapnel would fly everywhere. Worden said that he and Ramsay had entered the barnyard and shrapnel from one of the shells wounded the sergeant. When Worden had asked him if he were wounded badly, the sergeant said he was. So Worden went back to get some help, but could find no one who would help until he came to me.

"When we got to Ramsay, we found him unresponsive and discovered a wound the size of a dime in his neck just above his collarbone. Blood was slowly running from it. I attempted to stop the bleeding by placing my fingers in the wound. But the sergeant did not seem to be breathing. I turned the sergeant's head and saw that the piece of shrapnel exited his neck at the base of his skull. I held the wound in his neck to keep it from bleeding and asked Worden to put his ear to the sergeant's chest to see if his heart was beating. All this time the tank kept firing into the barn and shrapnel was tearing all about us.

"Worden said he could not hear his heart. His breathing had stopped. We concluded that Ramsay must be dead. We took his rifle and placed his bayonet on it and stuck the bayonet end into the ground. We placed Ramsay's helmet on the rifle butt. And, seeing that he was dead, we abandoned him and returned through the gate in the hedge as the tank continued to fire into the barn.

"I then went to a shed that was directly alongside the tank that was firing into the loft of the two-story barn. I don't know what prompted me to go to the shed. I don't recall having had any order or permission from my squad leader in this instance either, or even seeing him. I don't know how I lost contact with the squad. I believe someone had told me that one of our riflemen in the platoon had been hit there and the rifle squad needed some help. They said they had fired a bazooka into the tank and it had no effect on the tank. A small hole was visible where the bazooka shell hit. The tank, only thirty feet from the shed, was continuing to fire its big gun into the loft of the two-story barn. The problem was that one of the riflemen was hit in the knee and suffering a great deal of pain. I was under the impression that fragments from the bazooka shell explosion had struck him. He was afraid that the rest of us would leave him there. He could not walk. So, first I pulled out a morphine syrette and injected the contents into his thigh just above his knee. Then I found an old wooden ladder in the shed and we loaded him on it, all the while he was complaining that we were hurting his leg. Four of us grabbed the ladder and we hauled him back to the main street where medics took charge and evacuated him. By that time he seemed to be feeling little pain and expressed appreciation for our getting him the hell out of there.

"One of the men in our platoon said, 'Hey, there's a Kraut tank back here and some guys are trying to hit it with a bazooka.' Two of us walked on the east side of houses on the main street until we entered an open field. Four or five GIs were loading a bazooka. I do not believe these were men from my platoon. To the east of them about a hundred yards away was a small German tank. These men were standing up in the open in plain sight. I felt they were very careless, although quite gutsy, shooting at that tank. One man told us they had fired and missed the tank. As a bazooka man myself, I said that striking the tank at that range was unlikely. We watched as the group fired another round at the tank. The rocket arched high in the air, but skipped off the ground before reaching the target. It did not detonate. During all of this activity the tank never gave any indication that it would turn and fire at the Americans. My feeling was that there were some German infantry somewhere near the tank. That would be reason enough for the bazooka team not to approach the tank, to reduce the distance to a practical range. On the other hand, there was no small arms fire toward any of us even though we all were clearly visible. By then I felt that I needed to return to my squad. I think I must have been gone for about fifteen minutes.

"Our squad was well into town and assigned to a house on the main street. We were told to get some rest. The house was neat. There were beds with sheets on them. Also, in the basement we found a large supply of preserved purple plums in jars. Having had only three K rations for a couple of days I ate my fill of the plums. Several days later I had an extremely bad case of diarrhea, maybe dysentery. It took three weeks to get rid of it. Though exhausted, I could not sleep, even on the bed. Soon the members of our squad were told by Sergeant Capretta to get on alert because it looked like the Germans were beginning a counterattack. We began to hear very heavy firing to the northeast of our position in town. It was a mystery to me what the shooting was all about. It seemed to be a few hundred yards away."[15]

On the southern edge of town, Lieutenants Garneau and Reitano of the 23rd Tank Battalion had been injured that morning. Lieutenant Guitteau took command of the platoon at about 1100. Private First Class Andy Woods, loader for the Guitteau tank, described his first engagement with an enemy tank. "We were still at the Zorn River, waiting for orders. I listened to Lieutenant Guitteau as he explained to the other commanders his intentions. Guitteau was determined to find out for himself what was happening in the town. Sergeant Edward Vickless, commander of the number two tank, offered to charge into the town and see what was up, but Guitteau gave him a negative. Private First Class Frenchy Dubois, our driver, gunned the engine and *Cleopatra* rumbled eastward on a short side street called Rue de Balstein. Mortar rounds landed in the street and small arms fire came from the main street ahead. Halfway up the short street, Guitteau ordered Dubois to halt. The crew sat patiently as the lieutenant leaped up out of the turret hatch. I discussed with Dubois and Private First Class Cox, the gunner, the disposition of several cartons of cigarettes that had been stashed in the vacant bow gunner's position.

"Guitteau slid himself back down into the tank commander's seat. Dubois let the clutch out in low gear and *Cleopatra* crept forward. At the intersection of Rue de Gambsheim, Dubois swung the tank to the right and at Lieutenant Guitteau's order stopped opposite house number 36. We didn't know the location of the 17th Battalion command post, which was being set up only two houses to the south of our position.

"With engine idling, Guitteau tried to see what was happening in the south. I searched to the north from the loader's hatch, spotted a German tank about three hundred feet distant on Rue de Chateau, which came into the intersection from a diagonally north direction. The tank was painted white and its gun was pointed right at me. Flashing through my mind was the high explosive round in the breech. I shouted the direction to Cox who flipped the electric traverse switch and started swinging the cannon into position. I quickly extracted the H. E. shell from the breech, intending to replace it with an armor-piercing round. As I held the shell in my arms, a terrific explosion knocked me off my jump seat and onto my knees. A sheet of flame whipped through the tank body and turret, scorching my face and eyes. The concussion was so severe that I was unconscious for a few moments. I came to as machine-gun ammunition within *Cleopatra* began to ignite. It was a giant popcorn popper as bullets zinged around me. My mind concentrated on escape, but I could only see unfocused shapes. I dropped the shell and groped above me for the loader's hatch dogging handles. The hatch refused to open and flames were biting at my trousers.

"I slid on my back under the breech of the cannon and into the tank commander's seat. I saw daylight through the open turret hatch, but the .50-caliber machine gun blocked the way. I reached up and pushed the barrel to one side. Guitteau, who had jumped down from the tank, climbed back onto the engine deck to help me, but by the time I had pushed myself out of the burning tank Guitteau was nowhere to be seen. I leaped from the turret onto the engine deck, then down to the ground.

"The German Panther's coaxial machine gun continued to spray *Cleopatra*. Bullets pinged off the armor and ricocheted in random directions. I dodged the bullets as I ran to a shed at house number 36. I fell to the floor as Cox followed me in. Neither of us had a weapon. Pistols and hand grenades had been forgotten in the escape. We both lay on the floor waiting for the worst. I said that I couldn't see very well. Cox examined my face and said that my eyebrows had been singed.

"The house at 36 Rue de Gambsheim sat on a triangular island made so by a diagonal alley off of Rue de Balstein and Rue de Gambsheim. Cox and I waited for the machine gunning to stop, then we ran to the alley wall, jumped over it and almost into the arms of Dubois, who wanted to know what had held up his fellow tank crew members. Without answering, the three of us darted down the alley. Leaping over a fence into a field behind 32 Rue de Gambsheim, we dashed from fence to fence through pastures, heading south out of town. It was a footrace and I quickly regretted my cumbersome tank clothing. I tossed away garments at each fence and wall to be scaled. When at last I was safe I felt as though I couldn't run another step. We started walking back to Weyersheim, reversing the route we had taken earlier in our tank."[16]

George Hatt's job was to get to the center of Herrlisheim. He wrote, "I was sure my platoon was still ahead of me and so ran into a house on the east side of the street. There was Capretta and the others lounging as if there were no war. Men of another 3rd Platoon squad were in the house. The house hadn't been damaged. The beds even had clean linen. At least they had been clean before the members of his squad reclined on them in their dirty uniforms and muddy boots.

"I stepped into the cellar and heard the crack of a cannon. It was instantly followed by an explosion. It sounded as though it was about two blocks away to the east. I remembered seeing the steeple of a church in that direction and assumed that's where the action was.

Captain Erwin Bachmann, adjutant to Lieutenant Colonel Ernst Tetsch, who entered Herrlisheim on January 17, 1945, on a motorcycle and with two Panther Mark V tanks destroyed two Sherman tanks and captured 12 others with crews of the 43rd Tank Battalion (Bachmann collection).

"I remained in the cellar when others roamed about the house on Rue de Gambsheim. I thought I heard the sound of tank engines, but couldn't determine if they were German. Then I heard the ringing bells of a church. Three heavy strikes. My attention was distracted from the war by the incongruous sound of church bells. A few minutes later I heard two cannon shots that rose above the din of other explosions."[17]

The sounds of tanks and cannon fire heard by George Hatt had come from two German panthers commanded by Lieutenant Erwin Bachmann of the 10th Waffen SS Panzer Division. Zabecki and Wooster described Bachmann's patrol into Herrlisheim: "First Lieutenant Erwin Bachmann, Tetsch's battalion adjutant, rode into Herrlisheim on a motorcycle accompanied by two Panthers from the 2nd Battalion's 3rd Company. He ambushed and knocked out several Shermans, captured some 60 GIs and freed 20 German prisoners. Bachmann's force also captured intact four Shermans and their crews, which he sent back to Offendorf."[18]

Erwin Bachmann described how he managed to capture 12 Sherman tanks (in contradiction of Zabecki's number) of the 43rd TB: "That morning of January 17, I was in Offendorf listening to a report of Captain Pender's injuries in Herrlisheim. Pender had commanded a company of 10th Waffen SS panzergrenadiers who were attempting to hold back the Americans.

"I was itching to get into action, but I had never been a really aggressive officer. I was more the staff type, and on Lieutenant Colonel Ernst Tetsch's staff, I was a valued part of the regimental organization. I suggested with some temerity that in view of Pender's absence I should drive to Herrlisheim and take over command of 3rd Company. It was an impulsive offer that surprised not only Tetsch, but myself. I was not a large man and was quiet, even introspective. Born in 1921 and raised in Rostok, I had somehow been selected to go to Junkerschule, the military training institute. I had done well and in 1942 had become an officer.

"Tetsch agreed and assigned a BKrad (motorcycle with sidecar) and driver to me. Corporal Heinrich Sauerwein swung his leg over the motorcycle and I jumped into the sidecar. We shot up Rue de Offendorf and slowed when at the outskirts of town. We looked for 3rd and 4th companies, but couldn't find anyone. We chugged in low gear up the street toward the city center, all the while craning our necks, looking for some sign of life. We came to a fork in the road. To our left was a church with a tall steeple. Farther to the west I heard rifle fire coming from a few of the houses. Straight ahead was a street which seemed to dead-end in about sixty meters. To my right was the right side of the fork, but it had a curve and I couldn't see beyond the bend. I dismounted from the BKrad and walked up the street. It was the Rue Châteauneuf la Forêt, but I took no notice of the geography. Armed with only an officer's pistol in its holster I started to round the bend. A machine gun rang out and bullets ricocheted off the cobblestones around me. I turned tail and ran back to the BKrad where Sauerwein was waiting. I grabbed a panzerfaust and a few hand grenades, then shouted for Sauerwein to turn around and get back into Offendorf to bring up the two lead Panther tanks. I watched momentarily as the BKrad sped back down the Offendorf road.

"I then crept back up Rue Châteauneuf la Forêt. It was a short street which, like its left-hand fork, ended at about sixty meters. I peeked around the corner and saw several American soldiers standing in a cross street only about thirty meters from my position. Dashing across the street and into a protected space formed by a brick wall and corner of a house, I again observed the Americans. From this location I could see the nose of a Sherman tank. I knelt down on one knee and brought the Panzerfaust to my shoulder. I tried to remain calm as I went through the simple firing procedure. Sighting along the barrel I depressed the trigger lever. The whoosh of the rocket startled me and I jumped back into the protection of the house and wall. I thought I heard the shell explode against a tank, but I wasn't sure. Remaining still, I listened for the enemy reaction. All seemed quiet from the American Sherman tanks.

"Then I heard the squeaking of tank tracks from behind me. Only a few minutes had passed since I had sent Sauerwein on his way. It would have been impossible for the Panthers to have come up from Offendorf in so short a time. Again I looked out from my hidden position, this time to my rear. Amazingly, two Panthers came to a stop where I had left Sauerwein and the BKrad. I dashed back to them. Sergeant Heinz Berger, in the right-hand tank, jumped down and cupped an ear trying to listen to my directions. Sergeant Hans Mülradt, in the left-hand tank, stayed in his turret. I told Berger to cut his engine and hand-signaled Mülradt to do the same. The Maybachs throttled back and died. Berger explained that they had been in a small orchard outside of town when they saw the BKrad zip by them on its way back to Offendorf. Having observed the same motorcycle go into Herrlisheim with an officer in its sidecar less than a half hour before, they had decided to investigate. It had taken them only a few minutes to find the fork in the road where we now stood.

"While the tank commander talked, I was only half-listening. I was formulating in my mind a plan to attack whatever tanks may be on that road running perpendicular to the two streets before us. There was no time to lose. The Americans would shortly launch an attack of their own, if they knew just how puny the German forces were. I told Berger to take his tank up the right hand street (Rue Châteauneuf la Forêt), and when he got far enough around the street's bend to see the Americans, he was to open fire on whatever might present itself. I would stay with Mülradt's tank, and when we heard the shooting we would move up the left-hand street, called the Rue de l'Église. We would then charge the Americans from behind when they were engaged with Berger.

"The two tank commanders jumped up into their turrets and started the engines. Both roared into life simultaneously and as soon as I waved my hand, Berger drove his tank up Rue de Châteauneuf la Forêt. Meanwhile, I waved Mülradt on ahead. The tank crept up Rue de l'Église with me trotting at the left, just as a church bell a block away struck 3:00 P.M. When Mülradt's tank was only halfway up the short street, they heard Berger's cannon and his coaxial machine gun. Immediately, Mülradt accelerated, and before I caught up, he had blasted the engine housing of a Sherman at the intersection.

When I arrived, the tank was burning, but the crew members had not been injured. The Panther tank's menacing cannon swung in its turret to the next Sherman. Mülradt was anxious to destroy another American tank. As I took stock of the situation, an American officer waved something white.

"Simultaneously, Berger's tank at the front of the Sherman column swung around and faced the Americans. I quickly told Mülradt to radio Berger and tell him to hold fire. I walked out into the center of the east-west Rue de Capitaine Reibel and looked down the column of American tanks. There were six of them, not including the burning tank. The Americans were penned in and their guns were useless in their tight column disposition. It had taken only a few seconds for the commander of the American tanks to see the hopelessness of his situation. He waved what looked like a white undershirt, then stepped forward to greet his captors. I went forward to speak to him as he made hand signals, instructing the Americans to get down from their tanks.

"The American lieutenant spoke rapidly in English, none of which I understood. As he did so, the crew members were assembling in the middle of the street, while I pointed at the American officer's sidearm. The man unholstered his Colt .45 automatic and handed it to me, but I signaled him to throw it on the ground. I pointed to the Colt in the muddy street and instructed the Americans in German to lay down their arms where the automatic lay. The American tankers complied, keeping their hands in the air, although with what seemed to me to be the relaxed attitude of those confident of victory.

"Mülradt got down from his tank to assist me in the roundup. He brandished his Schmeiser submachine gun even though he was outnumbered sixty to one. Walking up the street toward Berger's tank, he scowled at the Americans and shouted at them to form a double rank knowing full well that the Americans couldn't understand what he was saying. Suddenly, he turned and ran back to me. He pointed to the side yards of the houses on the opposite side of the street. For the first time, I saw six other Shermans. Slowly walking away from them were the American crew members, who only minutes before had been casually eating their field rations. One of the American tankers spoke some German and stepped forward to interpret. I asked if there were any more surprises. The interpreter pointed to a side yard in which a group of German prisoners stood wondering what to do. Mülradt again dashed up the street and saw the Germans standing in a utility yard. He motioned for the German infantrymen to follow him. They approached me and stood at attention. Mülradt counted them and reported that these were twenty from the 553rd Volksgrenadier Division. I took charge of the group and ordered them to pick up the American weapons and to keep them as their own.

"I considered what to do with the windfall of American tanks at a time when Germany had so few of its own. Through the American interpreter I ordered the tank drivers to separate themselves from the other American tank crew members. The drivers stepped to the front of the American prisoners. I told them that they were going to drive their tanks to Offendorf. As motivation I would place a German soldier armed with a pistol behind each driver. The former German prisoners, now in charge of their former captors, volunteered to a man for the opportunity to ride in a Sherman. Berger selected the youngest and most eager of the group. The reluctant American drivers and their eager German escorts hopped up onto the high-sided tanks and disappeared down the turret hatches. I first made sure that all twelve of my captured tanks were ready, then the drivers started their engines. I walked to the other side of the street and signaled Mülradt who yelled that the side yard tanks were ready. I walked over to Berger's tank and inquired if his firing had caused any damage. Berger told me that he had only scared a couple of dead people in the graveyard across the street."[19]

The count of destroyed and captured 43rd Tank Battalion Shermans on January 17, 1945, has been variously reported. Engler states it thus: "Later inspection in February revealed the hulls of fourteen knocked-out tanks. Fifteen others were unaccounted for — moved by the Germans and in many instances used again as ordnance."[20] His tally of 29 tanks lost on January 17 is consistent with that of Ferguson, but not with that of Bachmann and the 12th Armored Division Inspector General.

George Hatt had heard the commotion on the Rue de Capitaine Reibel, less than two blocks from him. He decided that he had better report the noise to Capretta. He spoke of those hours: "I thought that the krauts might be coming toward us. I ran up the steps of the cellar and into the living room where Capretta was huddling with two members of his squad. The sergeant was giving orders to spot in all four directions from the house. I couldn't understand how the men on the main floor of the house could not have heard the engine noise, which was so distinct in the cellar. I started to explain, but it was clear that Capretta had other things on his mind. Capretta held up his hand for silence and ordered me to get to the rear of the house and keep an eye toward the east. I shrugged my shoulders and looked for a room with a window.

"I found the kitchen, which had a window facing east. Strangely, the window had glass panes. Somehow, this window had survived the concussion of cannon. By looking between buildings, behind the house I could see into the street to the east. I watched the street for movement. All seemed quiet, then I saw German soldiers running from left to right. They were coming from the north, getting into the houses behind the Americans. I broke the window glass with my rifle barrel and aimed it at a spot through which I knew the Germans would have to run. The next German ran into my line of fire and I pulled the trigger twice. Bullets skipped around the running German. I wasn't sure if I actually had hit him. Two more tried the transit and I again shot at them. Then all movement stopped in the street.

"Machine-gun bullets suddenly ripped into the kitchen-window frame. I jumped back into the shadows of the room. They had come from the house across the street to the east. I ran into the side yard, where a manure pile lay against a concrete block wall. I raised myself enough to the see the window from which the machine-gun fire had come. I saw muzzle flashes and pumped four rapid shots into it. When the men of my squad heard and saw what was happening they too opened up on the street to the east. It all happened in less than a minute. The machine-gun fire quit. I listened from my position outside. I heard moaning coming from down the street. It could be a German trick or it might be that we had hit the man with the burp gun.

"Behind the house was a barn and next to it was Sergeant George Drost, an old cavalryman now in the rifle squad, sharing the house with my squad. He had taken up a spotting position next to the barn where he could see out both ends. He waved me over to him and asked to be relieved for a short time.

"I took his position. I crouched down in the yard and listened to the sounds of battle. It seemed strangely quiet to the east. The firing seemed to ebb and flow in waves of explosions. This was one of those periods of relative calm. I sat to await the return of Drost."[21]

From the beginning, Major Logan had a difficult time with communications. He attempted to reach his outlying units, but the battery-powered radios would only transmit and receive to headquarters back in Weyersheim. The radioman called it "skip." The radios had crystal-set frequencies that seemed useless within the town itself. The radiomen called the 43rd and 23rd Tank Battalions, both of which were supposed to be in Herrlisheim, but Logan knew nothing of their location or condition. The radioman received no answer to his calls.

Bill Funke was called upon to carry messages to platoon commanders and squads of men scattered throughout the southwestern part of Herrlisheim. He was a rifleman and carried his rifle at port arms as he ran to various parts of the town. With paper messages stuck in his tunic pocket, he dodged from house to house, asking questions of those he met, then sprinting to wherever he was pointed. Since each platoon was on the move, Funke had to track each message recipient by running faster than the platoon was moving. It was exhausting and frustrating work. Most of the time, he was able to find the intended receiver of a message, but sometimes he failed.

Funke listened to Major Logan talking on the radio to CCA headquarters in Weyersheim. He explained the situation in Herrlisheim just as Funke entered the cellar. The major asked for the battalion to be removed from the town and to return to Weyersheim. He was told to wait. Funke heard the return radio call from CCA. The voice told Logan to stay in Herrlisheim and to attack the Germans at dawn of the next day. Logan was red-faced. The veins on his neck stood out as he tried to contain his rage. At least four times during the afternoon and night of January 17, Major Logan requested higher headquarters to send reinforcements into the town to help him hold his position. No positive action was ever taken on these requests.[22] The Battalion S-3, Captain Eugene A. Blackford, and the executive officer, Major John Cunningham, personally reported to CCA headquarters the precarious position the battalion was in as reported by Major Logan.[23]

As the sun went down on January 17, 1945, in Herrlisheim, France, the Americans hung on in the southwestern portion of the town. The men scattered in houses up and down the Rue de Gambsheim were being reduced in effectiveness by fatigue. In the barn cellar at number 32, the state of the 17th AIB officers deteriorated as the hours passed. Testimony to their condition was description from officers who visited the command post during the afternoon and night of that crucial day.

Second Lieutenant Dixon L. Warren, 2nd Platoon, Company A, 17th AIB, reported the following: "Major Logan said that he had orders to hold the part of the town they had. I never did get back to my platoon. I was very tired by this time, everybody was very tired. Major Logan was asleep, and after I had been in the CP about thirty minutes Lieutenant Muska fell asleep. About 0230 Captain Rowe brought his combat patrol in and asked if there was a mission for it. The Major told him no, to have them quartered in a house nearby to be available."[24]

Officers from various units came into the cellar and attempted to assess the situation. Major William R. Comfort, S-3, 23rd TB, was one such officer. He said, "During the several occasions that I talked to Major Logan it was obvious to me that he was what one might term 'punch drunk' due to lack of sleep. At this time dusk was beginning to fall. At this point I noticed American infantrymen running back down the street from the center of town and heard a lot of heavy machine gun fire towards the outskirts of town. At one time in talking to Major Logan he was very emphatic in expressing his opinion that the German strength in the town was very much underestimated. He made a statement as follows: 'I would like to get the son-of-a-bitch that said there were the number of Germans in the town that there were supposed to be."[25]

Major William A. Edwards, commanding officer of 23rd TB, when speaking of deploying his tanks in the town itself, said, "All the infantry were busy and if they were there the artillery hits around the tanks would have hit them anyway. So just at dark we pulled the tanks off the street to the west edge of town because of the artillery and snipers working through. I was at the 17th AIB CP when a runner came in telling Major Logan of the situation. The situation was about the same. Major Logan appeared to me to be just about pooped out. He fell asleep while we were talking to him. His last statement was that the 'sons of bitches were mixed up,' and if they wanted him to get men out of town he couldn't do it. He said he might get some out by crossing the canal. This was the last time I saw him. I went back to my tanks and sat through the artillery."[26]

At about 2100 Major Logan called Bill Funke for a messenger run. He told him to find every officer and man he could and tell them to get back to the Battalion CP. Bill Funke related his effort to find soldiers in the chaos of the hour. "I ran out into the darkness. I knew that it would be hard to find anyone in the burning houses. Flames to the north cast eerie shadows across the street as I ran from house to house yelling through windows and doorways. Through the vacant window of a house I saw an American helmet. I banged on the door. A shout from within demanded the password. My mind went blank. Again from within, the same voice asked his captain for permission to shoot through the door. The words have been with me all these years: 'Cap'm, you want I should blow that sneaky Kraut's head off?' In panic I remembered and yelled the password, 'Fisk.' The door opened. A filthy sergeant told me that I'd come close to getting my head blown off."[27]

Near the town's center, George Hatt left the barn after having been relieved by Sergeant Drost. When the sun had gone down, much of the firing had diminished. He related the events of that night. "Capretta told me to move to the adjacent house and stand guard in the upstairs rear bedroom. He wanted me to keep an eye out on what was happening to the east of our location. I crossed to the rear of the side yard and entered the back door of the house that faced the next street to the east, the Rue de Marais. I wound my way through the dark house into an upper-level room with a window facing the intersection of Rue de Marais and the curving Rue de Offendorf. I found a chair and pulled it to the window. The room was so dark I had to feel my way around in it. Looking out the window, I could only see the vague outlines of houses across the street. There was an intersection, more houses and behind them the white steeple of a large church to the northeast. As I settled down for the night, I heard voices and the downstairs door opening. I froze, then realized that the voices were speaking English. A soldier carrying boxes of ammunition came into the room. An argument immediately ensued. The soldier informed me that he and his two machine gun crew members had been ordered to set up their weapon at my window. I told them to get out and take their machine gun with them. I was tired and I had found a good place to rest. There were lots of windows in town and this one belonged to me.

"The Third Platoon machine gunners went into the adjacent room. I heard talking in whispers as they mounted the gun on a tripod. Their clicks and clangs and incessant whispering irritated me. I yelled for them to shut up. I heard nothing more from the next

17. Herrlisheim, January 1945

Severely damaged buildings were typical of the aftermath of combat in the Herrlisheim-Weyersheim area (National Archives).

room. I sat on the chair in front of my window. Finally, all was quiet. Even the three machine gunners in the next room were quiet. For a while I strained my eyes to see out the window. In the darkness nothing moved. I rose and felt around on the bed in the corner I pulled off the feather comforter and dragged it to the chair. Working the down comforter under my boots, around my legs, I pulled it up and over my body. Gradually, body heat filled the comforter and I was warm for the first time since leaving Geudertheim. I watched out the window, looking for movement in the darkness. Feeling an obligation toward my duty as observer, I vowed to steadfastly continue my watch out the window. In two minutes I was fast asleep.

"An orange glow came through my eyelids. Something deep inside me raised an alarm. I opened my eyes wide. The house across the narrow street to the east was blazing. It threw a flickering and harsh light into the room. I realized that anyone could see me from outside. I pushed the chair backward, the comforter caught under its legs and I crashed to the floor. A voice from the adjacent room told me to shut up. I was disturbing the machine gunners' sleep. I yelled for them to look out the window. In seconds I heard the clatter of the machine gun being dismantled. I grabbed my gear and followed the machine gunners down the stairs, through a yard and into the rear door of another house facing the Rue de Gambsheim. I had lost track of time and wasn't sure of where I was. The machine gun crew crept into the front foyer. Others were in the house and they crouched down where they were, but I found the front bedroom by the flickering light of burning houses coming through the vacant windows. I stuck my head out a window in time to see a Panther tank quietly making its way south on the main street. I watched, in rapture of its quiet motion. It stopped and its engine idled like a Cadillac limousine.

Suddenly, its cannon shattered the silence. The tank had found a target to the south. It reversed and started quietly to back north in the direction of the town center.

"I heard Bill Funke's voice hollering through the paneless window of the living room. He yelled that he was from Major Logan. The C.O. wanted all men to get back to the battalion CP. Lieutenant Owen, commanding officer of Second Platoon, was suspicious about the order. He stood in front of Funke on the opposite side of the glassless window and demanded to know a lot of detail. Funke repeated the order, then ran to the next house. I listened to the brief argument and tried to understand how Funke's information could be doubted. Then Lieutenant Owen hollered for everyone to assemble in the yard next to the street. I and the others inside the house scrambled out the door and down the steps into the yard. The entire platoon was standing there. The excited lieutenant ordered his men to get back to the Battalion CP. The men who had heard Funke stared at him, not knowing what to make of the order. The lieutenant repeated his order, this time in a falsetto screech. The soldiers milled around the yard, not knowing where the CP was. The lieutenant was obviously panicky about something, but he was a replacement and maybe just letting off steam. Again the lieutenant shouted for the men to take off.

"I had heard Funke and knew the CP must be to the south. I opened the gate to the street and took off, bending into a crouch as I ran. I turned left, heading south with others strung out behind me, each man trying to obey an order he didn't completely understand. The men were now running down the main street in the direction from which they had come that morning. Holding my rifle at port arms, I ran as fast as I could, keeping close to the houses on the east side of the street. I had run a few blocks when I heard a familiar voice from behind me. It was Sergeant Drost trying to catch up. He came alongside and I just waved at him to keep pace.

"Some of the soldiers were cutting across the street and into houses, looking for the CP. I just wanted to get out of the line of fire. I looked over my shoulder, but could no longer see anyone following. Drost's bent-over run resembled a quarterback sneak. I raced at top speed, but kept my eyes on what was ahead. Orange light from burning houses reflected off low clouds. I spotted a knocked-out Sherman tank (*Cleopatra*) directly in front of us. Its gun barrel pointed downward, and in the flickering light I could see that it had been a victim of the fighting earlier in the day. I made out a vacant field between houses on the east side of the street, slightly beyond the Sherman. The field was depressed from the road, and along the downslope parallel to it, white movement caught my eye. I instantly recognized a line of snow-camouflaged German infantry lying prone, side by side and perpendicular to the road. As we ran up to the tank, I instinctively began shooting my Garand from the hip. I quickly fired most of my clip into the Germans. Drost did likewise with his carbine and screams rose from those we hit.

"We ran forward, then stopped on the street side of the Sherman. Three German hand grenades exploded at the point where we had first started shooting. I frantically tried to grab another clip while Drost pulled a hand grenade from his belt and tossed the grenade into the field. I leaped out from behind the tank and fired two rounds at a silhouetted German soldier as the grenade exploded. Then my empty clip popped out of the rifle. I dodged back behind the tank and ripped a glove off my right hand. I pulled out a grenade, pulled the pin and tossed it into the Germans.

"We dashed from the protection of the tank in a serpentine track that took us south and out of town. As we ran, machine-gun tracers banged around us. Some of the bullets kicked up the pavement and the ricochets made a singing noise. The Germans were shooting wildly, temporarily blinded by the grenade. We kept running, then slowed to a walk. Neither of us could talk. We sucked in air and blew it out as fast as our lungs could work. Finally, after the houses had disappeared behind us and our breathing slowed to almost normal, I realized that our escape had been a miracle. I felt exhilarated and giddy. I laughed the laugh of a person who had won the Irish sweepstakes. We crossed the street to the west and ran into a high barbed-wire fence. I fumbled through my many pockets and pulled out the wire cutters. I held them up for Drost to appreciate and started snipping the wires. He was amazed and I felt a tinge of pride. We jumped through the pulled-back wire and ran across the field."[28]

As George Hatt and Sergeant Drost made their escape from Herrlisheim, Bill Funke knew that if he remained where he was he might get cut off himself. Many years later, he described his capture: "I picked my way south on the west side of Rue de Gambsheim. It was a race of running, stopping, listening, looking, then running again; all the time panting from the exertion. It took over an hour, but I finally reached the barn where the command post was located. If I had to make another trip I needed to catch my breath. Thinking that I would rest a moment before reporting back, I squatted down at the corner of the barn. It was made of stone and I leaned my back against it. The muscles in my legs cramped, pulling themselves like drawstrings. I rubbed them through my bulky two sets of trousers and long johns. From my right, came the blinding flash of a white phosphorus grenade. A chip hit my hand and I wildly flicked it away. It burned, but my body had been protected by the stone wall of the shed. I was stunned and temporarily blinded by the flash, and as I stood up to gain my balance, a German soldier threw a second grenade into the barnyard. It exploded, but caused little damage against the stone. I stepped around the corner of the barn into the muzzles of German Schmeisers. I threw up my hands without being asked as other Germans smashed in the door to the barn and headed for the cellar within.

"I stood in the yard as my eyes regained a measure of night vision. Officers and men emerged from the subterranean command post, looking glum in the failure of surrender. I turned and saw an immense German tank. I thought it was a Panther, but couldn't be sure in the flickering light. The Germans were brisk and business-like with flashlights whose beams flashed from face to face. The officer in charge gave sharp and quick orders to his men who pushed us into a line. He then marched past us like a general at parade inspection. The German seemed to be in no hurry as he examined the rank insignias on the collars of his captives. I thought the German wanted to survey his catch, like a fisherman with a string of trout. When the German looked me over, I saw his Waffen SS emblem. I had never seen a German soldier so close. The young man's face looked like any other soldier. In fact, he didn't look much different than me.

"We were ordered into the street. The tank had disappeared and in its place were a group of other 17th Armored Infantry captives who looked haggard and tired. The Germans nudged the Americans into a double line and we walked east up Rue de Château to Rue de Offendorf, where we turned southeast. For me it was the end of the battle and the end of the war. It marked the start of my internment as a prisoner of war."[29]

In Weyersheim, Andy Woods checked into the field aid station, where a doctor told him that his eyes would clear in a few days. The three *Cleopatra* crew members had hitched a ride back to Gries where C Company waited for the return of its Shermans. Woods had found a billet in the Gries schoolhouse. Dead tired after his terrifying moments in the Sherman tank and his long walk back to Weyersheim, he slept on the floor of the schoolhouse.[30]

January 17, 1945, has been called the turning point for the 12th Armored Division. Most veterans agree that the division never again faced such a desperate situation in the fighting that took the men through Germany. The events of January 16 and 17 were significant enough for VI Corps to instigate an internal division review. Of most critical importance was divisional refusal to accept reports of those in the field and to continue issuing impossible orders in the face of heavy losses. Lieutenant Colonel Cecil R. Hill, inspector general for 12th AD, conducted interviews incident to the division's formal board of inquiry. The 60-page testimony was headed *Headquarters, 12th Armored Division Investigative Report of February 1, 1945, Pertaining to Actions of Units in Combat on January 17 and 18, 1945, Submitted to Commanding Officer, VI Corps, U.S. Army.* Pertinent testimony included the following:

Testimony of Lieutenant Colonel Wells, commanding officer of the 66th AIB: "The 17th AIB CP was in the basement and I had to sneak in through the barn in the rear entrance of it. While I was there I talked to Major Logan and Lt. Muska and two or three other officers. From the talks with these officers and Major Logan I gathered that at that time the 17th AIB consisted of a little more than 200 men in Herrlisheim most of whom were apparently in basements and pretty well pinned down in there, that the Germans were superior and also that they were pretty hopelessly outnumbered at that time. The buildings along the street, which was more or less of a boundary between the German and the 17th AIB, were on fire. At the time I left, everything was quiet and they had no reason to believe that they wouldn't be able to hold the small portion of the town they had. On the morning of the 18th approximately 90 men of the 17th AIB who had escaped from Herrlisheim were organized into a battle group and employed in a defensive position south of town in conjunction with elements of the 66th AIB and 119 Engineers south of the town. This position was maintained until early in the afternoon of 18 January at which time the men were transported west to the town of Geudertheim.... I do not think higher headquarters understood the situation. It is my opinion that it was impossible for the 17th to continue the attack at all. There was no 43rd in the vicinity and the 23rd stated they had been in the vicinity of Offendorf and lost a considerable number of tanks in the same place they were required to go back to the next morning."[31]

Testimony of First Lieutenant John C. Lee, 17th AIB: "At no time during the entire operation was any accurate information concerning a disposition and strength of enemy troops given to me. I could not, consequently, give a clear picture to my platoon leaders, which in turn goes right down to the enlisted men and makes it extremely difficult for a man to fight when he doesn't know what he is fighting."[32]

Testimony of Lieutenant Mowatt, 23rd TB: "It seems to me that the higher headquarters issuing the orders should have had some knowledge of what the present situation was before issuing an order to attack the second objective which was Drusenheim."[33]

Testimony of Lieutenant Colonel Harry E. Lardin, executive officer to CCA: "The night of 17-18 January orders were received for the 17th AIB and 43rd TB to continue the attack on Herrlisheim early 18 January; the AIB to attack and seize Offendorf, the 23rd TB to attack and seize Drusenheim."[34]

Inexplicably, the 12th Armored Division staff in Brumath during the critical hours of Herrlisheim were oblivious of what was happening to the division due to lack of planning, poor communication, haste in organization and an underestimation of the enemy strength. Contributing causes may have included a rear area insulation, a feeling of invincibility and a zeal to impress superior officers at Corps and the Seventh Army.[35]

18

Weyersheim, January 1945

January 18 saw a lull in the Herrlisheim-area fighting. The Germans had cleared the town by dawn and the American soldiers who had managed to escape were recuperating in Weyersheim and towns to the west. The German 6th and 7th Companies of the 1st Detachment resumed their slow movement to the southwest in preparation of its primary mission, the assault on Weyersheim. In Offendorf, Lieutenant Colonel Ernst Tetsch kept observer Wilhelm Balbach out in no-man's-land to keep track of enemy movements between Herrlisheim and the Steinwald. This was an important source of information, because General Harmel intended to strike hard at the Americans on January 19 and he was fearful that the Americans would attack him on January 18 at a time when he was vulnerable.[1]

Wilhelm Balbach knew nothing of the German tactics. As light became visible in the east, he concerned himself with trying to stay warm and getting enough to eat. He was quite willing to do his job, but he hoped Sergeant Schmidt would not return to harass Jens and himself. He described his miserable circumstances, "I raised myself above the lip of the foxhole. Out in the snow-covered field were the dark mounds of equipment and tanks. It was quiet and ghostly.

"I pulled my head down into the safety of the foxhole and thought that the American drive had to be failing. At that moment I heard running footsteps, then Schmidt jumped into the hole. He pushed his two subordinates aside, ducked his head down as far as possible and breathed heavily while trying to speak. He bragged that the Americans had tried to take Herrlisheim, but were being mopped up by Tetsch's infantry. He felt it necessary to educate Jens and me on the superior quality of the German fighting man over that of the American soldier. He droned on for some time before realizing that his two listeners were dozing.

"Finally, he got down to business and kicked Jens' foot. He ordered him to go back to Offendorf for more wire. In response to my questioning look, he said that we were going to move west to a new position. Jens leaped out of the hole as though he had been released from prison while I sank deeper into the hole in dejection at having to dig another foxhole. I fully expected to never see Jens again. He ran off to the northeast without saying a word. I thought that I would miss the little fellow with the large, sad eyes. Now I would be alone and exclusively under the thumb of the sergeant.

"The morning hours were silent. I tried to sleep, but was pestered by the shuffling of the sergeant. When the day was at its brightest, Schmidt produced from a pack another

French ladies of Drusenheim pour hot tea for the soldiers of the 314th Infantry Regiment. The weather during January 1945 was bitterly cold, as indicated by the mittens on the soldiers (National Archives).

sausage and loaf of bread. I longed for an apple, carrot or even cabbage soup, but any food was better than none. I reached out and took a length of sausage that clung to the point of Schmidt's knife. The knife then circled the loaf of bread and the resulting piece was tossed to me. I shook my canteen. It was half full. As I alternately bit into the sausage and bread, I washed them down with water. It soon would be gone, but I planned that during the night to scoop a little snow into my mouth. It was dirty and ice-laden, but it would give me moisture.

"In the afternoon, Schmidt became restless and suggested that we examine the remains of the Sherman tanks in the field. I thought it was ghoulish, but also knew that a suggestion from him was tantamount to an order. We left our foxhole and ambled out onto the frozen ground.

"Schmidt and I approached a burned-out tank. Two other soldiers appeared and told us they had been in the field and had taken more equipment and food than they could carry. One of the soldiers said that the field was a gold mine of stuff. The Americans had left everything behind; food, blankets, clothing, cigarettes, weapons and ammunition, all for the taking. He held a huge .45-caliber automatic for me to take. When it fell into my palm it weighed twice that of a German P-38. The soldier told me to keep it as a souvenir.

"I didn't know what I would do with so large a pistol, but it seemed like a good idea to have a hand weapon. I stuffed it into my belt. Before we left, three other soldiers joined us. They were burdened with K rations, blankets and Chesterfield cigarettes. My bulky clothing bulged all the more from the American gifts. I could hardly believe it, but

Schmidt found the way back to the observation hole. He was obnoxious, but he seemed to have a quality of competence. For two hours we slept soundly in our new American blankets and, upon awakening, ate American crackers, cheese and candy.

"In the midst of eating our American rations Jens suddenly loomed above us. He dropped his reels of wire and stumbled into our hole. I tossed him a box of American K rations. Jens didn't question the source of the windfall. He simply started digging through the contents, examining each little packet and jamming crackers into his mouth. Schmidt looked at the chewing gum and threw it out of the hole, then lit an American cigarette. He sucked in the smoke and exhaled with satisfaction. He held the cigarette with reverence and made the philosophical observation that if a soldier has to fight, let it be against the Americans.

"I watched the sergeant spring like a gazelle from the observation hole. He was a bundle of nervous energy. Jens and I unwound our legs and straightened into a semi-erect posture. Schmidt's order to scout to the west was idiotic, but I had no choice and Jens had even less. Jens disconnected the telephone and spliced the wires. He lifted the equipment, and once again the wire began to spool out as we followed our leader westward. A light snow was falling. I held up my palm to capture a few flakes. I licked the moisture as we walked. I carried two of the heavy reels without an order from Schmidt. The sun set and it grew dark. When we reached the Zorn River we stopped, knelt in the snow and listened. Jens quietly laid his equipment down.

"Voices were not far off, but I couldn't tell if they were German or American. Schmidt called out and the voices stopped. At night we were invisible and remained quietly kneeling in the field. After an hour of torturous immobility Schmidt slowly started backing away. I placed one foot behind the other and the three of us extricated ourselves from the unknown threat.

"For the remainder of the night Schmidt aimlessly roamed about the frozen terrain with Jens and me stepping in the tracks of the sergeant and trying to keep the wire from fouling. As each hour passed I became convinced that Schmidt had no idea of where he was going.

"At last he lit upon a spot. It was as if he had a divining rod and had magically determined that this was the place for digging. Jens and I set our telephone equipment on the ground and once again began swinging our portable entrenching spades. I thought we made an excessive noise, but Schmidt seemed unconcerned. We were dog tired after a night without sleep, but the sergeant was just catching his second breath. In our hole, he shared with us his plan. We were close to a bridge over the Zorn, and if the Americans wanted to get east of the river they would have to go over that bridge. We would alert our artillery and it would stop the advance. I didn't express my thought that we would be right in the middle of our own target area."[2]

Hans Quandel's group of ten Panzer IVs and the accompanying infantry that made up the strike force of 6th Company had slowly moved southwest toward Weyersheim on January 18. Progress had been limited to the pace of the accompanying infantry. During the day Quandel had deliberately held his group close to Herrlisheim so that it would be available for the fighting in the town, should the Americans attack a third time. When it was clear that other units had the situation in hand, the tanks of 7th Company, which had been with Quandel's group through the fighting at the waterworks, moved northward toward Haguenau.[3]

By evening of that day, radio communication between the two companies had died. This meant that only 6th Company would be used in the Weyersheim attack from the west. Bernhard Westerhoff remembered the night of January 18: "I thought that 7th Company would likely attack Weyersheim from another direction and that the coming operation had been planned in such a way as to trap the Americans in the town. My perception was corroborated by Quandel, who said that the attack would be well coordinated.

"We had rested the night before in a clearing northwest of Herrlisheim, and, because of a heavy cloud layer, had been able to continue our advance to the southwest in daylight without fear of American aircraft. In late afternoon of January 18, we brought our Panzer IVs to rest in a depression of brush that provided a small amount of protection. It was otherwise open fields southwest of Rohrweiler.

"When the sun set, the night turned bitterly cold. The steel of my tank absorbed the winter temperature and its inside became a natural freeze box. The shortage of petrol prohibited us from running the engine for warmth. We staggered out of the tank and tried to find some shelter. While I and my gunner stuck close to the tank, the other members of the crew looked for anything that might give warmth. Soon they returned to the tank and in a whisper told me to follow them. I and my comrade ran after the others. In a farmer's field shed I was blinded by a blue-white flame coming from an acetylene torch. The tankers had left it burning to heat the shed. The nozzle was now held by my driver who had been a welder by trade.

"One of the crew ran back to the tank and brought several American C Ration packs. He put the torch to a can of pork and beans. In a minute it exploded, showering us with gooey food. Nevertheless, the smell was delicious and we punched a small vent hole in the next can before heating it. The night passed in relative comfort, with the flame flickering out just as the sun rose. We had been able to sleep in shifts and we had a belly full of heated American rations. We stuffed the hard candy into our pockets."[4]

On January 18 the Germans were in full control of Herrlisheim and the few Americans who had gathered south of the town for another attack had been told to return to Weyersheim.[5] The town was devastated by the battle, but it was quiet. The civilians who had remained in their cellars during the previous day emerged in midmorning to restore their lives and to attend to the few livestock which had survived the random shelling.

One such family was the owner and occupier of the house, barn and yard which had accommodated the 17th Armored Infantry Battalion command post. The head of the Zilliox family was Charles Zilliox, a 48 year-old farmer. He had served in the German Army during the Great War until its end. Thereafter, he returned to his French identity in Herrlisheim. When Germany invaded France in 1940 he fought in the French Army against the Germans, and in 1942 he was conscripted into the German Wehrmacht. He was captured by the Allies in 1944 and returned once again to his French origins and his little farm in Herrlisheim. Here he and his family had lived in relative peace until early January when the Germans returned as a part of the Northwind offensive. Family members remained in the cellar as much as possible during the German occupation of the town.[6]

Fernand Zilliox reflected on the harrowing days of January. "I was a strong-willed lad of fourteen and was hell-bent on shooting Germans. I hated them despite my father's service for Germany. During the fighting on January 17th we remained in our cellar under the kitchen. When the Americans arrived the morning of January 17, and entered the courtyard between the house and barn, my father, Charles Zilliox, offered the barn cellar as protection from the shelling. He had retreated back into the cellar under the house and was with us when the Germans captured the 17th Armored Infantry Battalion staff.

"On January 18, my father and I left the house to feed the family's single cow in the field behind our house. A German soldier approached us and told my father to raise his hands. Speaking fluent German, my father told him about his service to Germany during two wars. It failed to move the soldier, who was convinced that his duty was to remove all civilians to Offendorf. Father became furious and told the soldier what he thought of him. I yelled at the soldier telling him that if he took my father as a prisoner he'd have to take me too. Where my father went, so went I.

"The soldier didn't back down. He was a stiff-necked bully. I think he intended to take us to Offendorf, but another soldier intervened and told the hothead to calm down. Still insistent upon taking his prisoners, the soldier argued that as soon as he let us go we would help the Americans. He was right, of course. An officer came to the scene and didn't waste time on the petty situation. He simply ordered the two soldiers to release us and get back to fighting the war. The three Germans left us to the chores of civilian life.

"I have softened a bit over the years, but my wife, Yvette, hates the Huns to this day."[7]

George Hatt and Sergeant Drost had walked the distance from south Herrlisheim to the Zorn River, which they crossed about six hours before Wilhelm Balbach entered the area. The two Americans intercepted a jeep on the road to Weyersheim and hitched a ride for the remaining distance. George Hatt described the lost feeling he had when attempting to rejoin his unit: "Drost and I thanked the jeep driver who had brought us to the headquarters of CCA. We entered a brightly lit large room with clicking typewriters and efficient clerks. It was hard to tell the officers from the men. They all wore ties and creased trousers. We stood in the room for a minute or so, until it became apparent that no one had any time for us. We were filthy and unshaven and tired beyond belief. Drost left the formalities to me and stretched out on the bottom shelf of an empty bookcase-type cabinet. I remained standing for another minute then decided to join him. In the next minute we were both sleeping the sleep of the dead.

"It may have been our snoring that disturbed the routine of the busy office. Some sergeant shook me and asked what we thought we were doing. I thought it was a stupid question and said so. An officer approached and I crawled out from my berth. I saluted and told him that we had just returned from Herrlisheim and were looking for our platoon. This brought a fluster of activity and the officer whisked us up the stairs to a desk at which sat another polished officer. Soon we were before General Riley P. Ennis, commanding officer of CCA. He said, 'Where's my tanks? What happened to all my tanks?' I looked at Drost and shrugged my shoulders. Drost said, 'We ain't seen any tanks, General. Except that one knocked-out Sherman in Herrlisheim.' We stood for awhile, but the general didn't seem to notice us. I coughed. He said, 'You're dismissed.'

"We left and a nice sergeant took us to a house where we found an empty room. We went back to sleep. That's the way I spent January 18th."[8]

At the close of the day the effective combat strength of the 17th Armored Infantry Battalion was 150–170, including drivers, mechanics and all other available men.[9]

Andy Woods was one of those lucky soldiers to have made a successful escape from Herrlisheim. However, his eyes had been scorched and his vision was less than half its normal acuity. He relaxed in the Gries schoolhouse during the day and evening of January 18. He kept his eyes closed most of the time and although the doctor had assured him that his vision would return to normal in a few days, he worried about going through life with limited eyesight. In the afternoon he heard tank engines and rushed into the street to await his fellow tankers. The line of tanks gunned their engines and turned off the main street to the northeast. Andy was disappointed, but his job was to attend to his wounds. He withdrew back into the building where he could let his body recuperate.

Woods took the time to write a chronology of events that took place on Thursday and Friday, January 18 and 19. In his personal war journal, he wrote of those days as described by Lieutenant Wayne Guitteau and Corporal Frank Conway, who was gunner in Sergeant Edward P. Vickless' tank on both days. Two weeks later Woods became loader for Vickless and added to his journal the tank commander's narrative. The January 18 events described by Guitteau, Conway and Vickless were rewritten in 1946 from the perspective of Andy Woods as follows: "When C Company's tanks ran up the main street of Gries on January 18, Lieutenant Wayne Guitteau hadn't seen me waving my arms in front of the school. Guitteau had swung his tank column into a side street that led into a field just outside the town. Here the engines were cut and Guitteau traveled by jeep into Weyersheim to receive new orders. There, he found that his division had largely evacuated the town. When he entered the city hall where his battalion had made its headquarters, he was greeted by a colonel of the relieving division, the 36th Infantry, 'Texas' Division. The colonel explained that his division was slow in filling the gap and that, for the moment, Weyersheim was wide open to attack. What was needed was a company of tanks to keep the Germans at bay long enough for his division to get into place. It wasn't an order, because the colonel had no authority over Guitteau. The fact remained that C Company tanks were needed at this crucial time.

"Guitteau devised a plan that would best utilize his small force. He would station his tanks south of the Kurtzenhouse-Weyersheim Road. Three of his tanks needed repair and they were to stay in the field at Gries. Edward 'Pete' Vickless and Kenneth Detrick would station their tanks at the farthest eastern point of the defense line in a wooded area called the Bruchwald, about a half mile southeast of Kurtzenhouse. Guitteau would lead another tank to a position about a mile due east of Weyersheim. He examined a map of the Waldgraben Canal. It had three bridges. One was southeast of Weyersheim and

Stars and Stripes photograph of the Vickless tank crew standing before the Vickless Sherman tank. From left, Staff Sergeant Pete Vickless, commander; Private First Class Robert Grover, driver; Private First Class William Flemming, loader; and Corporal Frank Conway, gunner (Woods collection).

another due east of the town. He would position himself and his tank at the bridge due east of Weyersheim.

"In late afternoon of January 18, Lieutenant Guitteau assembled his tank commanders and went over the plan. He emphasized that tank commanders should be ready to roll to any problem point.

"Vickless started his engine and slowly rode through Gries on his way to Kurtzenhouse. Detrick kept right behind him and the remaining tanks followed, strung out along the Weyersheim-Kurtzenhouse Road. Vickless had only area maps. It was necessary to nose around the southeastern extremity of Kurtzenhouse to find a field access road that ran generally southeast. Leaving all the tanks except the two point-Shermans, he walked ahead of the two tanks to reconnoiter the best defense position. Farm tractor ruts were narrower than tank tracks, but the tanks maneuvered themselves into a dense wooded area and stopped. Vickless found a slight depression that suited their needs well. He waved the two tanks into position so that they faced southeast, with their gun barrels at the edge of the woods. Vickless was on the right and Detrick on the left. Beyond the woods, or Bruchwald as the Alsatians called it, lay an icy field that looked deserted.

"He radioed to Lieutenant Guitteau that all was set and that he would walk back to the road and guide the other C Company tanks into wooded positions along the same access road, but closer to the town. Vickless returned to his tank and the two crews settled in for the night with rotational watches set on the turret tops. Inside the tanks, crew members lit cigarettes and gabbed about life back home. They ran the engines ten minutes every hour for compartment heat. Vickless took the first watch."[10]

James Francis described the tank disposition as follows: "Charlie Company of the 23rd TB moved into the Bruchwald woods north of the Zorn in the afternoon of January 18 and spent the night there. One company of the 119th Engineers went with them; acting as infantry they set up a defense line along the southern edge of the woods for the night."[11]

19

The Bruchwald, January 1945

Private First Class Andy Woods and Corporal Frank Conway, gunner in the Vickless tank, described the events of January 19: "Just before midnight of January 18-19, Sergeant Vickless was standing on his Sherman's turret looking through his binoculars into the darkness beyond the edge of the Bruchwald. Little could be seen except light patches of snow and ice over winter fields. Suddenly, the peaceful scene was shattered by rifle fire. Vickless saw the muzzle flash as something ripped open his arm and chest. Both tanks blasted the field in front of them with fire from their coaxial and trainable machine guns. The engineers, acting as riflemen, shot at shadows on the brush-studded terrain in front of them. It was a withering staccato which stopped as suddenly as it had started.

"Vickless slid down into the tank and dropped into his commander's seat. He giggled at the bad luck of having placed his tanks almost on top of a German. He had instinctively held his binoculars to his chest by folding his arms as he dropped into the tank. Still in this position, I, Frank Conway, saw blood oozing from his left arm and chest. I lifted Vickless out of the tank and placed him on the engine deck. The loader, Private First Class Bill Flemming, tore open [Vickless'] jacket and poured sulfa powder into the [wound]. Sergeant Detrick radioed our platoon commander, Lieutenant Guitteau, and explained the injury. Soon a jeep came bouncing down the road. Sergeant Detrick directed the jeep to the two tanks, and Sergeant Vickless sat in the passenger seat of the little vehicle as it ran back up the access road to Kurtzenhouse.

"Two hours later the jeep returned with Sergeant Vickless at the wheel. The private first class driver sat in the passenger seat. Detrick saw Vickless and was ready to protest his fellow tank commander's disregard for his own safety. Vickless said that he had no use for hospitals and that was the end of the matter. Our two tanks resumed the night vigil in the Bruchwald.

"Meanwhile, Lieutenant Guitteau and a single remaining tank had set up shop exactly where his plan indicated. He found the bridge over the Waldgraben Canal as well as three long hay sheds. On the ends of the sheds were trees and brush, sufficient to give cover to his tank and command jeep. He and his radio operator climbed to the roof of the shed. They checked their communication with both the Vickless/Detrick team and the tanks held in reserve close to the Weyersheim-Kurtzenhouse Road. He would keep his tanks in position for whatever length of time it might take to reinforce Weyersheim."[1]

At first light on January 19, the German tankers of the 6th Panzer Company ate a hasty breakfast. Ernst Storch ate field rations that consisted of coffee made on a portable stove, bread and a hard-boiled egg. The men around him ate while standing next to their tanks. In 2006 he remembered the terrifying hours that followed: "Lieutenant Quandel's voice came over the radio which was monitored in each tank. He summoned his tank commanders for a last-minute review of the day's attack plan. I climbed into my tank and tried to find a little comfort in my loader's position.

"Second Lieutenant Stratmann, our tank commander, came back to the tank and told us that we were going to attack Weyersheim. It would be a major assault with 6th Company protecting the right flank of Lieutenant Colonel Fritz Richter's Panzergrenadier Regiment 21. We would cross a small stone bridge over the Waldgraben Canal, while the infantry of the 21st Regiment would cross the Zorn River on a bridge a half mile to the south. It was a declaration more than an explanation, leaving the impression that the town would be just another Drusenheim. The rest of the crew entered the tank and our driver started the engine. After a minute, our heating system kicked in and I was thankful for a little warmth. We moved ahead about a mile and again stopped. Our tank commander kept us informed, since we could see little outside of our tank. He told us that Lieutenant Quandel had stopped the tanks to confer with an officer from the 21st Regiment.

"Stratmann took the time to tell us what he knew of the coming attack. Weyersheim would be no Drusenheim. The Americans would fight for the town, but the Frundsberg Division intended to push the 21st and 22nd Panzergrenadier Regiments over the Zorn River and move into the town from its southeast. At the same time we would go over the Waldgraben Canal and attack from due east. He emphasized to us that from where we were to the west was likely to be defended by American forces and probably with tanks or antitank guns. I was convinced that we would have to be on our toes every minute of the time."[2]

The German plan of attack involved much more than just taking Weyersheim. According to Perny, "The 10th SSPD would continue on to Geudertheim and Brumath upon completion of bridges over the Zorn River. The 553rd VGD was to protect the left flank of the 10th SSPD as it advanced westward."[3]

Confirming the ultimate objective of the attack as Brumath was Michaelis: "On January 19th the 10th SSPD began its attack to take it to Brumath."[4]

While the 6th Company prepared to attack Weyersheim at noon, Wilhelm Balbach sat in his hole at the Zorn River with Jens and Schmidt. He related the day's events: "The sergeant called Offendorf and told his superiors that all was quiet on the western front. He seemed to enjoy his reference to Erich Maria Remarque's famous book. He then straightened as if coming to attention in the sitting position. He listened intently, said, 'Yes, sir!' and hung up the piece. The news was important. The division was going to take Weyersheim. The attacking infantry would be at our position shortly after noon. If the Americans used artillery it would be our job to spot its location and report it to Offendorf.

"I thought that this must be the big push all the way to Brumath. I slept a little, then ate another of the American K rations. It might be my last nourishment for a long time. About noon a telephone message came from Offendorf that the attack would be late in starting. Schmidt relayed the news to us.

"We waited until it was nearly dark. I couldn't understand what could have been holding up the attack, but knew that such a bold move required detailed planning. The sun was setting when advance engineers began to arrive at the Zorn River. They moved silently as they instructed men to dig and camouflage a command foxhole. Schmidt told us to stay where we were. He leaped from our hole and dashed to where the engineers were surveying the Zorn River. Offendorf called and I confirmed that our forces were on the east side of the Zorn.

"Artillery shells began exploding at infrequent intervals. It was difficult for me to tell from where the American shells were coming. I didn't wait for Schmidt to return. I called Offendorf and reported the coordinates for the area of Hoerdt, to our southwest. When our infantry began arriving, engineers ran forward with rubber rafts. These would be used in addition to the bridge that lay to the right of our position. I was impressed with the thorough planning of the attack. Even so, the men bunched up at the river's edge and American artillery concentrated on the area around the river. As the American artillery got the range the intensity of the barrage increased. After a few minutes shells screeched in from across the Rhine River. I made some corrections and shells continued to fall in the Hoerdt area."[5]

To the north of Balbach's position, the ten tanks of 6th Company traveled in formation across shallow ice and snow toward the Waldgraben Canal. It was just noon and Quandel had no reason to believe the general attack was not on schedule. They passed through fields where small stakes identified their ownership as Eisenrad and Sommerwald.

Shortly after noon on Friday, January 19, the ten Panzer IVs dispersed to both sides of a field access road running from east-northeast to west-southwest. Westerhoff's tank moved south, about two hundred meters from the road. His job would be to keep the northern elements of the 21st Regiment in sight. The other nine tanks stuck to the road in single file with Quandel in the lead. When the commander spotted scrub trees that lined the Waldgraben Canal he stopped the tank column. According to plan, he ordered five of his tank commanders to follow him to the right. This group of six tanks was to reconnoiter the Waldgraben to the north, then circle back and follow the canal south to cross the bridge where the group would join the waiting three tanks.[6]

In 2005 Bernhard Westerhoff spoke of January 19 as if it were the turning point of his life: "I kept the turret hatch open with my head and shoulders outside the tank. With binoculars, I scanned the frozen fields to the south, but could see no advancing infantry. This was disturbing and I wondered about the overall tactical situation. There was nothing I could do, except carry on as if the assault were proceeding on schedule. I turned the tank slightly to the left to position us closer to the infantry, assuming that they were out there and I just couldn't see them. I was careful to keep the other tanks in sight. I could see the line of brush ahead and to the right which marked the canal, so I stopped where I was. The engine idled and the crew was kept warm as I watched Quandel and the other five tanks turn off the field road and head north. All I could now see were the three remaining tanks which were to cross the canal not far ahead of them. A half hour went by and the three tanks on the road didn't move. I assumed they were waiting for the Quandel tanks to reach a point to the north where the company commander could order the waiting three tanks to cross the bridge. My driver yelled that we were burning fuel and suggested that we shut down the engine. I rejected his concern because of the uncertainty of the situation.

"The tanks in column on the field road were commanded by Corporal Reinhard Knappe, Corporal Horst Franke and Second Lieutenant Erik Stratmann. I could see exhaust coming from their tanks so I knew that those tank commanders were anticipat-

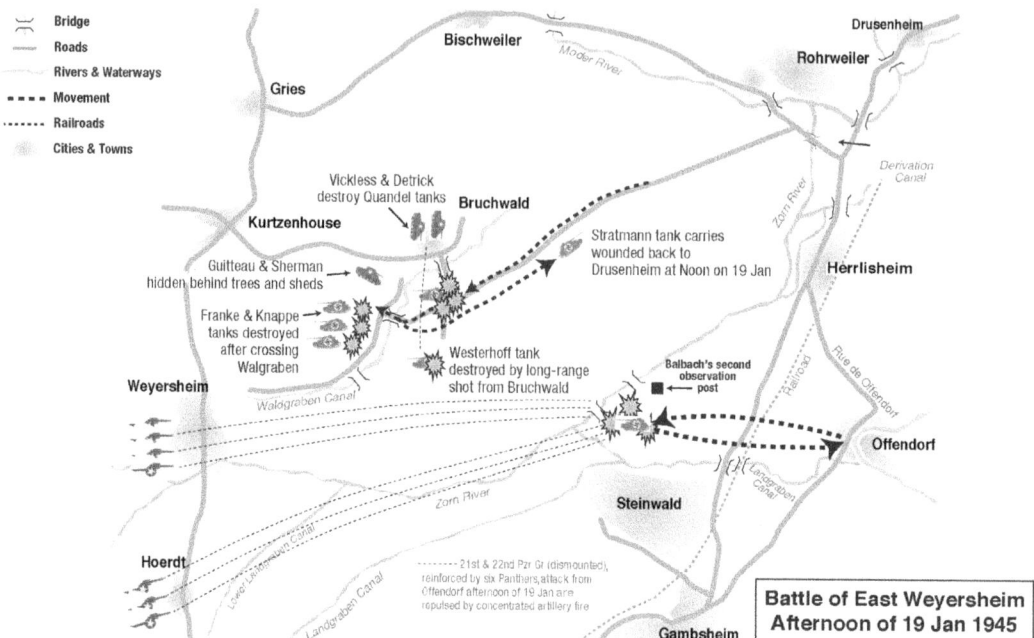

Battle of East Weyersheim
Afternoon of 19 Jan 1945

ing Quandel's order. My earphones were clamped to my head and my throat mike was attached. I heard Quandel's voice give the order and Knappe's tank lurched ahead. Franke and Stratmann followed close behind."⁷

Andy Woods continued, "Lieutenant Wayne Guitteau had lain hidden on the sloping roof of the farm shed just west of the Waldgraben Bridge. The Sherman tank which had accompanied him was below and to his left, hidden in trees and brush. With his radioman he watched the approaching German tanks through his binoculars. He informed Vickless and Detrick by radio that six Panzer IVs had turned north. Time went by, but the lieutenant was patient. As three other German tanks crossed the bridge and crept into a line abreast he gave his hidden Sherman tank commander permission to fire. The range was so short that missing was impossible."⁸

Ernst Storch could see little through his gunner's port, but his memory of the ensuing few minutes was vivid. "Stratmann heard Quandel's order and told our driver to follow on the heels of Franke. I could see the low iron rails of the bridge. The tanks ahead of us passed over the canal. It was solid and we crept over it without incident. Knappe's tank swung to his left, then stopped. Franke followed him and halted on Knappe's right side. We did the same. I saw a line of sheds to our right. We were in a line abreast with only about twenty meters separating each tank. Stratmann was high in the turret. I could see only his legs.

"The field road which we had taken over the bridge dead-ended where we were. A road led north to parallel the canal on its west side and the other ran south, probably into Weyersheim. I remembered having seen a church steeple a few miles to the west. Stratmann held his position as each tank commander assessed the fork in the road and the sheds in front of us. I was startled by the distinctive sound of tank cannon fire. It was about a half mile away and came rapidly from more than one tank. Stratmann dropped into our tank and slammed the hatch shut. He yelled for me to train right on the trees to the right of the shed. There was panic in his voice and I put my full strength into turning the hand wheel."⁹

Frank Conway described the action at the Bruchwald: "Pete Vickless stood on the turret seat with his upper body exposed. I watched a line of Panzer IVs approaching. My heart pounded as I realized that we had positioned ourselves for a perfect ambush. I trained on the last tank in column and hoped that Detrick would get the lead tank. Vickless gave the order to commence firing. I was looking at the right side of the German tanks as they passed in front of us about a hundred yards distant. Detrick's first shot hit the lead tank, but the projectile failed to explode. That tank drove itself into a depression, broke through the ice and sank into a bog. I had my hands full and didn't pay attention to what happened to the German crew. The tank I hit lost its track and smoke was coming from its rear. As the crew bailed out, our engineer-infantry's machine guns killed them. I trained right and, together with Detrick's tank, we quickly knocked out the remaining four Panzer IVs. I shot at the tanks with my coaxial machine gun, but most of the Germans were cut down by our engineer-infantry. As the loader and I pumped shells into the Germans, Vickless was hollering on the radio. I assumed it was with Lieutenant Guitteau."¹⁰

Ernst Storch described the carnage at the bridge: "As I frantically turned the turret training wheel, Knappe's tank exploded, sending parts flying into the air. My tank rocked from the blast. I trained on the dark place in the trees, but still couldn't see a target. Ten seconds later Franke's tank was hit. The blast was so severe I was thrown off my seat. Without waiting for an order, our driver reversed gears and we accelerated rearward. Stratmann opened the hatch and yelled direction orders to the driver. I have often thought of our luck in crossing the bridge without going into the canal. Once across, the line of trees and brush hid us from the view of the Americans on the canal's west side."¹¹

Frank Conway explained what was simultaneously happening at the edge of the Bruchwald. "I sat at my gunner's station. Lieutenant Guitteau was on the radio with Vickless. Our tank commander ducked his head into the turret and told me that a lone German tank was far to the south, but within range. The gun breech in the Sherman next to Lieutenant Guitteau had jammed. It was up to us to get the remaining German tank. Vickless peered through his binoculars, trying to locate the panzer. He picked it out only because it rose above the flat terrain and the normal haze had momentarily lifted. Coaching me onto the target, he estimated the range at 1,000 yards. I spotted the shape in the distance. I set the super-elevation for that range and the Sherman rocked backward as the cannon fired. Vickless watched smoke rise from the target. The loader had slammed home another AP round, but Vickless hollered to hold fire. One round had done the job. I thought that this single shot had to have been the luckiest in World War II."¹²

Bernhard Westerhoff watched the action at the bridge. He was so shaken by what he saw that he momentarily forgot the safety of his own tank. The lead panzer at the bridge had burst with a flash and a moment later another tank was hit. Without warning, his own tank exploded and he was blown out of the hatch and into the air.¹³

At the bridge, smoke billowed from Knappe's tank, and its gunner leaped to safety. On the east side of the bridge, Ernst Storch and Stratmann grabbed a tarpaulin and ran back to the smoking tank. Ernst Storch described the scene, "I looked to see if anyone else had managed to escape their burning tanks. There was one from Franke's tank and four from Knappe's tank. One other man died from massive bleeding, and Knappe lay beside his tank, bleeding from the groin but still conscious. While the other four wounded men staggered back across the bridge, Stratmann and I rolled Knappe onto the tarpaulin. We gripped the corners of the makeshift litter and dragged the still-bleeding man over the snow-covered bridge. I removed his belt and used it as a tourniquet. I glanced to the south and saw smoke rising from the Westerhoff tank. I didn't have time to wonder at Bernhard's status, but it looked grim. The wounded men were now lifting each other onto my tank. I recognized my comrades Horst Franke, Günther Hermann, Herbert Schulze, Erik Woita and Günther Groth. We all were hanging onto the engine deck. I helped lift Knappe onto the tank. The others made way for him. He looked in bad condition. I climbed up to the edge of the engine deck while Stratmann was in the turret with the hatch open. The tank commander again peered to the south to see if there was any movement around the Westerhoff tank. He could see none and so gave the order to drive straight to Drusenheim. We had to get the wounded men to an aid station. I gripped the engine compartment cover with one hand while keeping pressure on Knappe's thigh tourniquet.

"When our tank roared into Drusenheim and stopped in front of a building serving as an aid station, three medical orderlies ran to the tank, lifted the wounded men down and rushed them into a building. I dropped down into the tank and slumped onto my gunner's seat. My mind was a blank from the trauma of the preceding hours."[14]

Perny simply described the complicated event as follows: "Sergeants Vickless and Detrick opened fire. In a few minutes they put 10 German tanks out of action — eight consumed by fire. This however, did not stop the Germans."[15]

The exploding shell in Bernhard's tank had blown him into the air, then dropped him back to earth. He lay unconscious in the frozen field. In 2004 he described his situation: "Panic gripped me when I saw two 6th Company tanks shredded by fire. My comrades had been surprised by an unseen enemy. I yelled for my gunner to train right onto the sheds where I thought antitank guns must be hidden. At the same time I ordered the driver to reverse, but neither command was executed before an American shell ripped into the lower compartment.

"When my mind cleared I opened my eyes, but couldn't grasp where I was. I remembered seeing 6th Company tanks being destroyed by unseen American guns. That was all I could remember. Lifting myself on an elbow I tried to think. I looked at my own demolished tank. Smoke came from the turret hatch, the right side armor remained intact, but a jagged hole at the drive sprocket told the story. Still, I couldn't understand how my tank had been hit. I looked toward the bridge, but all I could see was black smoke curling into the air.

"I attempted to stand. My gloves had gone and I remember feeling the cold ice. I stood up and my feet under me remained anchored to the earth. I weaved as I tried to walk. Thoughts of my crew made me listen. I thought that perhaps they could be alive, only wounded. I waited for them to call out to me, but there was only the quiet. I knew that no one could have survived such a blast.

"I staggered northward, away from my tank. I began to think more clearly. The Americans were out there, on the other side of the bridge. I would be a sure target if I tried to get close to the destroyed tanks. I again stood motionless, uncertain of what to do. I strained to see the trees and sheds on the other side of the Waldgraben Canal. Nothing moved over there.

"I made my way to the access road and looked down at track marks left by a tank heading east. I remembered seeing Stratmann's tank. Perhaps, he had been able to run from the American guns. It was afternoon, but the sun was hidden by low clouds. Once again, I had no choice. I had to start walking to the east. I stumbled along, placing one foot in front of the other. I didn't think about what lay beyond my next step. I followed the ruts where Stratmann's tank had lifted the snow."[16]

The 6th Panzer Company had been destroyed, but after several delays the infantry of the 21st and 22nd Regiments had finally reached the Zorn River. The men assembled on the approaches to the bridge over the Zorn River as American shells exploded among them.

While the 12th Armored Division used what resources it still had in Weyersheim to fend off the 10th Waffen SS Panzer Division, the 36th Infantry Division began to take up positions within the town.[17]

Wilhelm Balbach watched the confused effort of trying to get across the river. He said, "The engineers threw rubber boats into the narrow river. Men and equipment piled into them. It was already dark as others lined up at the bridge and ran across at the commands of sergeants. The American artillery hammered our infantry. Rounds were coming from west of Weyersheim as well as from the southwest around Hoerdt. I shouted correcting coordinates into the telephone which miraculously kept working. Our infantry kept advancing to the west in spite of heavy losses from artillery striking our bottleneck area at the Zorn River. Not far from my foxhole was the 21st's command post. It was just another hole, like ours but much larger. Officers were crowded into the hole and were shouting orders to junior officers who ran out to their men. A phosphorus shell hit directly above the hole, turning it into a scene of nightmarish carnage."[18]

Private First Class Kurt Rademacher was a driver in a Mark V Panther tank, 2nd Panzer Company, Regiment 10. His tank was one of six Panthers that accompanied the 21st Infantry Regiment. He contributed his story of the attack on Weyersheim in the Westerhoff self-published book, *Kämpfe im Elsass, January 1945*. He wrote, "We moved westward toward the Zorn River about three in the afternoon. Sometime thereafter we reached the river. We turned left into an area of brush next to the river, where we took a tremendous blast from above us. Suddenly the tank's interior became very hot. The tank commander yelled for us to abandon the tank. When the radioman and I climbed out of our hatches we received phosphorus burns from the chemical clinging to the tank. We both dove into the icy river and splashed the chemical from our hands and ankles. We had to find some medical help so we ran east and found an ambulance that took us to Gambsheim, where we were treated for burns."[19]

Major Fritz Richter, who had commanded the 3rd Battalion of the 21st Regiment, took command of the regiment for the assault on Weyersheim. After the war he wrote of the attack in *Die Hellebarde*, "The 21st Infantry Regiment was accompanied by Panther tanks of the SS Panzer Regiment 10. We attacked on January 19 in the face of heavy American artillery fire. I was new to the Regiment, as we assembled for the attack at noon. As we moved close to the Zorn River, artillery fire took many lives. I directed the attack from my Kübel command car. I was a real target, but somehow evaded the shelling and bombs from airplanes. For so many very young soldiers, the experience of being strafed by American airplanes and having artillery explosions was terrifying. We were soundly defeated with heavy losses. We retreated to the Steinwald woods where some of our injured soldiers were treated. The sun set and General Harmel ordered another attack, this time at night. I was driven in a BKrad as I led the second attack on Weyersheim. We had no observers west of the Zorn River and we lacked communication. I was on foot. My soldiers had to step over bodies as we moved forward. There was no artillery and no airplanes this time. All was quiet. After crossing the Zorn, I ran across an abandoned American self-propelled gun, but had no landmarks to help us. I had my men shoot at shapes in the dark to flush out the Americans. Then, intense fire came upon us, killing many. We pulled back, but couldn't find the bridge over the Zorn. All my men seemed to have disappeared. I got back to Offendorf under a cloud of failure."[20]

While the American artillery had blunted the Frundsberg attack on Weyersheim, the town was still vulnerable to attack and the Americans expected the Germans to wait for dusk before hitting the town with full strength. Ferguson described the situation: "The tattered remnants of CCA assembled at Weyersheim and prepared to defend the town against an inevitable German attack. When the attack came on Friday, January 19, well-aimed artillery fire halted and turned back the German tanks and infantry."[21] Engler also praised the 12th Armored Division for its stand: "Super-human efforts stopped the German drives short of Rohrweiler and Weyersheim, inflicting heavy tank losses on the attackers and finally holding a line at the Waldgraben Creek just east of Weyersheim. Two American tanks commanded by Staff Sergeant Vickless and Sergeant Detrick of C Company, 23rd TB caught a column of panzers broadside."[22]

Woods wrote about the night action of January 19-20 by the Vickless and Detrick tanks: "Lieutenant Guitteau ordered Vickless and Detrick to get their tanks in position to the east and southeast of Weyersheim in order to stop any troops which might come across the Zorn River during the night. The remaining tanks at his disposal were to take up defensive positions to the north on the Kurtzenhouse-Weyersheim Road and to the south on the Hoerdt-Weyersheim Road. As Vickless placed his two tanks at the most favorable position at dusk, snow began fall. The white flakes conveniently covered the two Sherman tanks as they waited east of Weyersheim. Each Sherman had its coaxial machine gun, its trainable bow machine gun and a husky .50-caliber machine gun mounted on the turret. These six machine guns remained silent as Vickless and Detrick listened to the sound of German infantry coming nearer. Vickless was convinced that the Germans were sufficiently bunched up at the Zorn River bridge to make attractive targets. Then both tanks opened up with their weapons. The gunners operated both the cannons and the coaxial machine guns, while bow gunners operated their trainable machine guns. Standing on their turret seats, the tank commanders operated the fifties. The result was a devastating amount of firepower. The guns traversed back and forth west of the river without letup. Neither Vickless nor Detrick could see enough in the dark to estimate the effectiveness of the shooting. When they ceased firing they heard the sounds of wounded and dying men. Through it all, the snow had continued to fall. When light appeared in the east, signaling dawn, the two Shermans pulled out of their position and joined the other tanks of the 23rd Tank Battalion in Gries. Post action reports stated that more than 200 German infantry had been killed by the two tanks."[23]

During the night of January 19, the 36th Infantry Division completed its movement into Weyersheim to occupy positions previously held by the 12th Armored Division. The survivors of the preceding three days were able to move into a rest area. Edward P. Vickless received a battlefield commission, being promoted to second lieutenant as reward for

The Waldgraben Canal, a half mile east of Weyersheim, as it appeared in February 1945. The steeple of the town's central church can be seen in background. The dug-in soldiers along the canal's banks are those of the Texas 36th Infantry Division, which had relieved the 12th Armored Division in Weyersheim on January 20 and 21, 1945 (National Archives).

his leadership and skill on January 19 and 20, 1945, in destroying six enemy tanks and over 200 infantry.[24]

The attack on Weyersheim had failed and the 12th Armored Division had played a singular role in throwing back a part of Operation Northwind. But for Bernhard Westerhoff it was not quite over. He related in 2004, "I had no choice but to walk toward the east, toward our forces in Drusenheim. After having walked for a few hours I realized that I was surrounded by men shuffling along the same road. They were the wounded infantry, those who had not made it over the Zorn River. They were depending on me to reach safety. I straightened myself and remembered my rank. I kept a mental image of the map that I had studied. I skirted south of Rohrweiler, hoping to avoid the Americans that seemed to be everywhere. The infantrymen didn't question my judgment. They simply kept plodding along beside and behind me. When I crossed the La Breymuhl bridge I knew that we were close to Drusenheim.

"The road divided. I took the northern turn and the infantrymen stayed with me. At last, the houses of the town appeared. In the morning hours the town seemed deserted, but I knew that soldiers were sleeping in many of the houses. At the town's center I signaled for my fellow travelers to find their units. A single, lone sentry at the front of a building watched the approaching men. I watched my fellow travelers enter the building and I followed their example. I slept through the rest of the night and at dawn resumed my journey to Roeschwoog.

"I walked east, eventually coming almost to the Rhine River. The road turned north

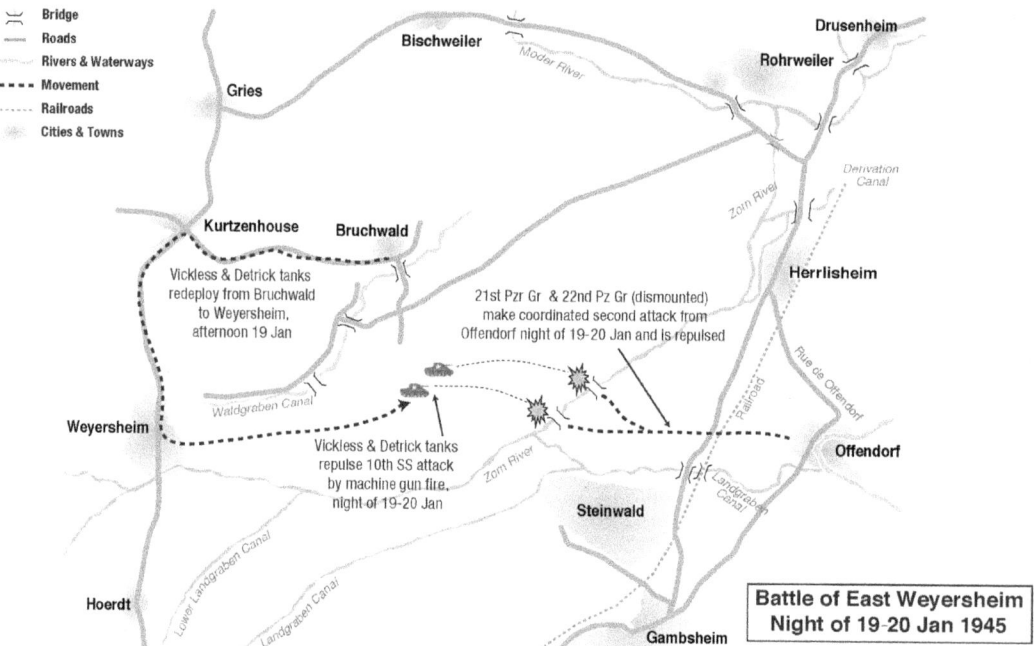

again and I followed it. My legs ached from the distance, but I knew that I would eventually find Roeschwoog. At noon I passed familiar streets, but the town seemed quiet. It had taken me over a day to walk the relatively short distance. I felt very old. If only I could reach the restaurant I would be able to find some comfort.

"I came to the restaurant and rang its bell. Manda saw who it was and was stunned by my appearance. I must have looked like another person. She pulled me into the restaurant and called for Frau Schneider. The elderly woman came from a back room and saw immediately who it was. They escorted me into the back room where they sat me at a table. Manda walked to the stove and took a steaming kettle to a pot. She dumped in several spoons of sugar and carried the pot and a mug to the table. Frau Schneider pressed my hands around it. Manda brought a tray of bread and sausage. I held the mug with both hands and sipped the steaming tea. I chewed on a slice of bread and wished the war would somehow end."[25]

Part III

Beyond Alsace

Introduction to Part III

In late January 1945, Oberkommando Oberrhein gave notice to General Harmel that the 10th Waffen SS Panzer Division should start pulling out of Alsace. It was to cross the Rhine River, then be transported by rail to the eastern front. At this time all that was known by division headquarters was that another massive march order meant more energy devoted to long-distance movement.

By February 1, Harmel and his staff were preparing the division's transfer to Pomerania, where it would fight as a part of the XXXIV Panzer Corps. The rail route took the men and material through Nürnberg, Saalfeld, Halle, Berlin and Stettin.[1] At this time the division had about 10,000 men. By February 10, transferees from other branches of the military began to arrive. Michaelis wrote, "Its (the Frundsberg Division) losses from the battles around Herrlisheim and Weyersheim were made up by men transferred from the Navy and Luftwaffe. By mid–February it was at full strength in terms of men, but lacking in equipment."[2]

Harmel received orders to take up positions in the area of Schlötenitz and Margartenhof. From there he was to immediately attack the Soviet forces.

At approximately the same time, the American 12th Armored Division was able to pull back from the Herrlisheim/Weyersheim area to regroup and refit. With its refurbished units, the 12th Armored Division drove south into the Colmar pocket. It attacked and seized Sundhoffen and St. Croix. CCB fought alongside French units pushing the Germans back across the Rhine River. American forces occupied an undefended Herrlisheim on February 4, 1945. The 12th Armored Division split its forces, with one group swinging north to block roads from eastern approaches into the Vosges Mountains and the other group attacking Rouffach, south of Colmar. On March 2, 1945, the division occupied Forbach and Stiring Wendel after the towns had been taken by the 70th Infantry Division. By the middle of March, all its units had been withdrawn from the Colmar area and were now attacking the Germans to the north of Alsace. The division received three infantry rifle companies on March 10 and one company was assigned to each of the armored infantry battalions and designated as D Company.[3]

The 12th AD was detached from the Seventh Army on March 17 and attached to the Third Army. The initial order for the biggest operation of the month was received at 0239 of that date. It ordered the 12th AD to move from the area near St. Avold to the vicinity of Sierck-les-Bains and to be attached to XX Corps under the Third Army.[4]

The 12th Armored Division occupied Ludwigshaven with CCA while CCB took Speyer. As its battalions rolled across fields and charged into small towns they never knew what resistance might be encountered. Sometimes determined Hitler Youth soldiers put up a strenuous fight. Some towns were simply abandoned and left to civilians, who hung white bedsheets from their windows. On March 24, CCA was given the mission of occupying and defending Ludwigshafen.[5] By this time the kinks had been worked out of the communications system and the division finally had plenty of radios.[6]

On March 27, 1945, the division crossed the Rhine River at Worms. It assembled itself on the eastern side of the river and attacked Wortheim, which put up a determined resistance. The division moved on to the large city of Würzburg, and here it met even stronger defenses. The division then bypassed Würzburg and drove eastward to take Hettstadt and Rottenbauer, returning later from the east to take Würzburg. On April 3, elements of the 222nd Infantry Regiment, originally part of the 42nd Infantry Division but temporarily attached to CCA, crossed the Main River in assault boats and secured a bridgehead on the east bank of the Rhine River near the town of Würzburg. The 12th AD, 119th Engineers, moved up and began construction of a Bailey bridge. Other elements of the division seized their assigned objectives in the area then consolidated their positions.[7]

Also in early April, the 12th A.D. took the towns of Schweigern, Sachsenflur and Edelfinger. George Hatt's A Company of the 17th AIB was in the van. He reported, "Able Company moved from the vicinity of Geisslingen to attack Hernberchtheim on April 3. The enemy had an excellent defensive position along a railroad embankment at the western slope of town which delayed the attack for a few hours.[8]

Far to the east, the Frundsberg Division tried to hold back the Russians on a line from Naugard to Gollnow. On February 6, the division fought along the banks of the Ihna River, then in the area to the west up to the Faule Ihna River.[9]

On February 19 the division attacked the Russians at Schlötenitz. Panzer Regiment 10 under Lieutenant Colonel Otto Pätsch had poor maps and poor communication. Thus the attack was poorly coordinated and resulted in heavy losses with no gain.[10]

Holding the most crucial positions were the 10th and 22nd Regiments. Harmel had inadequate maps of the Pomeranian terrain. They had little time to plan an effective defense line. It was simply a matter of throwing in regiments to hinder the Soviet advance. The division fought in the area of Damnitz-Warnitz, but it accomplished little, except to slow the Soviet pace westward.[11]

Many of the 10th Waffen SS Panzer Division's units were nearly surrounded in the Muscherin-Lübtow area on the Plöne See. It managed to break out in the area of Pyritz, but lack of fuel meant that most of the division's precious tanks had to be abandoned. During this period, the 10th Regiment (including 6th Company) was temporarily transferred to the 14th Waffen SS Panzergrenadier Division, which was fighting around the town of Dölitz.[12]

In the middle of March, Frundsberg units fell back to Stenitz on the eastern side of the Ostsee. Units of the Frundsberg Division used boats to ferry equipment and men south on the Damnischer See to Ziegendorf, a town close to Stettin. On March 16, Lieutenant Colonel Pätsch, commanding officer of the 10th Regiment, was killed by Russian artillery. Lieutenant Colonel Ernst Tetsch assumed command of the regiment. The town of Altdammer, on the eastern bank of Damnischer See, became the scene of a bloody street battle when the Germans fought fiercely to keep the Soviets from the city of Stettin.[13]

By March 20, the dispersed units of the 10th Waffen SS Panzer Division had fallen back to the eastern side of the Oder River. The division had suffered heavy losses, so Hitler Youth who had manned anti-aircraft guns across Germany now entered the division. It had nearly 15,000 men, but lacked supplies. On March 25, 1945, it had only 35 Panzer IVs, 47 Panthers, 18 panzerjägers, 8 flakpanzers and the 12 captured Shermans from Herrlisheim.[14]

During the same period the American 12th Armored Division crossed the Main River, striking southwest at Ochsenfurt. On April 5, the Germans counterattacked in the Würzburg area and the division played a critical role in the defeat of the German effort. Continuing its drive to the south, CCR entered the towns of Königshofen and Bad Mergentheim, where Shermans met heavy antitank emplacements. It pushed on to Schweinfurt along with other divisions and entered the city on April 12. Immediately thereafter, CCB attacked and occupied Ullstadt, then crossed the Aisch River. On April 13 the 12th Armored Division received orders to advance in the direction of Nürnberg and points south. Skirting around the large city, the 12th Armored Division took Ansbach to the southwest of Nürnberg. On April 19, units of the 66th AIB continued a house-to-house mop-up of Ansbach. The division then struck straight south to the Danube River. On Wednesday, April 25, the battalion led by Able Company followed the river's northern side. Its aim was the capture of a bridge over the Danube at Günzburg.[15]

By April 22, 1945, the division had taken Lauingen, but the bridge over the river had been blown up by retreating Germans. The 66th AIB and companies from the 43rd TB advanced rapidly to Dillingen, and just before noon on April 22 the force shot its way into the center of town and found a bridge that had not been blown. It took Dillingen and found a bridge still intact. The division crossed the Danube at this point. After CCA captured Dillingen and seized a bridge over the Danube River on Sunday, April 22, the 17th AIB column followed, then veered to the right (west) about five kilometers from the town. It moved into Horchstadt, then continued on the south side of the Danube River toward Austria.[16]

The lightning thrust across the German Rhineland was a model of mobile warfare, and showed what a well-equipped, well-trained and seasoned armored division could accomplish.[17]

On April 26 the 92nd Cavalry Recon Squadron led CCB as it advanced from Burgau to Hiltenfinger on the Wertach River. Here they captured an intact bridge and an airfield. At the airfield were some 50 Me-262 jet fighters. About half appeared to be in working order, but abandoned for lack of fuel.[18]

Combat Command A received orders to proceed toward Innsbruck, Austria, with all possible speed. The 66th Battalion passed through the 101st Cavalry Division and moved toward Weilheim, where it continued south, clearing Etting of German infantry and roadblocks. It then went on to Murnau against light enemy resistance. In the process it released 6,500 Allied POWs.[19]

In Pomerania, Stettin fell to the Soviets in early April, at which time the Frundsberg Division retreated to the south. This time its task was to defend the city of Dresden. Because of the lack of fuel, most of the division had to march the distance. It set up positions by the middle of April along the west side of the Neisse River, including the towns of Forst, Muskau, Penzig and Gölitz. The Soviets crossed the river in rubber boats at several points. Rushing forward in waves of infantry, the Russians pushed the Frundsberg soldiers back to the Spree River from Cottbus to Bautzen.[20]

Harmel discussed with his adjutant Colonel Remer plans for a breakout to the northwest to consolidate forces with the Wenk Army in Berlin. By the end of April it was apparent that all was lost and further fighting was futile.

The city of Spremberg, which lay mostly on the eastern side of the river, became the focal point of heavy house-to-house, street-by-street fighting. It was basically an infantry fight with men of former panzer units fighting as foot soldiers. By the end of April, remnants of the division had retreated farther southwest to Dippoldiswalde, but by that time, orders coming from Berlin were straws in the wind. The division existed only on paper. Its units had long since vanished. Since Stettin, decimated regiments had been combined to form independent fighting groups, but by Spremberg even these were uncoordinated bands of soldiers who kept resisting the Soviets to give time for thousands of civilian refugees to flee to the west.

On April 27, 1945, Heinz Harmel was accused of insubordination and treason. He was relieved of command and was replaced by Lieutenant Colonel Röstel, who had commanded Panzerjäger Abteilung 10. After Hitler had ordered his execution, Harmel fled to Traunstein and then to Klagenfurt, in Austria.[21]

In southern Germany, the 12th Armored Division crossed the Wertach River at Hiltenfingen, then crossed the Lech River on April 25. The division was now deep in southeast Germany between Munich and the Austrian border. It had moved so quickly that the Germans could not put up a coordinated defense. Inmates of the Dachau concentration camp had been pushed into boxcars and transported to hastily built camps in Germany's extreme southeast. One such camp was Number Four, near the town of Landsberg. On April 30, 1945, lead elements of the division surrounded the camp.

Near Pfraundorf the 17th AIB took a thousand German prisoners the night of May 1-2. On the second evening 7,000 more Germans surrendered. Fortunately, the Germans gave no trouble to the 17th AIB as it continued to roll into southeastern Germany.[22]

On May 3, 1945, the division crossed the Austrian border. The 17th Armored Infantry Battalion, which had fought inch by inch in Herrlisheim, now drove sixty miles in seven hours. The battalion was commanded by Colonel Douglas Cameron. Alongside the 17th was C Company of the 23rd Tank Battalion. Both battalions were instructed not to fire on approaching forces, as they probably would be Russians. The 12th AD became Seventh Army reserve on May 4 and moved back out of the front lines. That meant, barring any unforeseen circumstances, the fighting days of the 12th AD were over.[23]

Victory in Europe came on May 8, 1945. The 12th Armored Division became a part of a general security authority. Its various units were spread over a wide area, ranging from Weilheim and Heidenheim to Murnau. It was a time for showers, meals, lectures on nonfraternization, movies, and letter writing. The Army had put together a motion picture called *Two Down, One to Go*. It told the story of how the division, along with most other forces in Europe, would soon be sailing for the Pacific to fight the Japanese. The men of the division were not excited about that prospect.

Most soldiers spent time looking at the strange country. Some drove up the Obersalzberg to see Hitler's demolished home. They picked up souvenirs from the bombed-out building and dusted off the furniture, where they sat enjoying a magnificent view of the mountains. Others worked to alleviate the difficulties of the German people. They sorted out displaced persons, arranging transportation, identification and food for the thousands of wandering people in a land of chaos. Some worked on the release of German prisoners of war. This required background checks at a time when documents were lost, burned or otherwise destroyed.[24]

20

Oberhoffen and Heidenheim, February–May 1945

Despite being thrown back from Weyersheim, the Frundsberg Division took on a new assignment with equal determination. It was to be the division's last effort before being withdrawn from Alsace. Harmel swung his forces to the north, toward the town of Haguenau. His intent was to take several key towns along the Moder River. These included Bischwiller, Kaltenhouse, Oberhoffen and Schweighouse (not to be confused with Schweighausen). In the meantime, the American forces withdrew from the Haguenau Forest to take up positions southwest from Bischwiller to Weyersheim. The Americans adjusted their lines during the night of January 20-21. Engler explained, "The establishment of the new line was carried out despite icy roads which hampered tracked vehicles. The new line was actually a scattering of muddy holes, bathtub deep, behind an ice-filled creek with exhausted marchers still arriving to sprawl in prostrated stupor for a few hours in sheds, barns, school houses and any other structures offering shelter."[1] The 242nd Infantry held the little town of Kaltenhouse east of Haguenau, and the 314th Infantry held from Kaltenhouse through Oberhoffen and Bischwiller.[2] East of Haguenau, the Frundsberg Division prepared for an attack as the eastern prong of a planned double envelopment that would reach around the pivotal city.[3]

To the southeast of Haguenau along the Moder River was the town of Oberhoffen, which the Frundsberg Division took on January 25. This was a brief stab into the American lines because Bischwiller, only a mile to the south, and Kaltenhouse, a few miles to the northwest, were both held by Americans.[4] According to Engler, "American intelligence had been paying particular attention to the location and movements of the vaunted Frundsberg Division, which had added a number of Sherman tanks to its force in the battle of Herrlisheim and in spite of losses in moving west of the Zorn represented a sizable armored force."[5]

Private First Class Wilhelm Balbach, observer for the 13th Artillery Regiment of the Frundsberg Division, played an insignificant role in the thrusts and parries of American and German forces during the latter days of January. He described his small part as follows, "On January 22, I finally was recalled to Offendorf where I found a billet. The earth could have split in half and it would not have awakened me for the next ten hours.

"When I arrived at the company command post I was told that the division was withdrawing to the north. It was going to take Haguenau and the Haguenau Forest. During the march to the north, I noticed an old man wearing a Frundsberg uniform. He was walking beside me as if I was something special. He introduced himself as Private Ludwig Horcher. He was to be a telephone wire puller under Lieutenant Scholl and would be working with me. I accepted his word without comment, because it made little difference to me what our next assignment might be. Horcher had a pockmarked face and teeth that were stained from years of cigarettes. Still, his eyes had a youthful sparkle.

"When we arrived in the regimental camp area, Lieutenant Scholl informed us that the 13th Artillery Company was in the process of moving its command post to the northern border of Oberhoffen. We were to follow and await orders.

"On January 27, 1945, I and my newly acquired comrades followed our company into the perimeter of Oberhoffen. We, along with many others, crowded into houses on the northern border of the town. Horcher, Scholl and I found a billet in a house on the road to Usine. When we entered the cellar, looking for food, we found it occupied by a group of women civilians. The women offered to cook and Horcher offered to assist them. He singled out a lady, well past her prime and a product of too many potatoes. But she had rosy cheeks and a pleasant smile. I was nineteen and so watched the older man play his gentle game of amour. Much could be learned from Horcher and since my job was to observe, that is what I did. The old soldier's timing had to be admired. With winks and nudges he plowed the fertile ground of romance. When the other women were close, he chopped vegetables with zeal, but when they weren't looking, he found excuses to touch the lady's generous contours. She winked at Horcher's advances and, like a flower's scent to a bee, he pursued her with great vigor.

"The next day the company moved its command post to the center of town. This meant that Scholl's little group also had to move away from their billet, away from the house of women and away from Horcher's targeted lass. He cursed his bad luck. All that effort had gone for nothing.

"All was calm in the town even though the Americans were just to the south in Bischwiller. I found a small hotel and we set ourselves up in its cellar. The former inhabitants had left an abundance of coal near the furnace. I waited patiently for nightfall so that I could stoke up the furnace and warm the room. To do so during the day would have invited American artillery.

"Horcher shoveled coal into the furnace until the cellar was warm. I removed my boots and propped my feet close to the oven door. I was enjoying this newfound comfort when a young soldier entered the cellar. The boy introduced himself as Private Heinz Jenkel. I was too comfortable to move. I gestured for Jenkel to pull up a chair and get warm. The boy did as he was told. I was only a year older than he, but he looked so young and I felt so old. Then he started talking. For the next hour I listened to the boy while sometimes dozing from the luxury of warmth. Jenkel, it seemed, was the sole heir of Farm Number 17 in eastern Germany. His sister was working the farm while waiting for her brother's return. Jenkel described every detail of his farm boy childhood, which I have remembered over these many years. Finally, he fell silent. I slipped into a semiconscious bliss of warm feet.

"Horcher approached. The old man knelt beside me and whispered into my ear about his need to get back to our former billet. It was dark, he explained. He'd never be missed. It would only take a few hours. I abandoned my comfortable position so I could look at Horcher. The old man's eyes had the pleading look of a dog at mealtime. I waved my hand in agreement and Horcher, the amorous wire puller, disappeared up the stairs. After a few more exquisite minutes of warmth, the field telephone rang. I was tempted to ignore the thing, but upon further consideration, decided to answer it. On the other end of the line was Lieutenant Scholl, who excitedly demanded to know what was happening. According to him the Americans had occupied the southern half of the town.

"I wondered where Scholl might be. I hesitated, then listened. No noises came from the outside. Scholl ordered me to go into the street and observe. I laid the telephone on the floor, rushed up the stairs in my stocking feet and ran out to the middle of the road. My feet paid the price, as mud and snow squeezed into my socks. In the darkness, I heard loud voices speaking in English. I would have been heard by the Americans, were it not for my lack of boots.

"I ran back into the house, down the steps, into the cellar and grabbed the telephone. By then the line was dead. At that moment Horcher returned with a smile on his face. I couldn't believe it. I grabbed Horcher and signaled Jenkel that it was time to leave. Horcher took it all in stride. His amorous mission had been a success and the war had slipped into insignificance. I pulled my boots back on. It was a dreadful return to cold, wet feet in damp boots, but there was no time for complaint. Jenkel was on his feet, looking for guidance while Horcher gathered his gear. We climbed the steps and dodged out the rear door. We crept along a wall and hid in a shed.

"Meanwhile, three Panther tanks of the 10th Waffen SS Panzer Division rolled into town. They toured up and down the streets, blasting away at cellar windows. Americans who had infiltrated poured out of the houses and beat a hasty retreat to Bischwiller. German troops once again moved into vacant cellars and ground-floor bedrooms. We returned to our cellar. The windows were intact. The fire had gone out, but the furnace retained a bit of heat. Again, I removed my shoes. My filthy, wet socks had chafed my feet, which were now red and sore. I considered sticking my feet directly into the furnace, but compromised by pressing them against the warm oven door.

"Jenkel went up the stairs to relieve himself. All seemed to be settling into our comfortable cellar routine when a violent artillery burst blew dust and debris over us. Jenkel fell backward, down the cellar steps and into a heap on the dirt floor. Blood spurted from his neck. A shrapnel shard had cut an artery. Horcher held him as I tried to think of some first aid that might help. After a few moments Jenkel was limp. Horcher gently laid him down. It was a sad business and I thought of the boy's sister who had faith that her brother would return to help her with the farm. I have kept a brief record of him for all these years. Karl Heinz Jenkel was born on July 4, 1925, in Pomerania and died on February 2, 1945, in Oberhoffen. He is buried in the Soldiers' Cemetery in Bühl/Baden. The cemetery marker reads, 'In this cemetery are buried 153 soldiers of the former German Armed Forces.' Karl Heinz Jenkel had lived his short life in Bressagard on Farm Number 17."[6]

The American 12th Armored Division spent the latter days of January in refitting and replacing equipment and personnel in its various battalions. On February 2 much of the division moved south and prepared for an attack on German positions south of Colmar. Shortly thereafter, A and B Companies of the 17 Armored Infantry Battalion swept through Herrlisheim on February 5 while mopping up the town. Herrlisheim was cleared of the enemy by 10:00 in the morning. Six prisoners were taken. The companies then rushed south to join the division in operations in the Colmar area. On March 14, the 17th AIB closed in on Zimming, France.

The battalion assembled in the vicinity of Hofchen on March 18 as it prepared to pass through the 94th Infantry Division and push on to attack the city of Worms. Five days later the battalion acted with the 23rd TB to attack the towns of Hafsloch and Iggelheim. By March 29th, leading elements of 17th AIB were at Huitendal, again supported by the 23rd TB. On March 30 one half-track was destroyed as the battalion pushed forward. On March 31 the leading elements were located at a road junction two kilometers southeast of Buchen after having passed through Althausen.[7]

The towns of Althausen and Buchen were indelibly etched into Andy Woods' memory. He described those two days, March 31 and April 1, 1945: "After the demise of *Cleopatra* in Herrlisheim on January 17, 1945, I had spent a few days in Gries, during which time my damaged eyes healed. By the end of the month my vision was back to normal and I was ready for assignment to a tank in C Company of the 23rd Tank Battalion.

"I had first met Sergeant Pete Vickless while in tank training in Texas. The PX served soft drinks and what was known as 3.2 beer. Most of the tankers-in-training drank beer and sneered at those who didn't show their masculinity by drinking the foul-tasting brew. I preferred Coke, and the more I was ridiculed for my taste in beverages the more I stood my ground. Pete Vickless drank Coke, but none of the enlisted men were about to challenge the husky buck sergeant. He had played football for the University of Florida and brooked no disrespect. I, on the other hand, was a thin, intellectual type. I gravitated to the big man's table, believing that association with this Coke-drinking giant might be interesting. We two opposites struck a harmonious chord in the evenings at the PX. I learned much about Pete Vickless, and although the ex–football player didn't say much about it, I got the feeling he was a deeply religious man. So it was, that in January of 1945, Vickless demanded that I become his loader. And whatever Pete Vickless demanded was what happened. I really had no say in the matter, and even if I had, I wouldn't have had the temerity to say no to Pete Vickless.

"The commander in a Sherman tank sat in the right side of the turret compartment, the gunner was to the left of him and the loader was to the left of the gunner. The three turret occupants soon learned to work as a well-oiled team. Since I had been a gunner in the Guitteau tank, I fit into the routine quickly. Pete Vickless was not only a tank commander, he was a tank platoon leader with exceptional ability. His work in the Weyersheim area [earned] him not only decorations, but the respect of his fellow tank commanders. I regarded him as a fearless combat soldier. Having been a football quarterback, it was natural for him to lead the way. In tank combat the quality of fearless aggressiveness produced an ambivalent reputation of both admiration and trepidation. There were those who preferred a bit more caution when it came to engaging the enemy. I had no such reservations. I accepted Pete Vickless as a real warrior in a time when being such was an asset, not a liability.

"In the latter days of March 1945, the division started crossing the Rhine River near Worms. It was a single-file procession where tanks were navigated carefully along a narrow pontoon bridge. The division had been temporarily transferred from Seventh Army to Third Army. This Army's commander, General George Patton, had a reputation for speed and he was intolerant of those who needed sleep. The pace suited Vickless, who raced ahead from objective to objective. The transfer of the division back to Seventh Army had no effect on the tank commander's yen for speed. The objective was the city of Würzburg. Arising before dawn, Bob Grover, the driver, got into the tank and started the engine. He let it idle to warm as the rest of the crew assembled at the tank. Once again, the Vickless tank would be in the lead with the other C Company tanks following. I had grown accustomed to riding in the point tank, but it did carry its special burden. I was far more than a loader. With my head above the loader's hatch, I was another pair of eyes and ears for Vickless. The tank commander trusted me to look far ahead and to spot trouble as we raced across Germany.

"It was Saturday, March 31, the day before Easter Sunday. As the crew settled in for the day's journey, Pete Vickless was concerned about the possibility of him having to fight on Easter Sunday. He talked to me about his personal view of fighting on a religious day, but I didn't know how to respond. The column of tanks rumbled through village after village. In some towns our tanks and half-tracks met a token resistance which we blew off like swatting flies. The narrow roads meant single-file transport with Shermans alternately interspersed with half-tracks carrying 17th Armored Infantry. On a straight stretch of road with no Germans in sight, Vickless ordered Bob Grover, the driver, to pull the tank over to the side of the road. When the Sherman stopped, all the following tanks and half-tracks did the same. Vickless jumped onto the engine deck and hollered for me to have the carbine ready in case some sneaky German shot at him. As he jumped down onto the dirt road, I stood on the turret while holding the rifle. I scanned the field on both sides of the road. I knew Vickless was walking back to the battalion commander's vehicle to ask him to ease up on Easter Sunday. I watched my boss trot down the line of tanks toward the rear. Half an hour later Vickless climbed back up into the Sherman. He shook his head. His request to stand down on Easter Sunday had been denied.

"Bob Grover turned over the engine and let out the clutch. Vickless let it be known that he wanted speed. The engine roared as the Sherman plummeted up the dirt road. With Vickless and I searching for the enemy it wasn't long before German soldiers were spotted. A clump of them stood in an intersecting road to our left. Vickless swung the tank to head straight for them. They were about 350 yards distant when spotted, but at the sight of the approaching American tanks the soldiers scattered in panic. As the line of turning tanks stretched out behind our lead tank, a farm cart drawn by two huge draft horses entered the road halfway between us and the disappearing German soldiers. It was being driven by a small, whip-wielding German soldier who thought he could outrun the Sherman. The cart jockey looked over his shoulder as he shouted for his steeds to outrace the tank. The horses gave it their best as the little German lashed them with his whip.

"This insolence irritated Vickless, who ordered Frank Conway, the gunner, to cut the man down with the coaxial machine gun. Without a bow gunner, this was easier to imagine than to accomplish. The coaxial machine gun was mounted as a fixed gun to train with the cannon. As the Sherman rocked wildly in pursuit, Conway tried to train the gun on the bouncing German. Bullets flew but the cart kept going. The fleeing German soldiers farther ahead were forgotten in the heat of the chase. We were gaining, but the terrain was changing. Soon the cart picked up speed on a downhill run into the town of Althausen. With houses on both sides of the cobblestone main street, an incongruous echo of clopping horse hoofs and Sherman engine roar engulfed the sleepy village. German soldiers popped out of buildings and Conway took aim at these targets as the Vickless tank sped past them. Strung out behind the tank were half-tracks at maximum speed and the remainder of C Company's tanks. As these rolled through the little town, each blazed away at the few soldiers who thought it was their duty to defend the Reich.

"Ahead of us, in the midst of houses lining the street, a German staff car backed out of an alley. Grover went straight for it, clipping its trunk lid as the car's driver frantically tried to get it back into the alley. The .30-caliber machine gun had been firing in spurts since the cart chase had begun. I ducked back down into the loader's position to pull up another box of ammunition. In all the confusion of so many targets, the little German with his farm cart had vanished. Vickless ordered Grover to slow so he could search for the cart, but it was no use. The powerful horses had performed a miracle and I felt like cheering for the underdog.

"The town was left behind as quickly as it had been entered. Hills rose on the left of the road and one was high enough so that the road had been cut through it. The Sherman was brought to a halt and the trailing vehicles slammed on their brakes in response. The terrain ahead could be a trap. German infantry might have taken cover in the road cut through the nearest hill, behind other hillocks and in shallow ditches. If so, they would have panzerfausts, the nemesis of Sherman tanks. Althausen was behind us with many Germans still in the town. The next village was about a mile farther on and to the right of the hillocks. It too had many Germans who might well have one or more antitank guns.

"A flash from a cannon barrel in the town confirmed our suspicion. The resulting explosion was close, but did no damage. I could see movement in the foreground as German soldiers formed to attack us. I loaded the cannon with H.E. shells as fast as Conway could shoot at the guns in the town. After a few rounds they were blown into shrapnel. Only fifty yards distant, a German stood up and aimed his panzerfaust. Again, Conway fired the coaxial machine gun in long, uninterrupted streams of bullets. The man with the panzerfaust dropped, but Conway's coaxial machine gun was close to seizing.

"Other Sherman tanks were deploying to put down the German resistance. Infantrymen jumped from half-tracks and ran into fields on both sides of the road. American mortars went into action. It was turning into a nasty firefight. In the frenzy of spotting individual targets, Pete Vickless had kept his head just out of the turret hatch. Rifle shots had been pinging off the raised hatch cover and Vickless had been swatting the back of his neck as if being stung by bees. As the bullets splashed against the tank's steel they splintered and tiny shards pocked his neck beneath his helmet.

"The half-tracks and tanks had fanned out across the field to bring their guns to bear on targets in and around the village. I kept Conway's guns loaded, but I also acted as spotter for Vickless. Groups of German infantry were running along a ditch between our tank and the slope of the nearest hill. I thought they were trying to surrender, but couldn't be sure.

"Suddenly, the nearest half-track behind us blazed up. It had taken a hit in its fuel tank. Grover pulled the tank forward, away from the blazing half-track. I watched infantrymen jumping to the ground from the half-track inferno, but some had been splashed with fuel. They were running torches until the flames took their lives. A few who had escaped the burning fuel crouched behind our tank. Germans were now in close proximity to the American tanks and infantry. The half-track's assistant driver jumped from the disabled vehicle. His helmet had been blown off and his right leg was bloodied from the blast. His ripped trouser leg flapped as he hit the ground. A German soldier was nearly crushed by the sergeant's jump and the two immediately began a boxing bout which resembled the great John L. Sullivan. With dukes extended, the two opponents swung at each other. Finally, the German gave up, raised his hands and marched off to the rear, which probably had been his original destination before being jumped by the sergeant.

"The incongruous sight of fisticuffs in the middle of a brutal battle had distracted my attention. I now looked at Pete Vickless, who raised himself in the turret hatch. He sagged. His head dropped to his chest as he slid back down onto his seat. Blood streamed from a small hole in his forehead. Frank Conway didn't want to believe that his commander had been hit. He tried to stop the bleeding, but couldn't. He radioed for medical help and soon Brad Dressler, a company medic, leaped up onto the tank. He was determined to help Pete Vickless, but it was too late. Infantry saw what had happened and laid down an intensive covering fire. With Frank Conway and me pushing from below and Brad Dressler pulling from above, we were able to extricate the football player's heavy body. Dressler laid Vickless out at the road's edge close to an ambulance jeep he had parked directly behind the tank. Bob Grover remained in the driving compartment and so couldn't see the ambulance jeep just behind the tank's tracks. On the jeep were four stretchers, two over the hood and two over the rear seat. As Grover stepped on the gas to reverse, the Sherman rose up in the rear. The four injured men on the stretchers leaped off the jeep in spite of their wounds. Grover geared the Sherman forward, off the jeep, but it had been demolished. I used the radio to get more medical help and the injured were evacuated, with Dressler remaining alongside Vickless.

"Grover turned our Sherman around and we crept back through Althausen, which was now quiet. It entered a field and Grover shut down the engine. The company commander, Lieutenant Guitteau came to us and asked about Pete Vickless. I explained what had happened. Other tanks on the enemy side of Althausen kept attacking the Germans, but it was impossible for the Vickless tank to join them. On March 31, 1945, the day before Easter Sunday, Pete Vickless died. I sat in the dirt leaning against a track. I rested my head on my knees and arms. I couldn't understand it. Why had this magnificent warrior deliberately stood up in the hatch when it was certain death to do so? Was it bravery, recklessness, a feeling of invulnerability, or was it simply that he didn't want to fight on Easter Sunday?

"I felt very tired and fell asleep where I sat. Two days later Wayne Guitteau was killed between Königshofen and Bad Mergentheim."[8]

Robert Arrasmith was one of the infantrymen riding across Germany in half-tracks. He was one of the 18,000 men in the 12th Armored Division who fought small skirmishes and pitched battles in the villages and fields of the crumbling German nation. He told of his last days in the war. "I had returned to B Company of the 56th Armored Infantry Battalion when it was moving north from the Colmar area. I was among those who witnessed the liberation of Dachau's Concentration Camp Number 4, and it was difficult for me to reconcile what I saw with the decent German soldiers I had seen when performing guard duty during my transportation chores in America. Most German civilians I had seen in villages seemed not very different from the folks in my home state of Washington. They had stared at me in bewildered defeat. Some must have been resentful and others must have harbored a hatred of Americans, their enemy, but most simply accepted their lot without much rancor. I couldn't imagine any of them perpetrating the horrible crimes I saw at Camp Number 4."[9] The men of the 12th Armored Division had never before seen anything like Camp Number 4. Charred bodies and hundreds of skeletons in various stages of decay lay in the compound. Colonel Edward P. Seiller, head of the division's military government section, took charge. He summoned the civilian adults in the nearby town and ordered them to view the corpses. He directed the civilians to remove their hats in respect to the dead, and with the aid of an interpreter he addressed the crowd. "Like yourselves, these individuals were people who could see, feel, hear, smell and taste like other humans, but who were coldly and inhumanely murdered. You may say that you weren't personally responsible for all this, but remember, you stood for the government which perpetrated atrocities like these. I now produce for you the man who was commandant of this vile camp. Here's the man who was chiefly responsible for the tortures you see here with your own eyes which were inflicted on the unfortunates lying here."[10] The German commandant stood defiantly before the civilians, who hollered, "Throw the wretch down here, we'll finish him off and bury him along with the others." The 250 onlookers shouted German profanity and some spat at the man. The civilians then went to work to carry the corpses into a mass grave and bury them using only shovels and hand tools.[11] In a series of 11 separate camps in the vicinity of Landsberg, 40,000 to 50,000 Jews and political prisoners had been incarcerated, starved, beaten and mistreated in virtually unimaginable ways. Many hundreds of the inmates were murdered by the SS guards just before the Americans arrived to liberate the camps.[12]

Robert Arrasmith continued his story. "On May 5, 1945, only three days before the war's end, I was patrolling a quiet sector near Heidenheim in southeastern Germany. Suddenly, machine-gun bullets ripped up the street around me. A bullet ripped open my right leg and I crumpled to the ground. While I lay on my side in the street, others in my squad turned their rifles on the suspected window, then threw hand grenades into the house. A fellow squad member entered the house with his rifle at the ready. Three minutes later he emerged and held up two fingers. It gave me little satisfaction. Two of my buddies carried me to an aid station where I was again in the hands of doctors. The war ended on May 8, 1945, and we injured soldiers lying on our cots in a school room shouted with joy."[13]

In 1993 Heinz Harmel explained his last days of service. "In late April 1945, it was clear to me that it would be insane to continue the fighting. I formulated a plan to save as many of my men as possible from death and the Soviets. Hitler expected me to fight the Russians to the last man, but I knew that the time had come to give up. In Teplitz-Schönau I gathered my officers together and gave them my final order. They were to save their men and themselves. They were to extricate themselves from their positions as quietly as possible and flee to the west. Nothing more could be done. I had received the order from the Führer Bunker to fight to the last man and had sent a return message that I refused to obey the order. I told my officers that I had subsequently been told that an order for my arrest and execution had been issued from Hitler. My intent was to make my way south into Austria and lay low until the war was over.

"My officers were ashamed to comply with this final order, but they knew as well as I, that the end was at hand. I said good-bye and shook the hands of the officers I had known for so long. I was sad that I could not say farewell to all the others in my command who were willing to carry out whatever suicidal order I might give. I dismissed my driver and took the wheel of the command Kübel. I drove south to the Tyrol, to a section of Germany that was so remote I hoped no one would hear of Hitler's execution order.

"In a small Alpine town, I ran into a gauleiter who assumed that I was simply cut off from my troops. The times were chaotic and it was understandable that he might make such an assumption. The gauleiter, who had considerable authority as governor of his political district, ordered me to assume command of a large group of soldiers fighting the British to the southwest of his district. The British and Americans were advancing through the mountain passes into Germany itself.

"I obeyed the gauleiter's order with quick dispatch. I took command of the men and immediately ordered them to lay down their arms and surrender. They were relieved to have been given such a sensible order and started waving white flags. I surrendered along with them. I had no sword or pistol to give the British colonel who accepted my surrender. I knew not what awaited me, but I was confident that whatever it might be, it was better than what would have been provided by the Soviets. After several days of interrogation I was transferred to a prisoner-of-war camp under British control in northern Germany."[14]

The United States Army transported Robert Arrasmith to Paris, then to England where he underwent extensive surgery. Before his arrival in England, Dr. Lipmann Kessel, who had been at Arnhem in September 1944 and had made his way back to England, was performing his regular duties as surgeon. Arrasmith described his hospitalization and return to civilian life. "The doctors determined that my injured leg couldn't be saved and planned an amputation. One surgeon resisted. He was British with the unusual name of Kessel. The American doctors held him in high regard, so I did what he said. This doctor performed several operations over a six-month period. I was anxious to catch a ship back to America and pleaded with the doctor to let me go. The war ended with me still in a hospital in England. The doctor was insistent and I stayed put until the leg had healed enough for travel. Later in life I wrote Dr. Kessel a letter and thanked him for giving me a chance at a normal life. I don't know if he ever received the letter.

"England was at peace and I was allowed to leave the hospital grounds. We were in the country and I watched the townspeople going about their business as if the war hadn't existed. I wondered if the German soldiers with whom I had traveled in America were on ships heading back to Germany.

"Back in America, I entered another Army hospital where I underwent a long therapy to restore the use of the leg. The recuperation period was long. During this time, President Truman was elected to a second term and America had returned to a peacetime economy. After I regained my walking ability, I was declared healthy by the U.S. Army. Released from the hospital, I got a lot of back pay. I put on my uniform and boarded a train for the state of Washington. It was a long and enjoyable journey. I decided that I would never again think of the war. I had done my part and now I was going to be a civilian. I wasn't sure exactly what I would do, but right then I had a pocket full of money and a family waiting to greet me.

"I returned to Spokane, Washington. My parents were there at the station. I breathed clean, cool air sweeping in from the Cascade Mountains. For a week I did nothing. As the conquering hero of the Arrasmith family I was not allowed to do anything for myself. After of week of that, I formally declared myself a civilian, took off the uniform and started dealing with my new life."[15]

21

Stalag XI-B and Berlin, April 1945

In January 1985, Paul W. Rice, Jr., wrote of his German captivity, "My small world after capture and interrogation was involved with three other C-66 infantrymen: Charlie Fitts, Luke Scott and George O'Bryan. We became a group of 4, in 20 groups totaling about 100 individuals of the 12th AD and the 28th Infantry Division captured within five miles of the Rhine River. We were ferried across the Rhine River the evening of January 16th and passed through a small village as I remember called Moos. For three days we were herded into cattle cars so crowded we had to stand and take turns lying down. I remember we walked or pushed our way around inside the car most of the day and night, trying to avoid the area near the door where everyone relieved himself."[1]

Charlie remembered his experience as a prisoner of war: "As the Germans transported us to the rear in January 1945, I inventoried my belongings. I had my high school graduation wristwatch, my prayer book and the clothes on my back. After walking through Gambsheim my fellow prisoners and I were herded onto a pontoon bridge which the Germans had put up only a few days before. That evening, on the east side of the Rhine River, German guards stashed us in a barn for the night. I knew [some other prisoners from] C Company, and we stuck together, as did prisoners from other companies. More Americans came through the barn doors to be crammed into stalls, hay bins and loft. Some of the new arrivals had been captured elsewhere and were from the 106th Infantry Division. The next day we walked east, prodded by the snapping guards who believed they were in the midst of a great victory.

"For the next several days, we trudged along muddy roads. One night I was billeted in a school containing a [horse-riding] ring. I noted with passing curiosity the opulence of prewar Germany. Although the buildings had not been maintained, it was clear that they had once been objects of pride. As we walked through villages we were watched by the townsfolk with great curiosity. Some of the women and children hollered invectives and a few even threw rocks, but mostly they simply stared at the ragged column of dejected Americans. We entered a town and halted in a square facing a beautifully ornate building which had to be the town hall. We stood in sloppy ranks with guards at our perimeter facing the steps to the building. An elderly but low-ranking officer mounted the steps. He was an incongruous sight in his jodhpurs and shiny boots. With clipboard in hand, he called out three names. They all started with A, and I realized that someone had taken the time to arrange the names of the prisoners in alphabetical order. I found it amusing that even at war's end the punctilious Germans insisted on thorough organization."[2]

In 1984 Charlie Fitts described his interrogation. "I walked in and saluted a Wehrmacht colonel that spoke better English than I. He offered me a cigarette and a glass of brandy which I thanked him for but did not take. I had just turned 20 on December 18. He told me that he was happy that I was not wounded and he wanted to notify my parents that I was OK. He asked where he could write them. I gave him my name, rank and serial number. He assured me that he just wanted to help if I would cooperate. He then asked me whether I was in the 12th or the 106th. I answered the same as before. He then asked if I was in A Company or in C Company. Same answer. He became peeved, stood up, came from behind his desk and told me that I was the assistant squad leader of the 60-millimeter mortar squad of the Second Platoon of C Company, 66th AD and that I was from the southern part of the United States. Why wouldn't I let him notify my folks? I do not know who went in to the colonel before I did, but one of them must have tried to buy something by talking. That has bothered me more than any other one thing in the entire war.

"We came to prisoner-of-war camp V-A, near Ludwigsburg. Here we were told to strip down. The Germans took every piece of redundant clothing. It was winter and layered garments were needed for warmth, but that applied to Germans as well as Americans. In their mind it was better for Americans to suffer than Germans. The second pair of socks and second shirt went to the German war effort. We were then crowded into boxcars, and the slow-moving train rattled northward through the night to Stalag XI-B, near Fallingbostel. We left Stalag V-A and arrived at Stalag XI-B after a train ride we all remember."[3]

Edward Waszak described Stalag XI-B. "It was a very large prison camp. The barracks were large single-story structures, about 120 feet by 40 feet, elevated a foot or two above the ground on blocks. At that point in time there was no heat in our part of the building. The room was filled with bunks except for a small area near the windows that was used for tables with attached benches similar to picnic tables. There was a water spigot at our end of the barracks. There were a few single light bulbs hanging from the ceiling that were turned on after dark for an hour or so depending on the disposition of the guards. The windows had shutters on the outside that were closed by guards at nightfall and during air raids. There were no air raid shelters for the POWs."[4]

Paul Rice wrote about prison life with Charlie Fitts. "Here (Stalag XI-B) we met Canadian prisoners who had been there since their capture at Dieppe. These men were experts at prison survival. Their uniforms looked worn but neat, they were clean shaven and they wore their field caps as if on parade. We had much to learn from them. We learned to live the tough life of the prisoner. Those with diarrhea took the bottom bunks. The dismal barracks were almost the same temperature as the freezing winter outside. During morning and evening roll calls, blowing snow added to the prisoners' misery. We were fed twice a day, thin turnip soup. Charlie Fitts had a perpetual headache from lack of food. Red Cross packages were the difference between death and survival, but they were split between three or four men, and we knew the closer the Allies came, the worse prison conditions would become. During our captivity Charlie Fitts and I spent our hours designing crossword puzzles. We also made a game of battleship and played this from time to time."[5]

Charlie Fitts continued his narration. "At morning formation in late February, the presiding sergeant asked for volunteers to work in a brickyard. The enticement was extra food. I thought that it would have to be better than my present circumstances. I volunteered and, together with Paul Rice, we marched to a site near Misburg that had been a fuel refinery before being reduced to rubble by American bombers. I was assigned to the brick pile. My job was identical to that of a hundred others who swarmed over an immense mound of broken bricks. I was to chip the clinging mortar away from each undamaged brick and stack it in a rectangular form, the dimensions of which were defined by shouting guards with keen eyes for symmetry. At last, I had found a job worthy of my ASTP training. Out of the corner of my eye I watched the more senior prisoners as they chipped a single brick as though it were marble in the hands of Michelangelo. A few days on the pile and Paul and I became experts at pretending to concentrate on our work while whispering stories of home. Of course, talking among prisoners was forbidden, since the German guards tolerated no lollygagging, but the prisoners timed one another in a contest to see who could produce the least for the Reich while convincing the guards they were giving their utmost.

"The walls of fuel storage tanks began to take shape from the thousands of reclaimed bricks. I had a twinge of guilt when I thought that given enough time, the recalcitrant prisoners might actually complete the tanks, in spite of their foot-dragging. I brought this to the attention of more experienced prisoners, who reminded me that the storage tank walls were six feet thick. It became apparent that this was our work for the duration. I chipped in the cold, thought of food and waited for the next meal, which was turnip soup with an occasional foreign clump of indifferent taste. Still, it was far better than Stalag XI-B, and I congratulated Paul on making the right decision.

"In late March some of the men were reassigned to mixing fresh mortar and slapping the bricks into a circular form that [was] the rising walls of the previous tank. These men became instant journeyman masons by edict of German engineers who worked their fingers to the bone in fear of being sent to the eastern front. As the refinery began to take shape and my storage tank began to rise from the ashes like a phoenix, a single Mosquito reconnaissance plane flew over. Two days later, Allied bombers reduced the work of the masons to rubble. The bombers had come at night, which was considerate in view of the men's working hours.

"I had to admire the Germans' tenacity. The day after the bombing, the men started chipping bricks as though their work was on schedule. I figured that the war's end was so near that the Germans had given up and were only marking time until the end. Brick chipping was now only an exercise in habit. This was confirmed by the guards' apparent leniency toward talking. As we whispered among ourselves while going about our business on the brick pile, we were sometimes interrupted by Germans who added comments of their own to the subject of concern.

"On April 7, we emerged from our barracks and lined up in preparation for the march to the brick pile. We were not happy about the turn of events. The Germans yelled at us to start walking east. The order struck fear into us. We saw danger in every step we took to the east. Whispering as we walked, we agreed that the Allies must be close and that the Germans were becoming desperate. The relaxed attitude of the brickyard guards had been replaced by a look of defiance in the new trigger-happy Hitler Youth guards."[6]

Charlie Fitts wrote, "We started walking on 7 April. So I guess the raid was a few days before. We left the school at Hanover at 5:45 A.M. on 7 April and walked 19 miles to Remling. On 8 April we walked 14 miles to Urlman, rested on the 9th. We covered only 6 miles on the 10th, 3 and ½ miles on the 11th to a place called Lusche. Last entry in my prayer book was, '14 April, liberated by the British — taken by truck to Hildesheim to await a plane out. With God's help I made it."[7]

At least 84 enlisted men of C-66 were taken prisoner by the German forces between January 7, 1944, and May 8, 1945. One died of wounds and two were killed while escaping. All others survived in relatively good health, physically and mentally.[8]

Charlie made it to London while still recovering from the malnourishment he had suffered while a prisoner of war. He remembered an incident that left an indelible image: "The European war's end was officially announced over BBC radio on May 8, 1945. Immediately, people poured into the streets. I celebrated by milling about with thousands of merrymaking civilians. Every pub in England kept pouring pints of beer into men who had seen five years of war. When sufficiently tanked, they entered the streets to hug and kiss any willing lass regardless of age. It was a city scarred with mountains of debris from V-1 and V-2 bombs. Its windows were taped and its doorways sandbagged, but these were only reminders of what had been. A future of prosperity stretched into infinity, and those who had survived rejoiced at the thought of it. Among the surging throng of spontaneous fun was an elderly couple who stood apart from the rest. They held hands and watched others as tears ran down their cheeks. They said nothing to each other or to anyone else. I spoke to them. The husband said that they had lost all five of their sons in the war."[9]

In April 1945, Ernst Storch arrived in Pomerania to fight the Russians. He told of his reluctant trip to Berlin: "At Stettin I was assigned to a tank commanded by Bernhard Westerhoff. We shook hands and exchanged memories of our escapes at the Waldgraben Canal.

"I remember looking at a hill to the east. It was March and the hill was covered with little wildflowers. I was amazed that the delicate creatures bloomed while destruction was the order of the day. I surmised that without eyes to see the killing and without ears to hear the explosions, they were able to persist in their little lives.

"I was walking back to the tank when a motorcycle messenger approached. He handed Westerhoff a message. He read the message and handed it to me. It ordered me to report to the Reichskanzlei, Berlin, April 14, 1945. It was signed Harmel, commanding. I was shocked and thought a mistake had been made, but Westerhoff pointed to the paper. It was an order from Harmel. I resisted, but Westerhoff ordered me to get into the motorcycle sidecar.

"I bounced over an open field, then onto a road that took the driver and I back to division headquarters. I entered a modest house in front of which sat several vehicles. My battle dress was dirty and I felt out of place with all the officers scurrying about. Then an officer in camouflage dress approached. He smiled and thrust his hand into mine. He introduced himself as Erwin Bachmann. We were to go to Berlin and shake the hand of the Führer. It was the Führer's birthday and we were to represent the division. I was bewildered, but I knew that I had to obey this order without questions. Bachmann's exploit at Herrlisheim was already a legend in the Frundsberg Division, but the amiable fellow didn't look like he could have captured a dozen Shermans.

"I followed Bachmann into the rear seat of a Kübel. Our driver wrestled the little car all day, dodging artillery and frequently being stopped by Waffen SS military police who inspected our orders. After sunset, with no lights the driver negotiated his way around rubble and shell holes as we entered the outskirts of the capital. We wandered down streets in Lichterfelde, then to the Leibstandarte Kasserne. A lieutenant greeted us and escorted us to a reception room. I was taken to a long room with high ceiling. Single beds lined the walls of the room as if in a dormitory. This is where I would sleep. Bachmann was to have his own room, a status of his rank.

"The next morning we continued our journey into the heart of Berlin, to the center of the once great city. The trees of Unter den Linden were budding in spite of relentless bombing. I saw what was left of the Adlon Hotel. Bricks and rubble had been shoveled away from its doorway. The driver turned into Wilhelmstrasse. The Kübel crept along in low gear. Here too, the bombers had done their work. On the right was the bombed-out President's Palace, Foreign Office and the remains of the Alte Kanzlei with its added balcony from which Hitler had waved to his cheering admirers in happier days. We swung right onto Voss Strasse and saw the line of new government buildings.

"Then the Kübel pulled up in front of the Great West Entrance to the Neue Reichskanzlei. It too had severe bomb damage. Two Leibstandarte guards were standing with rifles beneath four columns. No other cars were to be seen. The driver rushed around the car and opened the rear door. Bachmann stepped out. I followed. The tall brass door opened and we strode into a once-resplendent foyer that seemed to stretch forever to the right and left. The giant door directly ahead was the entrance to the Führer's office. The inside of the Reichskanzlei was still rich in marble and gilt, but was badly scarred. An officer greeted us and escorted us into the state dining room. This had been a fine restaurant-like room with white cloths on long tables. The windows which looked out upon the garden had been blown out. In spite of this, the view was serene, as though the windows had been opened for the spring air. We ate sausage, potatoes and hard-boiled eggs.

"We were guided to a line of twenty or so other men to be received. The line of soldiers stood at attention, but not so rigidly as to be uncomfortable. Soon the door to what looked like a concrete shed in the garden opened and several high ranking officers stepped out. Dr. Goebbels was among them. Then the Führer himself emerged. The bent man shuffled to the line of soldiers. He started at the opposite end. I could not see him clearly out of the corner of my eye, but I heard muffled voices and the unmistakable baritone of Adolf Hitler.

"At last the Führer was in front of Bachmann. With stooped shoulders and crumpled hat, Germany's leader seemed undersized for the long overcoat that hung nearly to the ground. I listened to a few questions from the Führer. They seemed straightforward and sincere. Then Hitler was in front of me. The leader of Germany smiled, but it was an old man's tired smile. I tried to look into the man's eyes, but they were hidden under his cap visor. I was tall and he seemed too short. In answer to a question I said I was from Vienna. Again Hitler smiled, probably because I was a fellow Austrian. He shook my hand. I was surprised by his strength. He held my hand for a moment as he thanked me for my sacrifices to the Fatherland. In a moment the leader of Germany moved on to the next man in line. As he did so I saw the tremor in his left hand which he held behind his back.

"Bachmann and I left the Reichskanzlei in the same Kübel with the same driver. On the return trip we slept through the swerving and jolting of the speeding car. The driver was now less confident. Unknown to Bachmann and me was the rapid disintegration of the division. Harmel was in command of fractured units often without coordination or communication. The elements were fighting the Russians the best they could with little supplies or enthusiasm. Into this chaos we returned."[10]

It was Hitler's last birthday and his last appearance above the bunker in Berlin. Both Bachmann and Storch were unmoved by the ceremony. They were too busy trying to survive.

At about the same time, Andy Woods was not doing well. The death of his comrade and true friend Pete Vickless hovered over him like a black cloud. He described the days following his tank commander's death: "I could not bring myself to help with the task of cleaning blood from the tank's interior. It was a gut-wrenching chore that fell mostly to Frank Conway. I held back my emotions and tried to assist in some way, but I was psychologically staggered by the loss. The crew gradually regained its strength, and by the end of the first week in April the tank was ready to take its position in C Company's formation. With Frank Conway as new tank commander, the position of gunner was filled by a young soldier named Ralph Sipe. The tank would no longer be at point. It would take a station far back in the column.

"On April 9, the Conway tank sat on a bluff in central Germany. It was a sunny day and as far as I was concerned it was a good time to stand down and enjoy the afternoon sun. My idea was not to be. A radio order was received to pull back to Königshofen. The company would remain there for the night. The next morning the tanks of C Company started their engines and moved out of the village. Soon they were back on the bluff overlooking a vast field to the south. The tanks were spread out in attack formation, but the Germans had brought up some antitank guns. Fire was exchanged and while American shells hit the barricaded positions, three of the Shermans were hit.

"Kenneth Detrick's tank was close to the point. The Sherman had been rigged as a flamethrower with the gelatinous liquid stored in a neoprene-lined container mounted on the transmission. It, too, was struck by one of the antitank guns. Detrick was badly wounded, but pulled himself out of the tank commander's hatch onto the engine deck, then onto the soft earth. He was followed by the gunner, Jim Welch, but when Welch was on the turret he saw that the cannon barrel was blocking the driver's escape hatch. He quickly jumped back into the commander's hatch and cranked the turret to remove the obstacle. He saw the driver, Bob Miles, emerging from the front armor hatch. A moment later the courageous Welch was killed by machine-gun fire. Kenneth Detrick died of his wounds where he lay on the German countryside.

"C Company's tanks were spread out across a field with infantry out in front. The hedgerow ahead glittered with machine gun and rifle muzzle flashes. American infantrymen took cover as the tanks responded with all their combined machine guns. Every tank blazed away at the line of bushes and scrub trees. A lieutenant out in front of Conway's tank waved his arms and yelled for his infantrymen to keep going. It reminded me of Civil War officers encouraging their men onward by setting an example. Suddenly, the officer collapsed where he stood. His body seemed lifeless and the tanks slowly rolled passed him as two infantrymen of the 17th Armored Infantry Battalion stopped to give first aid. I turned my attention back to the Germans ahead of us."[11]

George Hatt, who was near the Conway Sherman, saw his platoon leader, Lieutenant Yarborough, fall. He rushed forward to render aid, then saw that one of the soldiers bending over the fallen lieutenant was a medic. George ran forward to join others in his squad.[12]

Andy Woods continued, "My head and shoulders were out of the tank as I helped to direct the gunner's coaxial machine gun. The medic who had attended to the lieutenant leaped up onto the engine deck and pulled himself to the loader's hatch. He hollered something to me and pointed to the wounded Lieutenant Yarborough. The noise of the .50-caliber Browning on the commander's hatch drowned out his voice. The medic's face turned instantly red. A German rifle bullet had ripped open his head. The medic's only intent had been to save an officer's life. He rolled off the tank and dropped to the ground as we moved ahead. I had no time to look after the shattered medic or to wonder about the lieutenant in the field.

"On May 8, 1945, the Germans capitulated, but C Company had difficulty in making the adjustment to sudden peace. I was jittery and jumped at any loud noise. When I slept I was back in battle, so I tried to stay awake by drinking coffee. In some ways, the quiet of peace was more difficult than battle. All the men were the same. Combat leaves scars that don't show. Even Frank Conway, the steadiest soldier I ever met, was jumpy and ill tempered. Time was the cure, and a week of plentiful food with comrades who tomorrow would not die helped me to slow down. I saw poplar branches with leaves that spun in the wind. I listened to the birds. Spring was, for them, a season of romance. Their songs mixed with the sounds of warm wind, and I took pleasure in closing my eyes and feeling peace around me.

"The ship that carried me and thousands of other returning soldiers berthed in the harbor of New York City. The Japanese surrendered two days later. By then it was August. The war was over, but it was hard for me to perceive what this might mean to me personally. I had been assigned to the 86th Infantry Division and would have surely not made it through the invasion of Japan's home islands. It was good to be back on American soil."[13]

In late April Ernst Storch had forgotten his trip to Berlin and was concerned only with trying to stay alive. He spoke of the months following Germany's surrender: "I joined other soldiers who were walking west. I had no sense of purpose. I only knew that the war was coming to an end. First, I would cross the Elbe River. As I walked, I began to think about Austria. To get there I would have to turn south. I hoped the Americans were in Vienna, but I wasn't sure. I asked several of the men who trudged along in silence. No one knew and no one cared. Finally, a man spoke to me. He had an Austrian accent. Theo Svobota was the Austrian's name. He was heading for Salzburg, where he had lived before the war. We agreed to make the trip together.

"As we headed west toward the Elbe River the roads were clogged with people fleeing the Russians. I looked at the civilians around me and I considered myself lucky. They had carts of belongings and children who cried with exhaustion. It was a stream of humanity fleeing in panic, driven by fear of the Russians. They were walking into the unknown, away from their homes. Their fear must have been great.

"Theo and I came to the Elbe River. Few bridges were intact, but we approached the river between a baby buggy stacked high with bedding and a donkey that wobbled under his load of furniture. Without food and shelter, we rested in a wooded area. We agreed that the time had come to rid ourselves of identification. We dug a pit and threw into it the patches and emblems that labeled us as men of the Waffen SS. The last items discarded were our *soldbuchs* that recorded all our accomplishments in the military, including rank, pay, qualifications and medals. As we continued on our journey we ate what we could find, slept in the open and avoided roads as much as possible.

"In May we were close to Enns, Austria. Theo was a practical young man and he saw that at some point in time we were going to have to trust someone. We were in a country where people would recognize our accent and perhaps give us food. We knocked on the rear door of a farmhouse. A rough-looking middle-aged man answered the knock. His huge, swarthy frame filled the doorway. The farmer said nothing. He stepped back into the house and gestured for us to enter.

"The farmer immediately recognized us as Waffen SS. He directed his wife to feed us. Soon, the warm kitchen and ample food took effect. I couldn't keep my eyes open. I fell asleep at the table where we ate.

"I awoke on the kitchen floor. It was the following morning and the smell of frying sausages was overwhelming. I looked into the stern face of the farmer who demanded work for food and board. Theo and I nodded with eagerness. We wanted to be useful. After years of causing destruction we wanted to produce something of value. What better place to start than a farm?

"We shook hands with the farmer whose fingers were as thick as the sausages on the kitchen table. Then we ate our fill of boiled oats, bread and hot ersatz coffee. The lady of the house showed the new farmhands our room with two heavenly beds, an oak clothes cupboard and a basin of water on a bureau with three drawers. She pointed out the window at an outhouse at the end of the courtyard.

"For two months we worked in the field and ate gigantic meals. For me it was ideal, as if I were back in my youth working in the fields outside of Vienna. Toward the end of June 1945, the farmer brought clothing. We took what we could find that might fit. I took a dark-colored pair of trousers, a blue shirt and an old Wehrmacht field jacket. In the kitchen, the farmer showed us a pair of American Army boots. The boots fit me and I walked about the kitchen like a new man. The boots were nearly new. We removed our shirts and the farmer's wife looked at the SS blood-type tattoos. She and her husband argued over the best way to remove the tell-tale marks. The farmer became impatient and told his wife to boil water. With a razor, the thick-fingered surgeon cut away the tissue. Blood ran down my arm, but I held the pain without complaint. The wife swabbed the wound with spirits, then dressed it with clean rags wrapped around my arm. The same operation was performed on Theo.

"The farmer suggested that it was time for us to leave. The next morning we set off for Salzburg where the farmer had said Americans were in control. We looked like traditional hobos, with sticks and folded rags holding hunks of bread, wurst and a bag of oats. We reached Salzburg, but had not walked far when diarrhea overtook Theo, who ran down an alley to relieve himself. I stayed discreetly around the corner at the front of the nearest house. As I waited for Theo to return, an American jeep with two soldiers drove by. It stopped in front of me. The two Americans jumped out and approached me. They jabbered in English, asking questions that I could not understand. The soldiers were suspicious because I could produce no papers. Theo returned to the front of the house and into the custody of the Americans.

"One soldier withdrew his Colt automatic from its holster. He pointed to the jeep. Theo and I sat on the rear seat. The jeep soon stopped in front of a church. I had no idea where I was and wanted to ask Theo, who knew Salzburg, but these Americans seemed to mean business. We were pushed into an alcove where an officer sat at a long table. He spoke fluent German with a lazy accent and demanded to see identification papers. I shrugged as I said they had been lost when swimming across a river. The officer didn't buy the lie, and wrote information about me on a form. He demanded to see our left upper arms.

"I did as I was told. On the inside upper arm was a raw, red patch where the farmer had done his work. I explained that I had been wounded in the arm. The same explanation came from Theo. The officer didn't bother to ask any amplifying questions. He simply wrote 'SS' on the form.

"The guard took us to the imprisonment house. Theo and I were marched through a cemetery to the opposite side of the church grounds. A sturdy stone rectory bordered the cemetery. It seemed depressingly appropriate. The windows were shuttered and a guard with a Thompson submachine gun leaned on the wall at the entrance. The guard saw my American GI boots. He cried out to his friend. The other guard looked down and saw my boots. No doubt about it. They were GI issue.

"The two Americans with a rifle and submachine gun walked us into the building's stone entryway. One pointed the gun at a door. Theo and I stumbled across a door rail and while trying to regain our balance were struck from behind by one of the guards. The savage blow landed on my head. I collapsed into unconsciousness.

"Two hours later I came to. Two other detainees propped me against a wall. I saw Theo, who was sitting in a corner with his bloody head in his arms.

"A day went by without food or water. Two Americans grabbed me under the arms and dragged me out of the room, through the stone hall and out into the daylight. I was blinded by the light and fell on the gravel path that traversed the cemetery to the church. The Americans waited for me to pick myself up, then they pushed me into the alcove where I had been two days earlier. Three officers wearing military hats sat at a long table. They talked and laughed. I stood in front of them, but could only see their outlines. The middle officer read from a sheet of paper. One of the others translated. I had been charged with having no identification. I was sentenced to six months in prison. No one spoke on my behalf. I said nothing; no protest, no admission.

"I was taken by jeep to a formal jail. It was in another stone building with metal grates covering high, narrow windows. I was thrown into a room with about a dozen other men. Most were older and all wore civilian clothes. In the corner was a bucket and lid which served as the latrine. The room stunk of stale urine, feces and body odor. The high, uncovered windows provided some ventilation and when an occasional breeze pushed fresh air into the room the men raised their heads to sniff the outside.

"For six months I lived among thieves, pimps, cut-throats, black marketeers, pickpockets, con men and every description of derelict. A few of the men were ex-soldiers who probably had been in the Waffen SS.

"In January 1946 I was released into another frigid winter. I was lucky and found a ride with a trucker going to Vienna. The grizzled driver had been in the Wehrmacht and had survived the eastern front. He had little use for those who had not fought the Russians. I told him a few of my experiences in fighting T-34 tanks and we bonded for the duration of the trip.

"My mother opened the door. She had not heard from me for a year. At first she didn't recognize me. I was emaciated, pale, with long hair and stubble. She cried great sobs of simultaneous happiness and distress. My father was at home. He and I embraced. It was the first time I could remember ever having embraced my father."[14]

22

Michigan, Texas, Mississippi, Niedernhal, Vienna and Fachingen Lahn

Edward Waszak recorded the 12th Armored Division's capture of Wernher von Braun at war's end. He said, "On May 2, 1945, the German rocket scientist Wernher von Braun was in a mountain home on the German-Bavarian border. He and his brother Magnus had escaped Peenemunde and brought 125 fellow scientists and records south to surrender to the Americans. OSS knew of the general location of von Braun and dispatched a Navy captain with credentials signed by General Patch, General Marshal, Admiral King and President Roosevelt. In effect the documents gave authority for the bearer to requisition whatever forces might be needed in the liberation of von Braun. Colonel Fields of the 12th Armored Division greeted the Navy captain and assisted him by lending a platoon from A Company of the 714th Tank Battalion. At the same time, Wernher von Braun instructed his brother Magnus to ride a bicycle to the nearest village to let the Americans know of their whereabouts. Not only were von Braun and his colleagues liberated, the Americans also became owners of the secret hyper-wind tunnel that was hidden in a cave."[1]

Andy Woods described his final days in the Army: "I went home. When the train pulled into the small station in Niles, Michigan, I stepped down into the darkness of early morning. My family was scheduled to pick me up at the station, but my parents wouldn't arrive for another two hours. I sat on the curb and stared into the darkness. For the first time I tried to come to grips with my future, but the images of all those who had lost their lives in Europe stayed with me. I would have a future, be married, would have children and grandchildren. But there were those I had known, who were still back there, lying in some forgotten grave.

"While I sat alone I thought that I could do something worthwhile as representative of my lost friends. It was only a vague abstraction without substance and without any noble intent. The nebulous idea produced a nervous tension. I stood up and began walking around the little station house, talking to myself.

"For the next six weeks I wandered around the farm and absently planned with my father our mutual future. But I didn't tell him of my vision. I knew that whatever I might do, it would have to somehow reflect the loss of so many young men.

"I found that my prewar girlfriend had met and married a doctor. This news failed to dent my spirit. I had too much on my mind. By now, the vague image at the train station had begun to crystallize. I determined that I would make the lives of others around me better, while not revealing the motive for doing so. I thought of how crazy my scheme would sound to the practical-minded farmers living around me. First, I must have a financial base from which to work. With my father, I bought 230 acres of good land to add to what the family already owned. We grew wormwood, a plant used in the making of liniments and other pharmaceuticals. Since very few farmers planted this exotic crop, the extracted oil fetched a good price. Additionally, the pharmaceutical concerns that used the oil in their products were eager to sign long-term contracts. After a number of years I invested in a bank and became its president. I was an officer of the bank for eighteen years, from 1961 through 1979. At the same time I quietly used my wealth and energy to fulfill my dream of bringing benefit to others in a perpetuation of those left behind in Europe."[2]

A May 8, 2006, Texas newspaper article read, "For American GIs, Victory in Europe Day was an emotional day filled with celebration, joy, relief, thoughts of going back to a normal life, and even some anxiety about getting home. But for many of the 12th Armored Division there was that small matter of occupying and rebuilding a defeated Germany before going home. During the occupation there was plenty of idle time to relax and be young men again, without the pressure and horror of combat. The young men played baseball and football, and got passes to Paris."[3]

George Hatt read the article and wrote an answer: "The war was not over for the 17th Battalion of the 12th Armored Division on May 8, 1945. On that day we were up against the Alps, having chased Hermann Göring and his private guard that far and then turning his capture over to the Texas 36th Infantry Division. On the 4th we had been in Fischbach and were stopped by a roadblock set up by Waffen SS troops in the Inn River Pass. Company B or C was in Nied Audorf and Ober Audorf. Company A was in Fischbach until the 6th at which time hostilities ceased and we left the village for the area of Augsburg for search and occupation duties. I don't remember any emotion or celebration in the 12th Armored Division on May 8th. Joy? Questionable. Relief? Absolutely! We were worn down by the many weeks of piercing into hazardous southern Germany. Guys wounded and killed day after day. We were just plain tired. I especially remember our squad's first postwar patrol. It was near the Danube River. I had my squad's half-track pull into a wooded area and said, 'Let's take a break.' Everybody got out and took an hour's nap. That was something we never did in combat. We played cards, took a bath and went swimming in a lake or river, fished a river with hand grenades, hung around the village tavern, got into fights over petty arguments, stood guard duty, patrolled the countryside and villages issuing military government orders to burgermeisters and people. One burgermeister walked to our half-track carrying a Panzerfaust. He then said, '*Wir haben viel.*' He pointed to a warehouse. We had to call for a special group to come pick up a hundred or more. On the fun side we shared our PX rations of chewing gum and chocolate bars with the kids."[4]

George Hatt was separated from the 12th Armored Division at the end of July 1945. He described his return to civilian life: "The Army sent soldiers home based on a formula that involved the number of days in combat and number of days in the Army. Those with the most went home the earliest. Late in the fall, my release number came up. The

Army sent me to Bremen to await a ship that would take me back to the United States from Bremerhaven. A sergeant major examined my records and discovered that my duty in the enlisted reserve corps had been erroneously counted into the total points. I dropped six points and was thereby stalled in Europe. I went south to Karlsruhe to spend Christmas 1945 not far from Alsace. I had time to visit Herrlisheim in December. The town was still a wreck from the fighting a year earlier. I walked the streets, circled the rusting tank *Cleopatra* and remembered those terrifying moments a year before. I looked at the houses in which I had sought shelter. People were in the town, walking the streets and making repairs to some of the rooms in half-demolished houses. For Herrlisheim the war had ended in January 1945, but the only expression on the faces [of those] who occupied the town was a grim determination to rebuild.

"I tried to locate the grave of my friend Adrian Mariluch, but without success. He had drowned in the Zorn River after getting out of Herrlisheim on January 19th. It was a melancholy trip back to the town that had been the turning point for the division and me personally.

"In early February 1946, the Army sent me to Camp Lucky Strike in France, and on March 13th I was handed my discharge papers at Fort Smith, Arkansas. From there I hitchhiked to my home in North Dallas just as I had done in December 1943. After the war, I was released from the Army. I completed my degree in 1947 in chemical engineering at Texas A&M University and became an aerospace engineer working with General Dynamics. After a little over forty-one years I retired in 1989. In 1949 I married Jacquelyn McElwee of Kilgore, Texas. We have four children, eleven grandchildren, and four great-grandchildren.

"I visited France and Germany in 1985 where I met residents of Herrlisheim and Weyersheim. They remain my friends to this day. In 1990 I met four members of the 10th Waffen SS Panzer Division, including Bernhard Westerhoff and Erwin Bachmann. I spoke to Heinz Harmel on the phone and received several honorary awards for my contributions toward reconciliation of the two former enemies.

"Upon retirement in 1989 I and my fellow 12th AD friends Maurice Glover and Marvin Drum helped Professor Vernon Williams at Abilene Christian University initiate the 12th Armored Division Memorial Museum in Abilene. Today I serve as an officer on the Memorial Museum's board of directors and enjoy the fellowship of those of my Second World War buddies."[5]

In the last days of the war the 12th Armored Division liberated over 50,000 non-military prisoners, including French premiers Eduard Daladier and Paul Reynaud; a former commander of the French Army; the son of Georges Clemenceau of First World War fame; and the sister of Charles De Gaulle. The division suffered 2,647 wounded, 351 captured and 870 men killed in action.[6]

On May 18, 1945, Wilhelm Balbach was captured by the Americans. On April 24, 2006, he recounted his experience subsequent to the war: "I was in a French prisoner-of-war camp until February 1947, when I escaped to a French farm. There, I worked in exchange for my safety until April 27, 1947, when I determined that a journey to my home would be feasible. I made my way to Groningen and returned to school. Majoring in public administration I obtained the credentials for public service, but my military background in the Waffen SS was a hindrance. I appealed to the authorities, stating that I had not volunteered for the Waffen SS, but had been inducted into the organization.

Since I had had no choice in the matter, the government gave me a clearance for public work.

"I became a government inspector in Crailsheim, then in November I moved to Niedernhall. There I became mayor and remained in that capacity for more than forty years. I retired in May 2005, and now enjoy a modest life with my wife in our little town of Niedernhall in central Germany."[7]

A year after Robert Arrasmith's return to the Spokane area, he married Jean Cordes. To this day the couple resides in a comfortable home in Liberty Lake, Washington. They have four children, all of whom live in the state. Jean Arrasmith described her husband as follows: "I have never known Bob to shrink from any responsibility or dedication to duty, whatever it might be. He was head of maintenance and new construction for Northrop Corporation. In addition to being a great father and husband he was a Scoutmaster, Little League coach, and president of the high school football team booster club. What greater praise can a wife have for her husband?"[8]

Charlie Fitts made it back to the United States in May of 1945. He described his postwar years: "I was given a sixty-day leave and set off for Meridian, Mississippi, where my family and friends greeted me with open arms. The end of the war came when I was a member of a military police battalion at Fort McPherson, Georgia. In November of that year I was discharged. I went back to college on the GI Bill of Rights. While in college I met Jane Keller Watts of Huntsville, Alabama, daughter of a prominent attorney. In December 1947 we were married. We went to Meridian to be with my family. After church on a Sunday, I had a conversation with an executive of the F. W. Williams State Agency, which represented the United States Fidelity and Guarantee Company in the state of Mississippi. On a handshake I was promised a job when I finished college. I graduated from Texas A&M University. I started work at $225 per month, worked for the company all my life and was proud to have contributed to its growth.

"I have four daughters, Harriet Elisabeth Fitts, Kathy F. Howard, Susan F. Davis and Martha F. White. They have given me eight grandchildren and one step-grandson. I consider myself blessed throughout my life because I was born into a Christian family of love and respect and reared to know the true meaning of character, honesty and love."[9]

Through 1946 and 1947 the Austrian and German nations struggled with economic chaos. Gradually the people began to dig themselves out of poverty. Ernst Storch went back to school. He studied graphic design in Vienna, then went to Stockholm to finish his university studies. He became a professor at Höheren Institute in Vienna and taught at the institute until 1984. He married Ilse May and has two daughters, Barbara and Ursula. Barbara became a recognized European designer of shoes while Ursula became the curator of the Vienna Museum. Both are intelligent, articulate and successful Austrian professionals. Ernst spends his summers in the country as he did when a boy. He still loves nature and the quiet of the Austrian landscape.[10]

By the first of May 1945, the war was over for Bernhard Westerhoff. He ran through woods and fields away from the Soviet forces, swam the Elbe River, and walked to the town of Mulde. Three American soldiers pointed to a truck. Other German soldiers sat on benches in the truck's rear. No one in it spoke a word. Its motor started, and it slowly made its way among the throng of fleeing people down a road that lead to the west. Bernhard described his captivity, "My existence in several prisoner-of-war camps administered by the American Army and later the French Government cannot be described. It was unspeakable cruelty spawned from the belief that all Waffen SS soldiers were responsible for the heinous crimes of the SS. In 1947 I was released from prison. It was only after I had been released from the French prisoner-of-war camp that I learned of the terrible atrocities perpetrated on millions of innocent victims by members of the SS organization.

"I walked from Reims, France, through Germany toward home. On a sunny day in July 1947, after having walked over 300 miles, I came to the little bridge over the Lahn River above which was Scheidt and my family.

"My neighbors who before and during the war had been kind and generous were unforgiving and hurtful. Their scorn injured me more than any war wound. I was known in the little town as 'that SS man.' I may have been able to suffer the arrows of ridicule, but I couldn't expect my wife and son to carry a burden that was mine to carry alone. I moved my family to Fachingen.

"I came before a French occupation tribunal. The five-member board asked me many questions, and at the end of the hearing I was officially designated as 'denazified.' I had never had an interest in politics or the Nazi Party. I had simply told the tribunal the truth. The French were satisfied that I had seen the error of my ways. My horrible years in a French prison camp were never mentioned.

"I had been a Christian before the war as a member of a religious family, and during the war my faith had intensified into a staunch belief that God would see me through. The guilt and humiliation of being a part of such a bestial organization has been a personal burden for me the remaining years of my life.

"I have received several letters over the years that blindly condemn me personally for being a part of terrible SS acts documented in film and print. I didn't blame the letter-writers who wanted to strike out at whomever was connected to the SS organization, no matter how remotely. In 1986 I received a letter from a young member of the clergy. I kept the letter for several days as I pondered what I might say in answer to questions that on the surface seemed simple. The letter I wrote to the young clergyman was as follows: 'You ask, Why did you stand for it? Why did you let it happen? Why did you not resist? Why did you not recognize the criminal regime? How could you have not seen through Hitler?'

"My answer was as follows: 'Many of your age have the same concerns. I cannot answer your questions in a way that will satisfy you. Someone who did not experience the time cannot understand it, and someone who has experienced it has difficulty explaining it. The youth of today learn about the Scholl children, about Bonhoffer and Gördeler.[11] But they were so few. How could their voices be heard over the party badges, the songs, the marching and the feeling of being a part of something important? If there were responsible people in the government who opposed Hitler they were invisible to us. One cannot alter the time in which one is born. I have been cursed to live with the collective debt of the many atrocities inflicted on so many by fellow Germans during the Nazi era. When Hitler came to power I was fourteen. Our church minister preached on Sunday mornings and in the afternoon put on his SA uniform. The Hitler Youth was an organization that appealed to boys. We traveled, camped, and played together. It was exciting and challenging, just like the youth groups of today. The older boys and adults didn't have to instruct us in politics. They knew that we would learn to follow a strong leader and we did, and, of course, the leader was Adolf Hitler. I was never a member of the Nazi

Party and none of my comrades were Nazis. We kept our Christian values, became soldiers and fought for our homeland just as did other soldiers in other armies. I believe that assigning guilt to all those who served in the Waffen SS is an overly simplistic view of history. You cannot condemn us all for the actions of those who really were war criminals and murderers. The men I knew in the Waffen SS had the same concern for humanity, justice and compassion for others that you do. We fought hard, but never crossed the line of honorable duty. Please do not judge us all for the actions of some. I know that my words have failed, yet at least I have tried. Let me end by saying that revenge is not the answer. Someone must have the forgiving heart to say, 'It is enough.'"[12]

Bernhard Westerhoff died at his home in Fachingen Lahn on December 17, 2008.

Chapter Notes

Chapter 1

1. Texas A&M University website, http://www.tamu.edu.
2. Charlie Fitts interview with author, Abilene, Texas, May 2005.
3. Nicholas Lee, Kristie Simco, *Chronicle of the 20th Century* (London: Dorling Kindersley, 1995), p. 497.
4. Fitts interview.
5. Texas State Technical College (West Texas) website, http://www.westtexas.tstc.edu.
6. Edward F. Waszak, *Hellcat Historian* (Chicago: Write, 2005) p. 27.
7. George Hatt interview with author, Fort Worth, Texas, May 2005.
8. Hatt interview.
9. Bernhard Westerhoff interview with author, Fachingen, Germany, September 2003.
10. Bernd Wegner, *Hitlers Politische Soldaten: Die Waffen SS 1933–1945* (Munich: Ferdinand Schöning Verlag, 1997), trans. Irmgard Diekmann, p. 127.
11. Westerhoff interview.
12. Gerald Reitlinger, *The SS: Alibi of a Nation, 1922–1945* (Cambridge, MA: Da Capo, 1957), pp. 190, 191.
13. Westerhoff interview.
14. George H. Stein, *The Waffen SS: Hitler's Elite Guard at War* (Ithaca, NY: Cornell University Press, 1966), p. 21.
15. Westerhoff interview.
16. Stein, p. 27.
17. Westerhoff interview.
18. Walter Görlitz, *Der Deutsche Generalstab* (Frankfurt am Main: Der Frankfurter Hefte Verlag, 1954), trans. Irmgard Diekmann, p. 349.
19. Westerhoff interview.

Chapter 2

1. Walter Görlitz, *Der Deutsche Generalstab* (Frankfurt am Main: Der Frankfurter Hefte Verlag, 1954), trans. Irmgard Diekmann, pp. 385, 387, 389, 395, 396.
2. *Ibid.*
3. *Ibid.*
4. *Ibid.*
5. Bernhard Westerhoff interview with author, Fachingen, Germany, September 2003.
6. Ilse Westerhoff interview with author, Fachingen, Germany, September 2003.
7. B. Westerhoff interview.
8. Robert Arrasmith interview with author, Liberty Lake, Washington, June 2005.

Chapter 3

1. Ernst Storch interview with author, Vienna, Austria, April 2006.
2. Bernhard Westerhoff interview with author, Fachingen, Germany, September 2003.
3. Werner Oswald, *Kraftfahrzeuge und Panzer der Reichswehr, Wehrmacht und Bundeswehr ab 1900* (Stuttgart: Motorbuch Verlag, 2004), trans. Irmgard Diekmann, pp. 164, 165. PKW, or PersonenKraftWagen, was the name of a variety of small utility cars used by the Wehrmacht and Waffen SS. One of these was the Kübel, which was the German equivalent of the American jeep.
4. Ilse Westerhoff interview with author, Fachingen, Germany, September 2003.
5. Bernd Wegner, *Hitlers Politische Soldaten: Die Waffen SS 1933–1945* (Munich: Ferdinand Schöning Verlag, 1997), trans. Irmgard Diekmann, p. 58.
6. B. Westerhoff interview.
7. Gordon Williamson, *The SS: Hitler's Instrument of Terror* (St. Paul, MN: Zenith, 1994), p. 39.
8. B. Westerhoff interview.
9. Storch interview.
10. John C. Ferguson, *Hellcats: The 12th Armored Division in World War II* (Abilene, TX: State House, 2004), p. 12.

Chapter 4

1. Nicholas Lee and Kristie Simco, *Chronicle of the 20th Century* (London: Dorling Kindersley, 1995), p. 551.
2. Michael R. Waters, *Lone Star Stalag: German Prisoners of War at Camp Hearne, Texas* (College Station: Texas A&M University Press, 2004), p. 3.
3. Arnold Kramer, *Nazi Prisoners of War in America* (Latham, MD: Scarborough House, 1996), pp. 17, 33, 35, 38, 39.
4. Robert Arrasmith interview with author, Liberty Lake, Washington, June 2005.
5. Bernhard Westerhoff, editor, *Wegeiner Panzer Kompanie 1943–1945, 6 Kompanie SS Panzer Regiment 10, Frundsberg* (unpub-

lished manuscript, 2001), trans. Irmgard Diekmann, p. 12.
6. Bernhard Westerhoff interview with author, Fachingen, Germany, April 2004.
7. Westerhoff, p. 24.
8. Ernst Storch interview with author, Vienna, Austria, April 2006.
9. Storch interview.

Chapter 5

1. Charlie Fitts interview with author, Abilene, Texas, May 2005.
2. George Hatt interview with author, Fort Worth, Texas, May 2005.
3. James Francis, *History of the 23rd Tank Battalion, 12th Armored Division* (Abilene, TX: 12th Armored Division Museum, 2004), p. 3.
4. Hatt interview.
5. Weston Lewis Emery, *C-66: A World War Chronicle of an Armored Infantry Company* (Abilene, TX: 12th Armored Division Museum, 1992), p. 366.
6. Hatt interview.
7. Ferguson, p. 38.
8. Francis, pp. 4, 5.
9. Andrew F. Woods letter to author, December 2006.
10. Fitts interview.
11. Francis, p. 4.
12. Hatt interview.
13. Ferguson, p. 33.
14. Hatt interview.
15. Andrew F. Woods letter to author, November 2007.
16. Bernhard Westerhoff, ed., *Wegeiner Panzer Kompanie 1943–1945, 6 Kompanie SS Panzer Regiment 10, Frundsberg* (unpublished manuscript, 2001), trans. Irmgard Diekmann, p. 36.
17. Wilhelm Tieke, *Im Feuersturm letzter Kriegsjahre*, Osnabrück, Germany: Munin Verlag GMBH, 1975), trans. Irmgard Diekmann, pp. 34, 35.
18. *Ibid.*
19. Gordon Williamson, *The SS: Hitler's Instrument of Terror* (St. Paul, MN: Zenith, 1994), pp. 154, 155.
20. *Ibid.*
21. Tieke, p. 45.
22. Tieke, p. 47.
23. Tieke, p. 57.
24. Westerhoff, p. 39.
25. Nikolaus von Preradovich, *Die Generale der Waffen SS* (Barg am See, Germany: Kurt Vowinckei Verlag, 1985), trans. Irmgard Diekmann, p. 153.
26. Tieke, p. 98.
27. Gerald Reitlinger, *The SS: Alibi of a Nation, 1922–1945* (Cambridge, MA: Da Capo, 1957), p. 86.
28. Williamson, p. 155.
29. Tieke, p. 99.
30. George H. Stein, *The Waffen SS: Hitler's Elite Guard at War* (Ithaca, NY: Cornell University Press, 1966), p. 219.
31. Bernhard Westerhoff interview with author, Fachingen, Germany, April 2004.

Chapter 6

1. John Keegan, *Six Armies in Normandy* (New York: Penguin, 1983), pp. 145, 147.
2. *Ibid.*
3. Bernhard Westerhoff, ed., *Wegeiner Panzer Kompanie 1943–1945, 6 Kompanie SS Panzer Regiment 10, Frundsberg* (unpublished manuscript, 2001), trans. Irmgard Diekmann, p. 39.
4. Gordon Williamson, *The SS: Hitler's Instrument of Terror* (St. Paul, Minn.: Zenith Press, 1994), p. 169, 171.
5. Samuel W. Mitcham, Jr., *Retreat to the Reich* (Mechanicsburg, PA: Stackpole, 2000), p. 23.
6. Wilhelm Tieke, *Im Feuersturm letzter Kriegsjahre* (Osnabrück, Germany: Munin Verlag GMBH, 1975), trans. Irmgard Diekmann, p. 127.
7. Westerhoff, pp. 41, 42.
8. Ernst Storch interview with author, Vienna, Austria, April 2006.
9. Bryant Perrett and Jim Laurier, *Panzerkampfwagen IV, Medium Tank, 1936–1945* (Wellingborough, U.K.: Osprey Military, 1999), p. 18.
10. Tieke, p. 128. Trans. Irmgard Diekmann, Hegemann's words were, "*Wir werden unser eigenes Stösschen machen!*"
11. Tieke, p. 129, and Mitcham, p. 71.
12. Bernhard Westerhoff interview with author, Fachingen, Germany, September 2005.
13. Tieke, p. 205.
14. Tieke, p. 207.
15. Rolf Michaelis, *Die 10. SS-Panzer-Division, "Frundsberg"* (Berlin: Michaelis-Lindlar Verlag, 2004), trans. Irmgard Diekmann, p. 67.
16. Westerhoff, p. 46.
17. Tieke, p. 293.
18. Westerhoff interview.
19. Keegan, p. 253.
20. Williamson, p. 173.
21. Westerhoff interview.

Chapter 7

1. James Francis, *History of the 23rd Tank Battalion, 12th Armored Division* (Abilene, TX: 12th Armored Division Museum, 2004), p. 10.
2. John C. Ferguson, *Hellcats: The 12th Armored Division in World War II* (Abilene, TX: State House, 2004), pp. 47, 48.
3. George Hatt interview with author, Fort Worth, Texas, May 2005.
4. Charlie Fitts interview with author, Abilene, Texas, May 2005.
5. *The 12th Armored Division Association Book* (Paducah, KY: Turner, 1985), p. 52.
6. Andrew F. Woods letter to author, November 2006.
7. Fitts interview.
8. Ferguson, pp. 49, 50.

Chapter 8

1. Ernst Storch interview with author, Vienna, Austria, April 2006.
2. Bernhard Westerhoff interview with author, Fachingen, Germany, September 2005.
3. Gerald Reitlinger, *The SS: Alibi of a Nation, 1922–1945* (Cambridge, MA: Da Capo, 1957), p. 195.
4. Bernd Wegner, *Hitlers Politische Soldaten: Die Waffen SS 1933–1945* (Munich: Ferdinand Schöning Verlag, 1997), pp. 52, 53, 99.
5. Heinz Harmel interview with author, Krefeld, Germany, July 1990. This interview was conducted as preparation for a previous work by the author.

6. Westerhoff interview.
7. George Hatt interview with author, Fort Worth, Texas, May 2005.
8. Charlie Fitts interview with author, Abilene, Texas, May 2005.
9. George Hatt interview.
10. John C. Ferguson, *Hellcats: The 12th Armored Division in World War II* (Abilene, TX: State House, 2004), p. 51.
11. James Francis, *History of the 23rd Tank Battalion, 12th Armored Division* (Abilene, TX: 12th Armored Division Museum, 2004), p. 11.

Chapter 9

1. Bernhard Westerhoff interview with author, Fachingen, Germany, September 2005.
2. Wilhelm Tieke, *Im Feuersturm letzter Kriegsjahre* (Osnabrück, Germany: Munin Verlag GMBH, 1975), trans. Irmgard Diekmann, p. 313.
3. Cornelius Ryan, *A Bridge Too Far* (New York: Simon & Schuster, 1974), pp. 218, 219.
4. Ibid.
5. Herbert Fürbringer, *9. SS Panzer-Division, Hohenstaufen, 1944: Normandie, Tarnopol, Arnhem* (Bayeau, France: Editions Heimdal, 1985), trans. Dennis Denholm, p. 442.
6. Ryan, p. 232.
7. Tieke, p. 315.
8. Ryan, p. 255.
9. Bernhard Westerhoff, ed., *Wegeiner Panzer Kompanie 1943–1945, 6 Kompanie SS Panzer Regiment 10, Frundsberg* (unpublished manuscript, 2001), pp. 51, 52, 53.
10. Ibid.
11. Ryan, p. 271.
12. Tieke, p. 464.
13. Theodor Pietzka, "Die Kämpfen Arnheim," *Die Hellebarde*, Number 22, January, 2003 (Bonn: Kameradschaftsvereinig, W. R. Weber AG), trans. Irmgard Diekmann, p. 135.
14. Rolf Michaelis, *Die 10. SS-Panzer-Division, "Frundsberg"* (Berlin: Michaelis-Lindlar Verlag, 2004), p. 94.
15. Ryan, pp. 468, 469.
16. Ibid.
17. General Sir John Hackett, *I Was a Stranger* (London: Chatto and Windus, 1978), pp. 20, 21, 22.

18. Ryan, p. 291.
19. General Sir John Hackett interview with author, Coberly Mill, England, July 1989. This interview was conducted as preparation for a previous work by author.
20. Westerhoff interview.
21. General Sir John Hackett, p. 9.

Chapter 10

1. George Hatt interview with author, Fort Worth, Texas, May 2005.
2. John C. Ferguson, *Hellcats: The 12th Armored Division in World War II* (Abilene, TX: State House, 2004), p. 52.
3. Hatt interview.
4. Andrew F. Woods letter to the author, November 2006.
5. Michael Green and James D. Brown, *The M4 Sherman at War* (St. Paul, MN: Zenith, 2007), p. 42.
6. James Francis, *History of the 23rd Tank Battalion, 12th Armored Division* (Abilene, TX: 12th Armored Division Museum, 2004), p. 11.
7. Woods letter.
8. Ferguson, p. 55.
9. Charlie Fitts interview with author, Abilene, Texas, May 2005.
10. Napier Crookenden, *Battle of the Bulge, 1944* (New York: Scribner's, 1980), pp. 6, 9.
11. Samuel W. Mitcham, Jr., *Panzers in Winter* (Mechanicsburg, PA: Stackpole, 2000), pp. 35, 43.
12. Ibid.
13. Ibid.
14. Wilhelm Tieke, *Im Feuersturm letzter Kriegsjahre* (Osnabrück, Germany: Munin Verlag GMBH, 1975), trans. Irmgard Diekmann, pp. 394, 395.
15. Ernst Storch interview with author, Vienna, Austria, April 2006, and Bernhard Westerhoff interview with author, Fachingen, Germany, September 2006.
16. Tieke, p. 396.
17. Bernhard Westerhoff interview with author, September 15, 2005.

Chapter 11

1. John C. Ferguson, *Hellcats: The 12th Armored Division in*

World War II (Abilene, TX: State House, 2004), p. 53.
2. James Francis, *History of the 23rd Tank Battalion, 12th Armored Division* (Abilene, TX: 12th Armored Division Museum, 2004), p.12.
3. "Landing-Ship, Tank." Wikipedia, http://en.wikipedia.org/wiki/Landing_ship_tank.
4. George Hatt interview with author, Fort Worth, Texas, May 2005.
5. Francis, p. 13.
6. Ferguson, p. 58.
7. Hatt interview.
8. F. George Hatt, Jr., *Journal of Operations, 17th Armored Infantry Battalion, U.S. 12th Armored Division, 1944–1945* (Abilene, TX: 12th Armored Museum, 2005), p. 3.
9. "History of the Seventh U.S. Army, 15 December 1944 to 25 January 1945," *Army and Navy Journal*, April 7, 1945, reproduced by the 56th Armored Infantry Battalion, 12th Armored Division, Nordingen, p. 9.
10. Andrew F. Woods letter to author, November 2007.
11. Ferguson, p. 57.
12. Charlie Fitts interview with author, May 2005.
13. Ferguson, p. 59.
14. Hatt interview.

Part II Introduction

1. Napier Crookenden, *Battle of the Bulge, 1944* (New York: Scribner's, 1980), pp. 54, 118.
2. Michael and Gladys Green, *Patton and the Battle of the Bulge*, Osceola, WI: MBI, 1999), p. 82.
3. James Francis, *History of the 23rd Tank Battalion, 12th Armored Division* (Abilene, TX: 12th Armored Division Museum, 2004), p. 15.
4. Jeffrey Clarke and R. Smith, *Riviera to the Rhine: United States Army in World War II, European Theater of Operation* (Washington, DC: Government Printing Office, Center for Military History, 1993), p. 52.
5. Richard Engler, *The Final Crisis: Combat in Northern Alsace, January 1945* (Bedford, PA: Aberjona, 1999), pp. 84–87.
6. Ibid.
7. Ibid.

Chapter 12

1. F. George Hatt, Jr., *Journal of Operations, 17th Armored Infantry Battalion, U.S. 12th Armored Division, 1944–1945* (Abilene, TX: 12th Armored Museum, 2005), pp. 3, 7.
2. *Ibid.*
3. George Hatt interview with author, Fort Worth, Texas, May 2005.
4. John C. Ferguson, *Hellcats: The 12th Armored Division in World War II* (Abilene, TX: State House, 2004), p. 60.
5. James Francis, *History of the 23rd Tank Battalion, 12th Armored Division* (Abilene, TX: 12th Armored Division Museum, 2004) p. 19.
6. George Hatt interview with author, Fort Worth, Texas, May 2005.
7. John C. Ferguson, *Hellcats: The 12th Armored Division in World War II* (Abilene, TX: State House, 2004), p. 60.
8. Hatt interview.
9. Hatt, Jr., p. 6.
10. Hatt interview.
11. Francis, pp. 19–20.
12. *Ibid.*
13. Hatt interview.
14. Francis, p. 21.
15. Weston Lewis Emery, *C-66: A World War Chronicle of an Armored Infantry Company* (Abilene, TX: 12th Armored Division Museum, 1992), p. 55.
16. Francis, p. 22.
17. Hatt interview.
18. Charlie Fitts interview with author, Abilene, Texas, May 2005.
19. John A. Nugent, *56th AIB Chronological History* (Washington, DC: Government Printing Office, 12th Armored Division Museum, 1948), p. 41.
20. Robert Arrasmith interview with author, Liberty Lake, Washington, June 2005.
21. Fitts interview.
22. Francis, p. 24.
23. Ernst Storch interview with author, Vienna, Austria, April 2006.
24. Wilhelm Tieke, *Im Feuersturm letzter Kriegsjahre* (Osnabrück, Germany: Munin Verlag GMBH, 1975), trans. Irmgard Diekmann, pp. 420, 421.
25. Rolf Michaelis, *Die 10. SS-Panzer-Division, "Frundsberg"* (Berlin: Michaelis-Lindlar Verlag, 2004), p. 117.
26. Karl Schneider and Bernhard Westerhoff, *Kämpfe im Elsass, January 1945, Weyersheim-Herrlisheim* (unpublished manuscript, 2002), p. 9.
27. Tieke, p. 454.
28. Richard Engler, *The Final Crisis: Combat in Northern Alsace, January 1945* (Bedford PA: Aberjona, 1999), p. 192.
29. Bernhard Westerhoff interview with author, Fachingen, Germany, September 2005.
30. Schneider and Westerhoff, p. 9.
31. Pierre Perny, *Hiver 1944–45 Les Combats de la Libération* (Drusenheim, France: Société d'Histoire et d'Archéologie du Ried Nord, 1990), trans. Dennis Denholm, p. 347.
32. Westerhoff interview. Westerhoff remained friends with Frau Schneider until her death. He visited her in Roeschwoog after the war on three occasions. Frau Schneider's son survived the war. The punishment for misuse of the Waffen SS postal service was severe.

Chapter 13

1. Weston Lewis Emery, *C-66: A World War Chronicle of an Armored Infantry Company* (Abilene, TX: 12th Armored Division Museum, 1992), p. 50.
2. F. George Hatt, Jr., *Journal of Operations, 17th Armored Infantry Battalion, U.S. 12th Armored Division, 1944–1945* (Abilene, TX: 12th Armored Museum, 2005), pp. 7, 12.
3. *Ibid.*
4. George Hatt interview with author, Fort Worth, Texas, May 2005, and Frank Conway interview with author, Greentown, Indiana, February 2006.
5. Hatt interview.
6. "History of the Seventh U.S. Army, 15 December 1944 to 25 January 1945," *Army and Navy Journal, April 7, 1945*, reproduced by the 56th Armored Infantry Battalion, 12th Armored Division, Nordingen, p. 12.
7. Richard Engler, *The Final Crisis: Combat in Northern Alsace, January 1945* (Bedford PA: Aberjona, 1999), pp. 127–129.
8. *Ibid.*
9. Pierre Perny, *Hiver 1944–45 Les Combats de la Libération* (Drusenheim, France, Société d'Histoire et d'Archéologie du Ried Nord, 1990), trans. Dennis Denholm, p. 198.
10. James Francis, *History of the 23rd Tank Battalion, 12th Armored Division* (Abilene, TX: 12th Armored Division Museum, 2004), p. 24.
11. Perny, p. 214.
12. David T. Zabecki and Keith Wooster, "Herrlisheim: Death of an American Combat Command," *World War II Magazine*, January 1999, p. 47.
13. John C. Ferguson, *Hellcats: The 12th Armored Division in World War II* (Abilene, TX: State House, 2004), p. 66.
14. Perny, p. 215.
15. Ferguson, p. 68.
16. Francis, p. 24.
17. Perny, p. 221.
18. Robert Arrasmith interview with author, Liberty Lake, Washington, June 2005.
19. Ferguson, p. 67.
20. Ferguson, p. 69.
21. Zabecki and Wooster, p 48.
22. Arrasmith interview.
23. Ferguson, pp. 70, 71.
24. Perny, p. 231.
25. Arrasmith interview.
26. Perny, p. 233.

Chapter 14

1. Wilhelm Balbach interview with author, Niedernhall, Germany, April 2006, and Wilhelm Balbach unpublished autobiographical paper, June 1947.
2. Wilhelm Tieke, *Im Feuersturm letzter Kriegsjahre* (Osnabrück, Germany: Munin Verlag GMBH, 1975), trans. Irmgard Diekmann, pp. 454, 455.
3. *Ibid.*
4. Balbach interview. The term "wire-puller" is a direct translation of the German *"Zieher,"* parlance for field telephone technician.

Chapter 15

1. Weston Lewis Emery, *C-66: A World War Chronicle of an Armored Infantry Company* (Abi-

lene, TX: 12th Armored Division Museum, 1992), p. 75.

2. Richard Engler, *The Final Crisis: Combat in Northern Alsace, January 1945* (Bedford PA: Aberjona, 1999), p. 139.

3. *12th Armored Divisional History Pertaining to the Action of January 1 through January 20, Weyersheim, France* (Washington, DC, National Archives, 12th Armored Division Museum Archives, 1946), p. 1.

4. Pierre Perny, *Hiver 1944–45 Les Combats de la Libération* (Drusenheim, France, Société d'Histoire et d'Archéologie du Ried Nord, 1990), trans. Dennis Denholm, p. 213.

5. Lise M. Pommois, *Winter Storm: War in Northern Alsace* as quoted in Perny, pp. 341, 322.

6. Richard Engler, *The Final Crisis: Combat in Northern Alsace, January 1945* (Bedford PA: Aberjona, 1999), p.249.

7. Perny, p. 214.

8. John C. Ferguson, *Hellcats: The 12th Armored Division in World War II* (Abilene, TX: State House, 2004), p. 76.

9. Charlie Fitts interview with author, Abilene, Texas, May 2005. Fitts called his winter boots Snow-Pacs. They are referred to by other sources as Snow Shoes.

10. Ferguson, p. 74.

11. Fitts interview.

12. Emery, p. 101.

13. Fitts interview.

14. Emery, pp. 99, 100.

15. Perny, p. 293, 294.

16. Fitts interview.

17. Emery, p. 102.

Chapter 16

1. James Francis, *History of the 23rd Tank Battalion, 12th Armored Division* (Abilene, TX: 12th Armored Division Museum, 2004), p. 27.

2. Andrew F. Woods, autobiographical paper titled *Personal Wartime History, 1945*, April 1946. pp. 6, 7.

3. George Hatt interview with author, Fort Worth, Texas, May 2005.

4. F. George Hatt, Jr., *Journal of Operations, 17th Armored Infantry Battalion, U.S. 12th Armored Division, 1944–1945* (Abilene, TX: 12th Armored Division Museum, 2005), pp. 15–18.

5. Andrew F. Woods letter to author, July 2006.

6. F. George Hatt, Jr., *My Herrlisheim Story with the US 12th AD, 17th AIB, A Company, 3rd Platoon* (unpublished autobiographical war journal, January 1947).

7. Wilhelm Balbach interview with author, Niedernhall, Germany, April 2006.

8. Hatt, Jr., pp. 19, 20.

9. Woods, p. 8.

10. Richard Engler, *The Final Crisis: Combat in Northern Alsace, January 1945* (Bedford, PA: Aberjona, 1999), pp. 232, 230.

11. *Ibid.*

12. *Ibid.*

13. Karl Schneider and Bernhard Westerhoff, *Kämpfe im Elsass, January 1945, Weyersheim Herrlisheim* (unpublished manuscript, 2002), p. 44.

14. Bernhard Westerhoff interview with author, Fachingen, Germany, September 2005.

15. Engler, p. 235.

16. Westerhoff interview.

17. Wilhelm Balbach interview with author, Niedernhall, Germany, April 2006.

18. Westerhoff interview.

19. Pierre Perny, *Hiver 1944–45 Les Combats de la Libération* (Drusenheim, France, Société d'Histoire et d'Archéologie du Ried Nord, 1990), trans. Dennis Denholm, p. 348.

20. Westerhoff interview.

Chapter 17

1. James Francis, *History of the 23rd Tank Battalion, 12th Armored Division* (Abilene, TX: 12th Armored Division Museum, 2004), p. 27.

2. Richard Engler, *The Final Crisis: Combat in Northern Alsace, January 1945* (Bedford, PA: Aberjona, 1999), p. 259.

3. William Funke letters to author, July and August 2006.

4. Engler, p. 262.

5. F. George Hatt, Jr., *My Herrlisheim Story with the US 12th AD, 17th AIB, A Company, 3rd Platoon* (unpublished autobiographical war journal, January 1947), pp. 7–13.

6. Francis, pp. 31, 32.

7. "Appendix to 12th Armored Division History," *Post Action Report, January 17, 1945*, compiled February 1945, reproduced by 12th Armored Division (Abilene, TX: 12th Armored Division Museum Archives), p. 42.

8. Fernand Zilliox interview with author, Herrlisheim, France, interpreted by Stephanie and Eric Zilliox, April 2006.

9. William Funke letter to author, August 2006.

10. *12th Armored Divisional History Pertaining to the Action of January 1 through January 20, Weyersheim, France* (Abilene, TX: 12th Armored Division Museum Archives, 1946), p. 4.

11. John C. Ferguson, *Hellcats: The 12th Armored Division in World War II* (Abilene, TX: State House, 2004), p. 76.

12. *History of the 12th Armored Division* (Paducah, KY: Turner, 1988), p. 77.

13. Pierre Perny, *Hiver 1944–45 Les Combats de la Libération* (Drusenheim, France, Société d'Histoire et d'Archéologie du Ried Nord, 1990), trans. Dennis Denholm, p. 315.

14. *History of the 12th Armored Division* (Paducah, KY: Turner, 1988), p. 6.

15. Hatt, Jr., pp. 7–18.

16. Andrew F. Woods letter to author, January 2006.

17. Hatt, Jr., pp. 14, 15.

18. David T. Zabecki and Keith Wooster, "Herrlisheim: Death of an American Combat Command," *World War II Magazine*, January 1999, p. 51.

19. Erwin Bachmann interview with author, Göttingen, Germany, March 2005, shorthand notes taken by Irmgard Diekmann and translated by her, and Erwin Bachmann biographical paper, 1947.

20. Engler, p. 260.

21. Hatt interview.

22. Funke letter, August 2006.

23. F. George Hatt, Jr., *Journal of Operations, 17th Armored Infantry Battalion, U.S. 12th Armored Division, 1944–1945* (Abilene, TX: 12th Armored Museum, 2005), p. 16.

24. Lt. Col. Cecil R. Hill, Inspector General for 12th Armored Division, *12th Armored Division Investigative Report of February 1,*

1945 Pertaining to Actions of Units in Combat on January 17 and 18, 1945 (Abilene, TX: 12th Armored Division Museum Archives), pp. 21–23, 25–27, 47.
25. Ibid.
26. Ibid.
27. William Funke letter to author, November 2006.
28. Hatt interview.
29. William Funke letter and Zilliox interview.
30. Andrew F. Woods, autobiographical paper, 1947, p. 7.
31. Hill, Wells testimony, p. 14.
32. Hill, Lee testimony p. 17.
33. Hill, Mowat testimony, p. 18.
34. Hill, Lardin testimony, p. 33.
35. Hill, Conclusions, p. 42.

Chapter 18

1. Wilhelm Tieke, *Im Feuersturm letzter Kriegsjahre* (Osnabrück, Germany: Munin Verlag GMBH, 1975), trans. Irmgard Diekmann, p. 458.
2. Wilhelm Balbach, "Herrlisheim," *Die Hellebarde*, Vol. 12, January 1978, pp. 32–35, and interview with author, Niedernhall, Germany, April 2006.
3. Karl Schneider and Bernhard Westerhoff, *Kämpfe im Elsass, January 1945, Weyersheim Herrlisheim* (unpublished manuscript, 2002), p. 27.
4. Bernhard Westerhoff interview with author, Fachingen, Germany, September 2005.
5. F. George Hatt, Jr., *Journal of Operations, 17th Armored Infantry Battalion, U.S. 12th Armored Division, 1944–1945* (Abilene, TX: 12th Armored Museum, 2005), p. 17.
6. Fernand Zilliox interview with author, interpreted by Eric and Stephanie Zilloix, Herrlisheim, France, April 2006.
7. Eric Zilliox, *Family History*, personal journal of the Zilliox family, Herrlisheim, France, transmitted by email, July 2006.
8. Hatt, Jr., pp. 18, 19.
9. James Francis, *History of the 23rd Tank Battalion, 12th Armored Division* (Abilene, TX: 12th Armored Division Museum, 2004), pp. 36–37.
10. Andrew F. Woods, autobiographical paper titled *Personal Wartime History, 1945*, and Frank Conway interview with author, Greentown, Indiana, May 2006.
11. Francis, p. 38.

Chapter 19

1. Andrew F. Woods autobiographical paper titled *Personal Wartime History, 1945*, and Frank Conway interview with author, Greentown, Indiana, February 2006. The descriptions of the Guitteau and Vickless action of January 19 correspond with two German accounts, those of Bernhard Westerhoff and Ernst Storch, both in the Quandel-led 6th Company. Gunner Frank Conway had entered the Army in January 1943. After basic training he was assigned to the 23rd Tank Battalion at Camp Campbell in Kentucky. He later became a tank commander and served until six months after the war's end.
2. Ernst Storch interview with author, Vienna, Austria, April 2006.
3. Pierre Perny, *Hiver 1944–45 Les Combats de la Libération* (Drusenheim, France, Société d'Histoire et d'Archéologie du Ried Nord, 1990), trans. Dennis Denholm, p. 330.
4. Rolf Michaelis, *Die 10. SS-Panzer-Division, "Frundsberg"* (Berlin: Michaelis-Lindlar Verlag, 2004), p. 114.
5. Wilhelm Balbach, "Wacht auf dem Zorn," Schneider and Westerhoff, *Kämpfe im Elsass, January 1945, Weyersheim Herrlisheim* (unpublished manuscript, 2002), p. 24, and Wilhelm Balbach interview with author, Niedernhall, Germany, April 2006.
6. Schneider and Westerhoff, p. 18.
7. Bernhard Westerhoff interview with author, Fachingen, Germany, September 2005.
8. Andy Woods letter to author of March 2007 and amplifying description by telephone.
9. Storch interview.
10. Conway interview.
11. Storch interview.
12. Conway interview.
13. Westerhoff interview.
14. Storch interview.
15. Perny, p. 364.
16. Westerhoff interview.
17. John C. Ferguson, *Hellcats: The 12th Armored Division in World War II* (Abilene, TX: State House, 2004), p. 77.
18. Balbach interview.
19. Kurt Rademacher, "21st Panzergrenadier Regiment," Schneider and Westerhoff, *Kämpfe im Elsass, January 1945, Weyersheim Herrlisheim* (unpublished manuscript, 2002), trans. Irmgard Diekmann, p. 21.
20. Fritz Richter, "Angriff auf Weyersheim," *Die Hellebarde*, Vol. 12, January 1978, trans. Irmgard Diekmann, pp. 29–31.
21. Ferguson, p. 76.
22. Richard Engler, *The Final Crisis: Combat in Northern Alsace, January 1945* (Bedford, PA: Aberjona, 1999), p. 264.
23. Andrew F. Woods letter to author, August 2007.
24. On February 12, 1945, general order number eighteen issued by the 12th Armored Division by authority of the president and provisions of AR 600-45 of September 22, 1943, awarded Staff Sergeant Edward P. Vickless the Silver Star Medal. The award reads, in part, "For gallantry in action in the vicinity of Weyersheim, France. In an attack by Company C, Vickless' section accounted for ten of the twenty-five enemy tanks that confronted the company. Later the same day, Vickless' two tanks (the other commanded by Kenneth Detrick) were acting as an outpost when an enemy attack was launched. Vickless directed the fire of his two tanks so effectively that approximately a company of enemy was killed and the attack was repulsed…. Vickless' courage, persistence and leadership ability exemplify the highest traditions of the Army of the United States." The action referring to the destruction of tanks took place on January 19, 1945, southeast of Kurtzenhouse. The action described as killing a company of enemy infantry took place east of Weyersheim in the early morning hours of January 20, 1945. Edward P. Vickless received a battlefield commission, being promoted to second lieutenant as reward for his leadership. (See Note 8 to Chapter 26.)
25. Westerhoff interview.

Part III Introduction

1. Rolf Michaelis, *Die 10. SS-Panzer-Division, "Frundsberg"* (Berlin, Germany: Michaelis-Lindlar Verlag, 2004), trans. Irmgard Diekmann, p. 117.
2. *Ibid.*
3. Weston Lewis Emery, *C-66: A World War Chronicle of an Armored Infantry Company* (Abilene, TX: 12th Armored Division Museum, 1992), pp. 223, 230, 242.
4. *Ibid.*
5. *Ibid.*
6. John C. Ferguson, *Hellcats: The 12th Armored Division in World War II* (Abilene, TX: State House, 2004), pp. 82, 99.
7. *Ibid.*
8. F. George Hatt, Jr., *Journal of Operations, 17th Armored Infantry Battalion, U.S. 12th Armored Division, 1944–1945* (Abilene, TX: 12th Armored Museum, 2005), p. 41.
9. Michaelis, p. 119.
10. Wilhelm Tieke, *Im Feuersturm letzter Kriegsjahre* (Osnabrück, Germany: Munin Verlag GMBH, 1975), trans. Irmgard Diekmann, pp. 523, 529.
11. Michaelis, pp. 132–139.
12. *Ibid.*
13. *Ibid.*
14. *Ibid.*
15. Hatt, p. 41.
16. Ferguson, p. 102.
17. Hatt, p. 48.
18. James Francis, *History of the 23rd Tank Battalion, 12th Armored Division* (Abilene, TX: 12th Armored Division Museum, 2004), p. 72.
19. Emery, p. 320.
20. Michaelis, p. 119.
21. Tieke, p. 543.
22. Hatt, p. 23.
23. Ferguson, p. 108.
24. George Hatt interview with author, Fort Worth, Texas, August 2006.

Chapter 20

1. Richard Engler, *The Final Crisis: Combat in Northern Alsace, January 1945* (Bedford PA: Aberjona, 1999), pp. 276, 277, 285.
2. *Ibid.*
3. *Ibid.*
4. Pierre Perny, *Hiver 1944–45 Les Combats de la Libération* (Drusenheim, France, Société d'Histoire et d'Archéologie du Ried Nord, 1990), trans. Dennis Denholm, p. 301.
5. Engler, p. 286.
6. Wilhelm Balbach interview with author, Niedernhall, April 2006.
7. F. George Hatt, Jr., *Journal of Operations, 17th Armored Infantry Battalion, U.S. 12th Armored Division, 1944–1945* (Abilene, TX: 12th Armored Museum, 2005), pp. 28–31.
8. Andrew F. Woods letter to author, August 2007, and Woods' 1946 autobiographical paper titled "The Day Pete Vickless Died."
9. Robert Arrasmith interview with author, Liberty Lake, Washington, June 2005.
10. Louis P. Lochner, "U.S. Officer Makes Germans View Horror Scene," *The Hellcats, 12th Armored Division Association* (Paducah, KY: Turner, 1986), p. 115, 116.
11. *Ibid.*
12. John C. Ferguson, *Hellcats: The 12th Armored Division in World War II* (Abilene, TX: State House, 2004), p. 105.
13. Robert Arrasmith interview with author, Liberty Lake, Washington, June 2005.
14. Heinz Harmel interview with author, Krefeld, Germany, September 1991. Interview conducted for previous work of author.
15. Arrasmith interview and Lipmann Kessel, *Surgeon at Arms* (London: Sidgwick and Jackson, 1965). Dr. Kessel had been taken from St. Elizabeth Hospital in Arnhem and transported to the former Dutch barracks at Apeldoorn. The barracks were being used as a prisoner-of-war camp for the many British and Americans who had surrendered during Operation Market Garden. He and several other officers escaped from the barracks and were able to get back to England with the help of the Dutch underground. Upon his return, Dr. Kessel resumed his duties as a surgeon.

Chapter 21

1. Weston Lewis Emery, *C-66: A World War Chronicle of an Armored Infantry Company* (Abilene, TX: 12th Armored Division Museum, 1992), p. 377.
2. Charlie Fitts interview with author, Abilene, Texas, May 2005
3. Emery, p. 369.
4. Edward F. Waszak, *Hellcat Historian* (Chicago: Write, 2005), p. 111.
5. Emery, p. 370.
6. Fitts interview.
7. Emery, pp. 397, 398.
8. Emery, p. 369.
9. Fitts interview.
10. Ernst Storch interview with author, Vienna, Austria, April 2006. During this interview Mr. Storch telephoned Erwin Bachmann in Göttingen, Germany. They spoke for only a few minutes, but Bachmann remembered some details about the trip to Berlin. Irmgard Diekmann interpreted.
11. Andrew F. Woods letter to author, November 2006.
12. George Hatt letter to author, February 2007. Lieutenant Yarborough survived the wound he suffered on that day. He returned to his home in Texas after the war, and he and George Hatt remained friends.
13. Andrew F. Woods' autobiographical war journal and three amplifying letters to author, March and April 2007.
14. Ernst Storch interview with author, Vienna, Austria, September 2007.

Chapter 22

1. Edward F. Waszak, *Hellcat Historian* (Chicago: Write, 2005), pp. 92, 93.
2. George Hatt, interview with author, Fort Worth, Texas, August 2006.
3. Spencer Dumont, "V-E Day for the 12th," *Abilene Reporter-News*, May 8, 2006.
4. George Hatt, "Response to Dumont Article," *Abilene Reporter-News*, May 15, 2006.
5. Hatt interview.
6. John C. Ferguson, *Hellcats: The 12th Armored Division in World War II* (Abilene, TX: State House, 2004), p. 106.
7. Wilhelm Balbach interview with author, Niedernhall, Germany, April 2006.
8. Jean Arrasmith interview

with author, Liberty Lake, Washington, June 2005.

9. Charlie Fitts interview with author, Abilene, Texas, May 2005.

10. Ernst Storch interview author, Vienna, Austria, April 2006.

11. Maria and Hans Scholl were university students in Munich during the 1930s and became activists in student discussion groups where the evils of the Nazi government were described. The two youngsters wrote pamphlets decrying the war, saying, "The eyes of even the most stupid Germans, these eyes have been opened by the terrible blood bath in which Hitler and his confederates are trying to drown all Europe in the name of freedom of the German nation." The Gestapo confiscated the printing press, arrested the youths, and sentenced them to concentration camps where they subsequently died. Carl F. Goerdeler was a nationally known economist and mayor of Leipzig during the 1930s. When Hitler came to power he supported the Nazi government while never actually joining the NSDAP. During the course of the Third Reich's early years Goerdeler provided economic advice to Hitler and met with him on several occasions. For various reasons he became disillusioned with the government and ran afoul of Goering, who worked against him. After losing his position as mayor, he conspired with Generals Beck, Halder and Brauchitsch as well as Admiral Canaris to overthrow the government. By 1943 he was an integral part of the plan to assassinate Hitler. When the July 20, 1944, plot failed he was arrested on August 12, 1944, tried and found guilty of treason. He was executed by hanging on February 2, 1945, at the Ploezensee Prison. Dietrich Bonhoeffer was a recognized theologian and a lecturer at the University of Berlin. When Hitler became dictator of Germany Bonhoeffer denounced him in a radio broadcast. He saw no compromise between Christianity and Nazi ideals. He spent some time abroad, but returning to Germany continued to denounce the government. He was the leader of a group of Christian intellectuals who met regularly and plotted against the government. The Gestapo gathered some evidence, put him on trial where in 1943 he was sentenced to the Tegel Military Prison. While in prison the aborted July 20, 1944, plot involved his name. He was subsequently tried for treason, found guilty and was executed on April 8, 1945.

12. Bernhard Westerhoff interview with author, Fachingen, Germany, September 2005, and Westerhoff's letter of June 1986.

Bibliography

Arrasmith, Robert, and wife, Jean. Personal interview, Liberty Lake, Washington, June 2005.

Bachmann, Erwin. *Elsass Erlebnisbericht: Ich Habe 12 Sherman Erbeutet.* Bayeau, France: Editions-Heimdal, 1947.

———. Personal interview, Göttingen, Germany, March 2005.

Bacque, James. *Other Losses.* Toronto: Stoddart, 1989.

Balbach, Wilhelm. "Elsasseinsatz," unpublished manuscript, 1986.

———. Personal interview, Niedernhall, Germany, April 2006.

Beschloss, Michael. *The Conquerors.* New York: Simon & Schuster, 2002.

Bradstreet, Ken. *Hellcats, 12th Armored Division Association.* Paducah, KY: Turner, 1987.

Clifton, Daniel, ed. *Chronicle of the Twentieth Century.* London: Dorling-Kindersley, 1995.

Conway, Frank. Personal interview, Greentown, Indiana, February 2006.

Cooper, Belton Y. *Death Traps.* New York: Random House, 1998.

Cunningham, John W. *Division Operations in France, Combat Highlights, 12th Armored Division.* Abilene, TX: 12th Armored Division Museum, 1945.

———. *Journal of Operations, 17th Armored Infantry Battalion, 12th Armored Division.* Washington, DC: U.S. Government Printing Office, 1945.

Elson, Robert T. *Prelude to War.* Alexandria, VA: Time-Life, 1965.

Emory, Weston Lewis. *C-66: A World War II Chronicle of an Armored Infantry Battalion.* Abilene, TX: 12th Armored Division Museum, 1992.

Engler, Richard. *The Final Crisis: Combat in Northern Alsace.* Bedford, PA: Aberjona, 1999.

Ferguson, John C. *Hellcats: The 12th Armored Division in World War II.* Abilene, TX: State House, 2004.

Fitts, Charlie. Personal interviews, Abilene, Texas, May 2005, and Jackson, Mississippi, September 2007.

Francis, James. *A History of the 23rd Tank Battalion.* Abilene, TX: 12th Armored Division Museum, 2004.

Funke, William. Telephone interviews and letters, July-August 2006.

Fürbringer, Herbert. *The 9th Waffen SS Panzer Division, Hohenstaufen.* Bayeau, France: Editions-Heimdal, 1985.

Görlitz, Walter. *The German General Staff.* New York: Praeger, 1953.

Hall, Scott W. *Unit History from December 1944 to May 1945 of the 43rd Tank Battalion, 12th Armored Division.* Abilene, TX: 12th Armored Division Museum, 1949.

Harmel, Heinz, personal interview, Krefeld, Germany, July 1990.

Hastings, Max. *Das Reich: Second Waffen SS Panzer Division.* New York: Holt, Rinehart and Winston, 1981.

Hatt, George, Jr. Personal interviews, Abilene, Texas, and Fort Worth, Texas, May 2005.

———. "17th Armored Infantry Battalion Historical Information." Abilene, TX: Abilene Christian University Press, 1998.

Die Hellebarde, Nachrichten der Kameradschaftsvereinig. Suchdienst Frundsberg, Cologne, Germany: W. R. Weber Verlag. Published semi-annually since 1983 and distributed to Frundsberg veterans who subscribe to it.

Keegan, John. *Six Armies in Normandy.* London: Jonathan Cape, 1982.

Kessel, Lippman. *Surgeon at Arms.* London: Sidgwick and Jackson, 1968.

Krammer, Arnold. *Nazi Prisoners of War in America.* Lanham, MD: Scarborough, 1996.

Leleu, Jean-Luc. *The 10th SS Panzer Division "Frundsberg."* Bayeau, France: Editions-Heimdal, 1985.

Lucas, James. *Das Reich.* London: Cassell, 1991.

Michaelis, Rolf. *10th SS Panzer Division "Frundsberg."* Berlin: Michaelis Verlag, 2004.

Miller, David. *Tanks of the World.* Osceola, WI: MBI, 2000.

Mitcham, Samuel W., Jr. *Retreat to the Reich.* Mechanicsburg, PA: Stackpole, 1997.

Oswald, Werner. *Kraftfahrzeuge und Panzer, ab 1900.* Stuttgart: Motorbuch Verlag, 2004.

Perny, Pierre. *Hiver 1944–45: Les Combats de la*

Libération. Drusenheim, France: Société d'Histoire et d'Archéologie du Ried Nord, 1990.
Perrell, Byron, and Jim Laurier. *Panzerkampfwagen IV Medium Tank, 1936–1945*. London: Osprey, 1999.
Phibbs, Brendan. *The Other Side of Time*. Boston, MA: Little, Brown, 1987.
Pommois, Lise M. *Winter Storm: War in Northern Alsace*., Paducah, KY: Turner, 1991.
Preradovich, Nikolaus von. *Die Generale der Waffen SS*. Berg am See, Germany: Kurt Vowinckel Verlag, 1985.
Reiteninger, Gerold. *The SS: Alibi of a Nation*. New York: Viking Penguin, 1957.
Ryan, Cornelius. *A Bridge Too Far*. New York: Simon & Schuster, 1957.
_____. *The Longest Day*. New York: Simon & Schuster, 1959.
Shirer, William L. *Berlin Diary*. New York: Alfred A. Knopf, 1941.
_____. *The Rise and Fall of the Third Reich*. New York: Simon & Schuster, 1959.
Stein, George H. *The Waffen SS: Hitler's Elite Guard at War*. Ithaca, NY: Cornell University Press, 1966.
Storch, Ernst. Personal interviews, Vienna, Austria, April 2006, and September 2007.
Suemondt, Jan. *Wehrmacht Fahrzeuge*. Stuttgart: Motorbuch Verlag, 2004.
Tieke, Wilhelm. *Im Feuersturm Letzter Kriegsjahre, II SS Panzerkorps mit 9. und 10. SS Division*. Osnabruech, Germany: Munin Verlag, 1981.
Turner, John F., and Robert Jackson. *Destination Berchtesgaden*. New York: Scribner's, 1975.
Voltzenlogel, Joseph M. *Berichausüge über die Kämpfe in Herrlisheim und Umgebung in Rahman der Operation Nordwind*. Drusenheim, France: Société d'Histoire et d'Archéologie du Ried Nord, 1990.
Waszak, Edward F. *Hellcat Historian*. Chicago: Write, 2006.
Waters, Michael R. *Lone Star Stalag: German Prisoners of War at Camp Hearne*. College Station: Texas A&M University Press, 2004.
Wegner, Bernd. *Hitlers Politische Soldaten: Die Waffen SS, 1933–1945*. Munich: Schöning, 2008.
Westerhoff, Bernard. "Kämpfen in Elsass," unpublished manuscript, trans. Irmgard Diekmann.
_____. Personal interviews, Fachingen, Germany, September 2003, April 2004, September 2005 and September 2006.
_____. "Wegeiner Panzer Kompanie 1943–1945, 6 Kompanie SS Panzer Regiment 10, Frundsberg," unpublished manuscript, trans. Irmgard Diekmann.
Whiting, Charles. *The Second Battle of the Bulge*. Lanham, MD: Scarborough, 1990.
Williamson, Gordon. *The SS: Hitler's Instrument of Terror*. St. Paul, MN: MBI, 1994.
Woods, Andrew, letters to author with amplifying telephone interviews, January 2006, July 2006, November 2006, December 2006, March 2007, April 2007 and November 2007.
Zabecki, David, and Keith Wooster. "Death of a Combat Command." *World War II Magazine*, January 1999.
Zilliox, Fernand. Extracts from family history.
_____ and family (Charles, Fernand, Ivette, Jean-Marc, Stephanie and Eric). Personal interview, Herrlisheim, France, April 2006.

Index

Abilene 31, 35
Adlon Hotel 189
Afrika Korps 24
Allen, Maj. Gen. Roderick R. 46, 65, 115
Altdammer 172
Althausen 179
Althusheim 108–111
Andover 54, 59
Argantan 42
Arnhem 49, 56, 57
Arrasmith, Pfc. Robert 17–20, 25, 26, 45, 85, 86, 96–106, 182–184, 197
ASTP 8, 10, 30, 31, 35, 36, 187
Auenheim 128
Auffay 65, 66, 67
Aunay sur Odon 42
Avon River 61

Bachmann, Lt. Erwin 136, 141–143, 188, 189, 196
Bad Saarow 56
Bailey Bridge 128, 130
Balbach, Pfc. Wilhelm 107, 125, 152, 153, 160–165, 176–178, 196
Baton Rouge 35
Beach, Capt. 97
Bec Hellouin 11, 29
Bendler Strasse 50
Benestroff 87
Berger, Sgt. Heinz 142–144
Berlin 21, 22, 50, 56, 171, 188–191
Bettviller 83, 91
Bining 69–71, 78, 84, 91, 93
Bischweiler 95, 97, 176
Bittrich, Gen. Willi 55–57
Blackford, Capt. Eugene A. 145
Bochman, Georg 38
Bocholt 52
Bradley, Gen. Omar 75
Braun Haus 12
Brewer, Maj. Gen. Carlos 23, 32, 35
La Breymuhl 95, 97–101, 104, 127, 129–131, 167
British 1st Airborne Division 56, 57

Bromley, Maj. Gen. Charles V. 23, 32, 35
Bruchwald 157, 159, 163
Brumath 151, 160
Buchen 179
Buczacz 36, 38
Buehl 87, 107
Burgau 173

Caen 39
Calvados 43
Cambrai 44
Cameron, Col. Douglas 174
Camp Barkeley 31–36, 39, 45, 46, 60, 69, 85
Camp Campbell 23
Camp Chaffee 24
Camp Polk 35
Camp Robinson 24
Camp Shanks 24, 36, 45, 46
Caplinger, James M. 124, 126
Capretta, Harold Cpl. 54, 94, 122, 125, 127, 131, 132, 138, 139, 144, 196
Château de Bosmelet 66
Châteauneuf 39
Cherbourg 35
Collier, Pfc. Raymond 94, 124
Colmar 171, 178, 182
Cologne 63
Comfort, Maj. William R. 145
Conway, Cpl. Frank 90–92, 157–159, 163, 180, 182, 190
Costlow, Lt. Owsley 134
Cox, George 123, 139, 140
Crosby, Bing 9
Cunningham, Maj. John 145

Dachau, Camp #4 182
Daladier, Eduard 196
Dalhunden 128
Damnischer See 172
Danube River 173
Davis, Susan 197
Debes, Gen. Lothar 26
Denelsheim 128
Derivation Canal 105, 106
Das Deutschland Regiment 15, 37

Devers, Lt. Gen. Jacob L. 94
Dietrick, Sgt. Kenneth 79, 91, 92, 157–159, 162–166, 190
Dietz 63
Digny 39
Dillingen 173
Dnjestr River 36
Doetinchen 55, 56
Dölitz 172
Dorchester 65
Dressler, Brad 121, 182
Dreuy 39
Drost, Sgt. George 146, 148, 149, 150
Drum, Lt. Marvin R. 196
Drusenheim 94, 97, 100, 116, 127, 128, 150, 160, 164, 167
Dubois, Cpl. Frenchy 123, 139
Duelman 63
Düsseldorf 63

Edwards, Maj. William A. 146
Eifel 62, 87
82nd Airborne Division 56, 57
Eisenhower, Gen. Dwight D. 75
Elbe River 191, 197
Elbeuf 44
Elten 52
Empress of Australia 48, 52–54, 59, 94
Ennis, Gen. Riley P. 45, 116, 131, 155
L'Épine Orbière 42
Epsom (operation) 39
Erhard, Edmund 26
Erkelenz 62
Eterville-Maltot 40
Évrecy-Bach 40
Eyweiler 83, 84

Fachingen 49, 198
Fallingbostel 22, 23
56th Armored Infantry Battalion 31, 95, 96, 101, 102
1st Panzer Army 36
Fitts, Pfc. Charlie 8, 9, 30, 33, 34, 45, 46, 52, 53, 61, 67, 85, 86, 91, 115–119

Fitts, Harriett Elisabeth 197
553rd Volksgrenadier Division 76, 95, 112, 115, 131, 133, 143
Flemming, Pfc. William 157, 159
Forbach 171
Fort McClellan 8, 30
Fort McPherson 197
Fort Ord 24
Fort Smith 196
43rd Tank Battalion 31, 78, 115, 116, 121, 122, 126, 135, 143, 144, 145
Francis, Pfc. James 31, 33, 65, 78, 158
Franke, Lt. Leopold 26, 27
Freistett 87, 107, 110
Frost, Lt. Col. John 57, 58
Frundsberg Division 11, 14, 23, 27, 28, 38–42, 55, 87, 146, 148, 172, 176, 188
Der Führer Regiment 37
Funke, Pfc. William 31, 145

Gambos, Capt. Steven M. 91
Gambsheim 76, 87, 95, 96, 112, 115, 116, 120, 125, 131, 132
Garand, M-1 Rifle 25, 33, 80, 148
Garneau, 1st Lt. Ernest 82, 134, 139
Gestapo 13, 51
Geudertheim 122, 147, 150, 160
Goebbels, Josef 88, 90, 189
Gölitz 174
Gollnow 172
Göring, Hermann W. 195
Gries 195
Groningen 196
Groth, Günther 164
Grover, Pfc. Robert 157, 180–182
Guitteau, 1st Lt. Wayne 78, 79, 121, 123, 127, 134, 139, 157–159, 162, 163, 166, 179

Hackett, Brig. John 57, 58
Hafsloch 179
Haguenau 176
Haguenau Forest 88
Halberstadt 38
Halicz 36
Hamburg 37
Harmel, Maj. Gen. Heinz 37, 39, 43, 56, 50, 51, 57, 62, 63, 88, 112, 113, 152, 166, 171, 174, 183, 184, 188
Hartzer, Col. Walter 56
Hatt, Pfc. George 9–11, 31–35, 45, 52–54, 59, 65, 66, 69, 78–81, 83, 84, 92, 93, 122–127, 131–133, 140–141, 144–146, 155, 190, 195
Hatten 76
Hausser, Gen. Paul 23
Hayna 89
Hayner, Capt. Robert 47, 48, 91
Heatter, Gabriel 9
Heelsum 55
Hegemann, Lt. Theo 40–42

Heidenheim 174, 183
Hellcat News 32
Helm, Pfc. Willi 27
Helton, Capt. Carl J. 91, 133
Henderloo 52
Hermann, Günther 164
Hernberchtheim 172
Herrlisheim 77, 95, 98, 100, 103–106, 112, 116, 121, 127, 132, 135–151, 152, 155, 171, 179, 196
Hexheim 89
Hicks, Brig. Pip 56
Hildesheim 188
Hiltenfinger 173
Himmler, SS R.F. Heinrich 11, 50, 88
Hitler, Adolf 12, 18, 22, 36, 38, 39, 61, 62, 76, 174, 183, 189, 190, 198
Hochfelden 95
Hoerdt 116, 117, 161, 165, 166, 174
Hoeweller, Robert 120
Hofchen 179
Höling 83
Hölscher Regiment 115
Hönstaufen Division 39, 40, 56, 87
Horcher, Ludwig 176–178
Houghton, Sgt. William 84
Howard, Kathy 197
Hungerford 59

Iggelheim 179
Inswiller 93
Irlenbusch 87

Jelna-Bogen 16
Jenkel, Pvt. Heinz 177, 178
Jensen, Jack 94
Jodl, Gen. Alfred 36, 63
Jüttner, Maj. Gen. Hans 56

Kaltenhouse 176
Kampfgruppe Euling 57
Kampfgruppe Reinhold 57
Karlsruhe 196
Keitel, Gen. Wilhelm 62
Kessel, Dr. Lipmann 184
King, Adm. Ernest J. 194
Klagenfurt 174
Kleingraben Canal 119
Klingenberg, Fritz 38
Klinkmann, Capt. 37
Knappe, Cpl. Reinhard 162, 163, 164
Königshofen 173, 182, 190
Korherr, Dr. Richard 50
Kramer, Lt. James 91
Krass, Hugo 38
Krebs, Lt. Gen. Hans 55
Krefeld 62
Krölls, Cpl. Ludwig 40
Kulm, Otto 38
Kurtzenhouse 96, 157–159

Landau 89
Landgraben Canal 94, 95, 125

Landsberg 174, 183
Lardin, Lt. Col. Harry E. 150
Lathbury, Brig. W. 56, 94, 95
Lazzari, Sgt. Nello 84, 86
Lee, 1st Lt. John C. 150
Le Havre 65, 67
Leibstandarte 12, 21, 53, 189
Le Madeleine 39
Le Mage 39
Lemberg 36
Limburgerhof 88
Linnich 62
Linz 62, 87
Little, William 94
Liverpool 54, 59
Lochem 52, 56
Logan, Maj. James W. 91, 131, 134, 135, 145, 146, 150
Loire River 39
London 61
Longny 39
Lubbock 9
Ludwigshafen 88, 172
Luneville 66, 78
Lüttichau, Lt. Col. Charles 105, 115

Maas River 56
Maginot Line 78
Main River 173
Maltot 34, 41
Marbach Regiment 115
Mariluch, Pfc. Adrian 94, 125–127, 194, 196
USS *Marine Raven* 48
Marshall, Gen. George C. 66
Matheny, Pfc. Dale 117, 120
McElwee, Jacquelyn 196
Meigs, Lt. Col. M.C. 123
Meurth-et-Moselle 66
Miles, Pfc. Robert 190
Minsk 16
Model, FM Walter 55, 57
Moder River 96, 97, 129, 130, 176
Mont Ormel 43
Montgomery, FM Bernard 35, 39
Moos 185
Müller, Irmgard 37
Müller, Pfc. Jens 112, 113, 155, 156
Mülradt, Sgt. Hans 142, 143
Murnau 174
Muska, 1st Lt. Michael J. 91, 150, 174

Nargard 172
Nazi Party 13
Neerpelt 55
New York 46, 52, 60, 191
Niedernhall 197
Niederscheffoldsheim 115, 117
Nijmegen 56, 57
92nd Cavalry Recon Squadron 35
Nordwind 76, 77
Normandy 38, 39, 41, 42
Novosel, Lt. Col. Nicholas 135, 136
Nürnberg 171, 173

Oberhoffen 176, 177
O'Bryan, Pfc. George 85, 117, 119, 120, 185
Odeons Platz, Munich 12
Odon River 35, 39, 40
Offendorf 87, 95, 111–116, 121–127, 131, 132, 142, 143, 152, 155, 160, 161, 166, 173, 176
OKW 36
Old Fort Lewis 128
101st Airborne Division 56
Oosterbeek 55, 58
Oran 23, 24
Orne River 35, 39, 40
Ostrach, Pfc. Edward 125
Owen, Lt. 133, 148

Pätsch, Lt. Col. Otto 26, 42, 56, 57, 172
Pannerden 57
Panzer Lehr Division 39
Patch, Lt. Gen. Alexander M. 66, 75, 76, 194
Patton, Gen. George 35, 60, 75, 179
Peischl, SSgt. Charles 100–102
Penning Tent Camp 59, 61
Perdido Bay 9
Perkins, Lt. Francis 121
Plöne See 172
Podhajace River 36
Pomerania 171, 173, 188
Pöppel, Lt. Martin 42
USS *Porpoise* 47, 48
Purple Heart Lane 100

Quandel, Lt. Hans 26, 51, 52, 56, 62–64, 87–90, 128–130, 154, 160–162

Rademacher, Pfc. Kurt 165
Rahling 75, 76, 78, 82
Ramsey, SSgt. William 138
Regiment 21 and 22, 10th SS 160, 165
Das Reich Division 36
Reichskanzlei 189
Reinhold 63
Reisenberger, Sgt. Ludwig 27, 28, 40
Reitano, 2nd Lt. 134, 139
Renkum Heath 55
Reynaud, Paul 196
Rheinbach 87
Rhine River 95, 110, 116, 128, 161, 167, 171, 172
Rice, Pfc. Paul 117, 120
Rich, Pfc. George 120
Richter, Lt. Col. Fritz 160, 165
Roeschwoog 89, 90, 128
Rohrbach 78, 80, 81, 82, 84, 91
Rohrweiler 95–98, 104, 127, 130, 131, 150, 155, 166, 167
Roosevelt, Pres. Franklin 9, 194
Röstel, Lt. Col. 174
Rouen 43, 44, 65
Rouffach 171

Rue de Balstein 139, 140
Rue de Bischweiler 103
Rue de Capitaine Reibel 136, 143
Rue de Château 139
Rue de Châteauneuf la Forêt 141, 142
Rue de Gambsheim 139, 140
Rue de l'Église 142
Rue de Marais 146
Rue de Offendorf 146
Rue de Village 103, 104, 105
Ruma, SSgt. Charles 32, 33, 69
Rumohr, Joachim 38

Saarfeld 171
Sadler, 2nd Lt. James 134
St. Elizabeth Hospital 57, 58
St. Lambert 43
St. Malo 39
St. Pölten 62
Salisbury Plain 59, 60, 61
Salzburg 22, 192
Sarum 61
Sauerwein, Cpl. Heinrich 141
Scheffler, Cpl. Ludwig 107–110
Schehle, Pfc. Albert 27
Scheidt 13, 63, 198
Schifferstadt 89
Schmidt, TSgt. Hans 112, 113, 125, 152–154, 160–161
Schönau 183
Schröder, Sgt. Paul 51, 52
Schultz, Ilse 16
Schweighausen 87, 92, 93
Schweighouse 176
Schwemmlein, Cpl. Rudy 40
Schwimmwagen 43
Scott, Luther 120
Scott, Pvt. Robert L. 100, 185
2nd Cavalry Division 23
II Waffen SS Panzer Corps 23
Sedelhausen, Lt. Gustav 55
Seifert, Sgt. Reinhard 91
Seiller, Lt. Col. Edward P. 183
Sessenheim 76
714th Tank Battalion 31, 95, 96, 102, 194
17th Armored Infantry Battalion 31, 32, 35, 69, 78, 84, 91, 115, 121, 131, 135, 146, 149, 150, 174, 178, 195
Seventh Army 66
Seymour, 1st Lt. Robert 78
SHAEF 84, 91, 94
Sherman Tank 31, 41, 65, 66, 78, 92, 95, 121, 130, 148, 153, 179–188
Siddam 52
Siene River 39, 43, 44, 65
Sixth Army Group 94
6th Company, 10th SSPD 28, 36, 37, 40, 62, 87, 88, 129, 155, 165
VI Corps, Seventh Army 95
66th Armored Infantry Battalion 31, 34, 45, 66, 67, 84, 91, 115, 116, 120–122, 131, 150, 186
Smith, Kate 9

Smith, Pvt. Thomas 139
Somme River 39
Souprosse 29
Spree River 174
Staatmatten 128
Stalag XI-B 186, 187
Stars and Stripes 67
Steiner, Felix 12
Steinwald 76, 114–121, 125, 126
Stettin 171, 172
Stief, Sgt. Fritz 28
Stiring Wendel 171
Stonehenge 54
Storch, Pfc. Ernst 14, 21–28, 40, 49, 52, 62, 159–163, 188, 189, 191–193
Strasbourg 75
Stratmann, 2nd Lt. Helmut 87, 129, 160–165
Strypa River 36
Stuart Tank 31, 61
Svobota, Pfc. Theo 191–193

Tafelberg Hotel 55
Task Force Power 96
Task Force Rammer 96
10th Waffen SS Panzer Division 26, 36–39, 62, 76, 88, 107, 128, 131, 160, 165, 171, 173, 178
Tesch, Lt. Col. Ernst 112, 141, 152, 172
Texas A&M University 8, 30, 35, 36, 46, 141, 196, 197
13th Heavy Artillery Company 107, 111, 176
36th Infantry Division 165, 166
Tidworth Barracks 54, 59, 60
Tilset 22, 27
Tishcoff, Pfc. Marvin 124
Toulouse 39
Truman, Pres. Harry 184
12th Armored Division 23, 31, 34–36, 39, 45–47, 59, 61, 66, 77, 83, 91, 94, 106, 115, 127, 136, 150, 151, 165–167, 171, 172, 185, 196
23rd Tank Battalion 31, 34, 45, 61, 65, 66, 78, 79, 121–123, 132, 139, 145, 146, 166, 179

Uhlweiler 121
Ulbrich, Karl 38
Uniszki Zawadsky 12
Unter den Linden 189
Urquhart, Maj. Gen. Roy 56
Utweiler 84, 86

Verfügungstruppe 12, 37
Vickless, Sgt. Edward "Pete" 79, 91, 92, 139, 157–159, 162–166, 179–182
Vienna 37
Villers-Bocage 39
von Bock, FM Fedor 15
von Braun, Wernher 194
von Reitenstein, Freiherr 12
von Schlieben, Gen. 35

von Treuenfeld, Gen. Karl 36, 37
Voss Strasse 189

Waal River 56
Wacht am Rhein (operation) 62
Waffen 11, 14, 21, 22
Waldgraben Canal 157, 160, 161, 162, 166, 188
Ward, Cpl. Arlo 83
Warren, 2nd Lt. Dixon L. 145
Waszack, Edward 10, 194
Waterworks 98, 99
Watts, Jane Keller 197
Wenning, 2nd Lt. Herbert 40
Westerhoff, Sgt. Bernhard 11–15, 22–23, 26–28, 37, 38–43, 49–52, 55–58, 61–64, 87–89, 128–130, 161, 163, 164, 167, 188, 196
Weyersheim 77, 94–96, 112, 116, 122, 149, 152, 155, 157–162, 165, 166, 171, 176
Weymouth 65
White, Martha 197
Wilhelmstrasse 189
Wisch, Theodor 37
Wisembourg 76
Woita, Erik 164
Wood, Pfc. Thomas 120
Woods, Pfc. Andrew F. 33, 35, 45, 47, 61, 121, 127, 133, 139, 149, 156–159, 179–182, 190–195
Worden, Pfc. Irving 137
Worms 179
Wortheim 172
Wrobel, Herbert 27
Würzburg 23, 172, 173, 179

Yarborough, Lt. 190, 191

Zeller, Lt. Col. William 94, 95
Ziechenau 16
Zilliox, Charles 134, 155
Zilliox, Fernand 134, 155
Zimming 178
Zorn River 94, 95–101, 105, 115, 117, 121, 124, 127, 129, 130, 132, 134, 139, 153, 155, 158–161, 165, 166, 176, 196
Zutphen 49, 50, 52, 63

www.ingramcontent.com/pod-product-compliance
Ingram Content Group UK Ltd.
Pitfield, Milton Keynes, MK11 3LW, UK
UKHW050528150426
5217IPUK00026B/1845